have mother, will travel

For Kathy — who's been along for the journey from the beginning.

♡ Claire
Mia

Also by Claire and Mia Fontaine

Come Back: A Mother and Daughter's
Journey Through Hell and Back

have mother, will travel

will travel

A Mother and Daughter
Discover Themselves,
Each Other, and the World

Claire and Mia Fontaine

wm
WILLIAM MORROW
An Imprint of HarperCollins*Publishers*

HAVE MOTHER, WILL TRAVEL. Copyright © 2012 by Claire Fontaine and Mia Fontaine. All rights reserved. Printed in the United States of America. No part of this book may be used or reproduced in any manner whatsoever without written permission except in the case of brief quotations embodied in critical articles and reviews. For information address HarperCollins Publishers, 10 East 53rd Street, New York, NY 10022.

HarperCollins books may be purchased for educational, business, or sales promotional use. For information please write: Special Markets Department, HarperCollins Publishers, 10 East 53rd Street, New York, NY 10022.

A hardcover edition of this book was published in 2012 by William Morrow, an imprint of HarperCollins Publishers.

FIRST WILLIAM MORROW PAPERBACK EDITION PUBLISHED IN 2013.

Designed by Jamie Lynn Kerner

Library of Congress Cataloging-in-Publication Data has been applied for.

ISBN 978-0-06-168842-3

13 14 15 16 17 OV/RRD 10 9 8 7 6 5 4 3 2 1

For our own mothers, and for all mothers

Contents

CLAIRE'S PACK LIST

Passport with extra photos
Visas and immunization records
Travel insurance, important numbers
Video camera, camera, tape recorder
Batteries, cords, adapters, converter
Flashlight, pens, notebooks
International cell phone, language translator
$800 cash (50 singles), credit cards
Emergency contact info, freq flyer #s
Money belt, empty tote
Light jacket and pocket poncho
2 capris, 1 pair shorts
3 pants, 1 nice
7 tops: 2 long sleeve, 3 tees, 2 tanks
1 long skirt for Muslim countries
Cardigan
1 scarf and 1 pashmina
2 shoes: walking, sandal
Undies, bras, jammies
Swimsuit, sarong, flip-flops
Makeup and toiletries
Eye mask and earplugs
Travel towel, duct tape, sewing kit
Portable laundry line, Woolite packets
Tamiflu, antimalarial, chlorine tabs
First-aid kit, sanitizer
Antidiarrheal, Dramamine, aspirin
Medication, extra glasses and contacts
Sunglasses, sunblock (SPF 50)
Bug spray—30% DEET
Vitamins, PowerBars

MIA'S PACK LIST

Passport
Visa
Mother

Introduction

O ne word, Mia—*schistosomiasis.*"

An occupational hazard of writing is research; you look up the risk of eating sushi and five hours later you're an expert on the *Loa loa* eyeworm and the *E. japonica* flatworms that are teeming in rivers like the one my grown daughter, my only child, wants to plunge into today.

I'm holding the bathroom stall door closed for Mia at Kuala Gandah, an elephant rescue sanctuary located in the rain forest of Malaysia's Pahang region, where we've come to ride the elephants and learn about their rescue program. They allow a handful of visitors to ride the big gals into the muddy river and cavort with them as their handlers scrub them down. My devil-may-care daughter is among the select.

Look, I'm a big risk-taker, an intrepid traveler, but I stop at taking home larvae as souvenirs.

"You don't even have to swallow it," I whisper loudly, "they bore right through your skin and make a beeline for your liver."

She comes out, rolling her eyes. "There are fifty other travelers here, Mother. Do you see anyone else worried about it? By the way, these are probably the only sit-down flush toilets we'll see all day, I'd try to go if I were you."

"No one who gets it worried about it before they got it! It lives in rivers in the tropics. That," I point emphatically out the window, "is a river, and this is the tropics. What are you not getting here?"

"Mom, if you're going to be like this the whole trip, the only pain

I'll have in my butt won't be from traveler's diarrhea. You don't avoid London because people get hit by buses! How many opportunities will I get to swim with elephants?!"

I follow her out of the welcome center to a clearing in the jungle where a group of people, mostly stout, sturdy Brits, are wandering down a dirt trail through the dense flora toward the elephant area.

She hurries ahead to catch up, with me in tow trying to figure out a way to do what every mother of an adult daughter does when left with no recourse—bribe, threaten, or frighten.

"Exactly thirteen-point-nine percent of the field police officers of this country have tested positive for it!" I call out after her.

The Brits turn to look at me, not sure if they should be worried about the Malaysian police force or me.

Mia gives me a surprised look. "How the hell did you remember *that*?"

Given my lack of sleep and estrogen, it *is* impressive. "Actually, I have no idea why that stuck, but it's true. And don't swear."

She just shakes her head and scoots around the bend so she doesn't miss her "opportunity." I personally know people who struggle with parasites decades after trips to places like this. But she's twenty-five; I can't stop her. Once upon a time, when she was under eighteen, I had options.

My mom's hardly one to talk about parasites. The first thing she did when we arrived in China was drink three glasses of water—from the tap. It's not every day one gets to swim with elephants. In all fairness, however, I should probably add that her being overprotective doesn't exactly come from out of the blue.

Part I

HUNTING

chapter one

The Big Bang

I was on my way home from work when I got the call. The one that would make me quit my job, sublet my apartment, and take off for the great unknown alongside my mother. The call that led to the book you're now reading, an around-the-world adventure that's intended to entertain, educate, and, above all, explore the changing dynamic between mother and adult daughter.

But before you pack your three-ounce liquids, buy a trashy magazine you'd never otherwise read, and settle in for a cross-continental flight, allow me to hit the pause button. This isn't the first journey my mom and I have taken together, and you might need some background information so that, for example, if I refer to spending some of my teenage years locked up in the Czech Republic, it won't come from left field.

If you've read our 2006 memoir, Come Back: A Mother and Daughter's Journey Through Hell and Back, *this will be a brief refresher, and if you haven't, well, you may want that $10 cocktail because it gets a bit intense.* Come Back *was like a darker version of* The Runaway Bunny; *baby bunny hops away from home, mama rabbit follows in "dogged" pursuit until her runaway offspring's back home for good.*

I wasn't a baby so much as I was an extremely self-destructive teenager, and my mother's version of dogged involved putting her little bunny in a lock-

down boot-camp school for nearly two years. In the Czech Republic. In a place where (for the first several months) you ate food with no condiments, bid shaving and makeup adieu, communicated with the outside world solely through letters to your parents, and spoke only during group therapy or to ask questions in class. And when the school in the Czech Republic closed, I was sent to a similar facility in Montana, a part of the world where "She Thinks My Tractor's Sexy" was then a hit song.

Granted, my behavior warranted it: dropping out of high school, repeatedly running away, heavily abusing hard drugs, felony drug charges. My relationship with my mom had shattered, we alternated between not speaking and big fights, and by my last disappearance we were completely estranged. She tried everything she knew of: traditional therapy, the psych ward, an alternative school, my aunt's house in rural Indiana (thinking cows and fresh air would be more wholesome than L.A. was erroneous; in small towns, there's often the 4-H and the other H, heroin). Hearing about the school in the Czech Republic was a miracle to her. Everyone, of course, thought she was crazy, but my grandmother is from that region, so it wasn't quite so alien, it was pre-euro and therefore a fraction of the cost of stateside treatment programs, and, mainly, she'd have sent me to Mars if she thought it'd help me.

No sane teen would trade driver's ed or prom for draconian rules and confrontational therapy, but, considering how many people I knew who ended up dead or in prison, I'm glad she did because the school saved my life. My behavior stemmed from being sexually abused by my biological father when I was a small child (anyone who thinks small kids will "forget" about abuse sorely underestimates how durable a trauma it is), and over the course of my time there I healed from it, and became accountable for the role I played in my self-destruction. I also reconnected with my mom and my stepfather, Paul, whom I now consider and call Dad.

It was February 2000 and I was seventeen when I came back home from Montana and started community college. There was a learning curve; while I was gone, something called e-mail and the Internet had exploded, Bill Clinton's name had become synonymous with cigars and a blue dress, adults had become obsessed with some children's book about wizards, and white rap had advanced from Vanilla Ice to Eminem. I couldn't reminisce about first dates or prom with my peers, I dressed like a lumberjack, and ninth grade was the last time I'd actually paid attention in class.

But I threw myself into my schoolwork, and thanks to a 4.0 GPA and a rather unique college essay, Georgetown University offered me a partial scholarship. I transferred there my sophomore year and spent the next three years pinching myself to make sure I wasn't still high—I had phenomenal teachers and classes, interned at the Smithsonian Institution and National Geographic, and made lifelong friends.

I was a senior when my mom and I decided to tell our story, something that, because my mom was a screenwriter, we'd been encouraged to do. I was scared to share my life's nitty-gritty details, but I also wanted to help break the silence surrounding incest and let people who are struggling see that change is always possible. When you're at rock bottom it can be hard to see past it, and if you can't imagine feeling or acting differently than you currently do, what's your incentive to change?

So while my friends were off finding first jobs and apartments, I turned down a job offer at National Geographic to sequester myself in a room with my mother and a computer. A year and a half later, Come Back was released and met with enough success that we spent an additional few years speaking about and promoting it. In person and via e-mail, we connected intimately with thousands of people, and, to my total surprise, I loved public speaking. My mom and I both were continuously inspired by the work that dedicated individuals and organizations were doing to prevent and treat child abuse. It was an amazingly fun and rewarding experience.

It also came with unique challenges, and once publicity died down, I felt lost. I'd been living in the past for a living—and a radically different past at that. At twenty-four, I was more comfortable speaking to hundreds of people about drug and sexual abuse than mingling with other young professionals during happy hour. I loved every element of being an author, but I was also beginning to wish my sole identity wasn't as recovery's poster child. I wanted to be just a regular twentysomething.

*Few places allow you to reinvent yourself so easily as New York, and in April
2006 I moved to the Upper West Side and dove into city life. A day in Manhattan will leave you feeling either invigorated or like a drowned rat; like a
high-strung and intelligent dog, if you don't take charge New York will end up
walking you. But for a curious person with a short attention span, its endless
supply of restaurants, museums, parades, and parties made me feel like a kid in
the ultimate candy store.*

*It took a few weeks to decode Craigslist's rental euphemisms: cozy = expect
to live in a closet; character = you may eat, sleep, and bathe in the same room;
bustling neighborhood = you'll hear the noise level through earplugs. So where
am I currently living? In a cozy room in a bustling Brooklyn neighborhood and
a building with more character than Dame Edna. Buildings don't typically
have facial expressions, but the bricks in the center sag so much that from across
the street my building appears to be smiling. And because it's above a popular
local bar, weekends mean pushing through a drunken mob, explaining to them
yes, I live here and no, you can't use the bathroom.*

*Basically, it's your quintessential first apartment (and the $750 a month
price tag was too good to pass up).*

*Like most first apartments, I share it with roommates whom, thankfully,
I adore: Guenn, a spunky blonde who bakes sugar-free cookies for her grandmother and zips around town on a Vespa, and Alanna, a redhead who looks
and acts as though she stepped daintily from the pages of a Jane Austen novel.
Plus the cozy room overlooks a beautiful courtyard and a bustling neighborhood
means everything I need or want is within walking distance.*

*I work as a literary publicist in Union Square, an area known for outdoor
markets, rallies and protests, a great dog park, and a fleet of leggy models.
There's even a modeling agency on the same floor I work on, so my five-foot-
three self often rides the elevator sandwiched between two women whose chests
are level with my head, one breast on each side of me like earmuffs.*

*I often commute home from work with Soraya, a close friend from college
who lives three blocks away. I noticed her in my senior writing class because
she was unusually poised and mature, not to mention physically striking, with
delicate features, high cheekbones, and beautiful Persian coloring. Once she
started talking about Adam Gopnik and growing up reading issues of* The

New Yorker *lying around her grandmother's house, however, I knew I'd found a lifelong friend.*

Soraya's one of several college friends of mine who now live in Manhattan, and while they entered the workforce two years earlier than I did, we all seem to be on the same page with our ambivalence toward the adult world. Your first period may unequivocally announce puberty, but your first 9–5 doesn't definitively mean you've grown up. Just last week I passed a group of college girls and was taken aback, saddened even, to realize that I didn't relate to them anymore. But nor do I feel like I fit into the world of my older colleagues.

Some of our ambivalence is probably just disappointment; adulthood's no more or less fun than college, but the levels of stress and responsibility skyrocket. And my weight seems to have done the same since my metabolism came to a grinding halt about a year ago. The only thing decreasing in size is my bank account; after taxes, my boss's caffè latte costs about what I make per hour.

Angst about adulthood aside, however, I'm having a lot of fun and am generally happy. But there's one thing missing, and it's a big one: my mother. Sure, we wrote a book together, talk often on the phone, and see each other regularly for speaking engagements. But much as working together has brought us closer, it's also driven us apart, creating a disconnect because it deals with who we were rather than who we are. Some days I'm not sure she really knows me, or at least the "me" I am now. Ever since I moved to New York and she moved to Florida a few years ago (completely out of the blue, mind you), we've been wrapped up in our individual lives.

Lately I've found myself letting her calls go to voice mail, because if they're not about work, they're filled with unsolicited advice. Now that I no longer have a lunchbox to leave notes in, she uses my inbox, sending e-mails with subjects like "Link Found Between Stress Levels and Belly Fat," "Six Subtle Career Moves That Hold Women Back," and "Cell Phones May Cause Salivary Gland Tumors!" Then she'll send me Frédéric Fekkai samples from Sephora, "because the ends of your hair are like straw."

I don't know if she's bored in Florida without her old friends and colleagues, or if it's turning fifty and this is motherhood's last gasp, but something's up with my mom and I wish I knew what it was.

"Mom," Mia asked halfway through a recent call, "is this how you pictured your life would be when you're fifty?"

I opened my mouth to rattle off a packaged answer, but nothing came out. It was one of those defining moments (nothing coming out of my mouth is always a big moment, if not for me, for *someone*).

"This isn't going to sound very good," I said after a moment, "but I've never actually had a concrete vision of my life at fifty."

"Well, what do you *want* to be doing with your life now?"

That answer wasn't any better. "Not what I'm doing right now."

That call prompted a solitary trip to the beach at sunrise the next morning. I sat in the sand, my brain still lit up with all the mind chatter that accompanies my waking and tends to hang around most of the day. I wanted to contemplate my life, but I couldn't get a word in edgewise.

"Sit up, old girl, and focus on your breath." (My inner instructress has always been veddy English, probably because deep inside I'm far more Victorian than New Age. I hear a brass *gong* in a dim yoga studio and wish not for surrender but for a butler.)

The horizon yawned up the sun and I watched its yellow arms stretch across the sea, frosting the waves and warming my face. I opened a book I grabbed randomly from my bookshelf on the way out, Eckhart Tolle's *Silence Speaks*. My eyes fell on this paragraph: *"To lose your inner stillness is to lose touch with yourself. To lose touch with yourself is to lose yourself in the world."*

Which shut my mind up immediately. I had a good cry, took myself home, and set an intention before bed for the first time in three years, for clarity and vision. To find myself in the world.

Which means finding myself in my own life first. Because there are few things the world can throw at you that will cause you more grief than what you manage to throw at yourself. The last few years my aim has been deadly. Determination is one of my strongest traits. Unfortunately so is impulsivity. It can be a bad combination.

Four years ago I woke up and decided that it was high time to buy a house. *We're throwing money out the window every month!* I told my husband, Paul. *Prices just keep going up!* One week we were in our huge, beautiful apartment in L.A., three weeks later we were making an offer, not on a charmingly decrepit farmhouse under the Tuscan sun, oh, no—on a historic fixer-upper money pit under the blistering Florida sun. At the peak of the market. With no central air-conditioning and a moldering guesthouse so jerry-rigged that you turn the kitchen light on by turning on the *oven.*

Paul flew out for the inspection, sat on the hearth, which was covered in lizard droppings, hung his head, and said, "Claire, this is too much work, it'll bury us."

"It's all cosmetic! You always see the problems instead of the possibilities! The *New York Times* is raving about this neighborhood! We'll flip it at a big profit!"

Two weeks after closing, a category-five hurricane made a direct hit on our neighborhood . . . followed by a category four . . . then we found mold in the bathroom walls . . . then two more hurricanes hit us . . . and "cosmetic" turned out to be around one hundred fifty grand in needed repairs. Oh, and I'm not even going to mention the hot flashes that started the day we signed the mortgage. Not that I think it's a coincidence or anything.

And then the market tanked. We owe more on the house than it's worth. That Paul hasn't killed me is a miracle.

On the plus side, a 1920s Mediterranean is not without its charms. Most of the walls have their original hand-plastering, each an evocation of culinary delights: frosting in one bedroom, grits in the other, ricotta cheese (my dining room looks like it has cellulite), and the pièce de résistance, one-inch pie peaks on the top half of the living room, with the bottom half paneled in rare pecky cypress. Pecky beams run up through the plaster and across the cathedral ceiling. My living room looks like Noah's Ark meringue pie.

The rest of the walls lean to the creatively repurposed: asbestos floor tiles on the kitchen walls (useful in a meth lab) and, as God is my witness, kitchen-counter *Formica* not in the kitchen but on all four bathroom walls, from floor to eleven-foot ceiling. The bathroom mold actually turned out to be a blessing. Paul got to swing a sledgehammer really, really hard, for two whole weeks, knocking out the bathroom walls instead of me.

More significant than the house, however, was that in my excitement at finally being a homeowner (of a piece of architectural history!) I didn't fully consider the life I'd be leaving behind. I was a working screenwriter; I had a personal and professional network of people I dearly loved that had nourished and supported me for fifteen years; I lived in a city buzzing with culture, major research libraries, perfect weather, and mountains where I hiked three times a week. I had a life I pretty much loved.

I managed to avoid the full impact of my choices for several months by spending all my time in a library studying to get a real estate license. Writers have an unpredictable income, and I got the harebrained idea that I actually had the sales skills needed to make a killing in our *hot-hot-hot!* area, thus earning extra money to pay for renovations. Just before the exam (thank God, because I would have flunked) we got the book deal and I was able to get out of Dodge for much of the next year and a half. I wrote at a friend's home in a much cooler state to escape heat, house, and husband.

Once *Come Back* was published, I was away even more for book promotion. Two years later that tapered off and there I was, sitting on the hearth as Paul once did, reality fully settling in. Not much fixing, and no flipping, had occurred, because Paul and I agreed on absolutely nothing about the house or yard. It took us a year to agree on bathroom fixtures, but because the city wouldn't let us touch a thing until we rewired *the entire house,* we still had a bathroom with a brand-new tub and fixtures, but no walls, meaning no showers, only baths.

That I haven't clobbered him by now is an even bigger miracle. Unlike most men, who are happy to let their wives handle decorating, Paul, being a graphic designer, refuses to do a *single* thing until he has a

perfect blueprint for *everything*, down to the last detail. I can't even plant
a single shade tree in front till I know the genus and species of the border
plants in the alley.

And I always thought infidelity and canoeing were the biggest dangers in a marriage.

Every woman's circumstances vary, but I imagine a midlife crisis feels
pretty much the same for most women—boredom, fear, self-doubt, rest-
lessness, dissatisfaction. I can't seem to meditate anymore and, worse,
have lost the discipline and focus to write anything other than blog posts.
Writing has always been so central to my identity. Aside from replying to
reader e-mails and plotting how to kill our neighbor's ficus tree, which is
picking up the foundation of our house, my greatest joy is that my daughter is happy and healthy.

Not that my relationship with Mia is where I'd like it to be. It's good,
but far from what we enjoyed in the first years following those dark days
when even her physical survival wasn't assured, much less our relationship.

A woman's relationship with herself is mirrored everywhere in her
life, but no place more than with her daughter. In the last couple of years,
I've gone back to some of the old fears and habits of a controlling, perfectionist mom. The kind of mothering I'm doing sends daughters to
postcardsfromyomomma.com. Everything else I'm doing sends *me* to
fmylife.com.

The darnedest thing is that until a few years ago, I knew better. Because
there's no point sending an evolved kid home to unevolved parents, Mia's
school put parents through the same brutal process of self-examination
and growth.

And let me tell you, transformation is hard work. And then you have
to *keep* working on it, every day. Which I did. After Mia went off to
college, I took more courses and workshops, on vision, on leadership, I
got great coaching, and I eventually helped counsel others. I was com-

mitted to evolving. I *knew* how to choose a life consciously rather than by default, and through my forties, I did just that. I made a vision map years before most folks had heard of such a thing. I asked myself what my wildest dreams were and found images of all of them.

I'd completely forgotten about the map until I unearthed it last year while clearing out a closet. I opened it up, flattened the wrinkled, pasted-on images and words, and realized that I'd made all my dreams come true, *every single one*. Trust me, they were all *big* stretches. Being fit and strong (I'd never exercised till then), inner stillness, connection with God, travel to Europe with Mia, using my writing to help others. My biggest dream was in the center—my daughter home, healed, and happy.

It was a vision for who I was then: a woman whose purpose and identity was bound up in being a mom. Once Mia was on her own, I never bothered to dream up a new life for a post-motherhood, midlife me. Leave it to my daughter to get me to acknowledge out loud that I am fifty-one going on *the rest of my life* and I don't really know where that is.

I'm not exactly sure how I'm going to hit my life's restart button, but after a couple of weeks of sunrise meditation on the local beach, of just sitting still with my discomfort instead of denying or dodging it, I feel something I haven't felt in ages—trust, a feeling that delights me in the extreme. Genuine trust has always felt to me like fairy dust. Like God's magic wand is hovering and about to touch me but meanwhile, here, have some of *this*.

And, voilà, life delivered.

I'm standing in line at a café and see the travel section of *USA Today* on a table. There's a short article on a Global Scavenger Hunt, accompanied by a photo of a man on a camel in strange headgear, in front of the pyramids at Giza. Their motto is "Trusting strangers in strange lands," and the main goal for each team is to raise money for charity through sponsorship.

I love to travel! I love surprises! A chance to help others! I'LL BE ABLE TO TAKE A REAL STAND-UP SHOWER FOR ALMOST

A MONTH! Ten minutes later I'm on the phone to Mia, literally jumping up and down on the sidewalk.

The heck with renovations. Putting money into the house makes no sense anyway; the mortgage is almost double what it's valued at. Most of the royalties I earned from *Come Back* went to moving and to finish paying off loans from Mia's boot-camp schools. I've used almost none of it on anything nice for myself (unless you count a new dental crown). What self I have left is going to celebrate the success of the one thing I *did* get right in the last few years, writing *Come Back*. Before I hang myself from the fake-candle chandelier, or worse. Because Paul really is a very nice man. He doesn't deserve the noose.

My mom's so breathless with excitement that all I can make out is "article! have to go! four continents!" It doesn't help that I'm trying to listen to her while walking through the Union Square farmers' market, my eyes peeled for samples of artisanal cheese and piping-hot apple cider.

"Mom," I forcefully interrupt, "I can't understand a word of what you're saying! Slow down and start from the beginning."

She sighs impatiently before launching into her second try at explaining what sounds like an intriguing, if utterly random, trip around the world called The Global Scavenger Hunt. Beginning in China, we'd circumnavigate the globe over the course of twenty-four days, visiting no fewer than four continents and ten countries. Each leg of the trip has scavenges to find, often requiring riddles to be solved first; basically, The Amazing Race *without cameras, prize money, and staged drama stunts. It all sounds very mysterious and adventurous, which is very like my mom. However, her final reason, "We never really did anything to celebrate our first book," is very* unlike *her.*

My mom's not a celebrator. Growing up, I had to practically bribe her around the holidays so we could decorate the house or get a Hanukkah bush (we're Jewish, Paul's not). She has numerous unopened "special occasion" bottles of champagne despite having had ample occasions when it would have been fitting to pop one open.

"Are you kidding me, Mom? I'm thrilled you want to do something fun—I

almost feel like celebrating your celebrating. And I haven't used any of my vaca-tion time yet, so it's perfect."

"This is great! Okay, I'll e-mail you all the information. Oh, and I'm spending the summer in France afterward, my friend Chrystelle's going to find me a cheap rental. I need to get away for a while, and if you weren't working I'd ask you to join me."

I really should be used to her springing things on me by now; she announced she was moving to Florida the same way. Hi, honey, we bought a house in Florida, the movers are here, gotta run! I have no more idea why she left L.A. so suddenly than I know where her out-of-the-blue urge to celebrate and travel is coming from, but I do know this is the first time in ages I've actually heard her engaged and excited.

We tend to think of our mothers as anchored in a time and place, and it's a strange thing for me to not be able to picture the specifics of her life. When I think of my mother, I see her back at our old apartment in L.A., black apron tied over a simple but elegant dress, kissing dinner guests in greeting while dressing the salad. I see her writing at her antique desk, music from The Hours *playing in the background.*

I can't picture her life now. I don't know what cafés she works at; heck, I don't even know what she works at because I don't think she's been writing much, if at all. Something in her changed ever since she moved to Florida.

She rarely talks about her feelings and I can't tell if she's avoiding saying certain things out loud, of admitting them to herself, or if she's avoiding saying them to me. *Maybe I haven't been there for her, maybe there were times she wanted to open up and I missed the cues. The last time I'd lived with my mom I was eighteen and obsessed with proving my independence, hardly a time to think about her as, you know, an actual person. If my mother were to die today, I don't think I'd be able to say I knew who she really was as a woman, apart from being my mother.*

It dawns on me that I want to go with her to France. I'll have to quit my job, and the price of both trips will put a major dent in the royalty money I put away, but when else will I be able to do something like this? I'm not wild about working in publicity (I'm really only in it because it pays the bills and I have no clue what else to do), it's easy to sublet in New York, and, strange as it feels to admit, at some point I'll settle down and traveling for four months won't be so easy.

Provence is my mom's happy place. It brings out a very sensory part of her otherwise very cerebral existence. When she showed me pictures from her last trip there, I didn't see my mother in them. I saw a confident and sexy woman who was at peace with herself and loving life. I want to get to know that woman, the woman always glowing in photos. I want to meet my Provence mother.

Travel empties out everything you've put into the box called your life, all the things you accumulate to tell yourself who you are. Women tell themselves who they are through their career, marriage, home, social life, style, through our face and body, by how well we please; we often mistake our lifestyle for our life and others liking us for us liking ourselves. As mothers we define ourselves by how we mother, how well our kids turn out. Their needs come first for so many years that acting purely on our own desires and impulses can become a forgotten skill.

Who am I minus all of the above? What really matters to me at this stage of my life? What will I leave behind? And because I believe in being fully accountable in life, I want to examine the choices I made that created my current reality. More important, I've got to unearth the underlying, probably unconscious, beliefs that drove those choices.

And I better do it fast. Because I'm sorry, folks, but fifty will never be the new thirty; you can have your face injected, filled, or stitched tighter, but you can't stitch on more time. *This* is my biological ticking clock.

I was actually surprised that Mia agreed to join me in France. I knew she was thinking of quitting her job, but she loves her life in New York—I wouldn't have thought she'd want to leave for four months. And I suspect she was just as surprised that I asked her. It really drove home how much

disconnect there is between us. We worked too hard to find our way back
to each other to settle for a relationship by default, to live in the shallows.

Once upon a time we made it to hell and back; the scavenger hunt
will be a way to celebrate an amazing chapter of our life by taking a very
different kind of journey, this time not so far south, so to speak. The
extra time in France will be a rare opportunity to take stock of where we
are and chart a new course for ourselves, as women and as a mother and
daughter. And because we'll already be in Europe, we're going to take a
side trip to Budapest; I want Mia to see where my mother, her Bubbie,
is from.

The trip is also an opportunity for me to examine my relationship
to motherhood in general. How do you mother an adult daughter, *do*
you still mother her? What's motherhood like in other cultures? I think
there will be much to learn in France, where women seem to incorporate
motherhood into their lives more easily than we seem to. They also treat
women *d'un certain age* differently.

We've reached out to friends and readers for donations to the charities
the scavenger hunt will support and we've been overwhelmed, though
not surprised, at their enthusiasm and generosity. Several thousand has
already been pledged, and counting.

And so, a dozen shots and a carry-on full of pharmaceuticals for
third-world maladies later, we're off for the swirl and chaos and beauty of
the world, for the sound of crowded cafés, of foreign tongues and cellos
in ancient cathedrals, for the sun on gilded warriors and gods frozen in
time in the middle of traffic, for farmers' markets with rows of deeply
colored spices.

Mia's detour ended my youth with a dreadful, unexpected bang. Now
I'm beginning the second half of my life with a different kind of bang.
I'm so excited about our upcoming journey, I'm telling everyone about it.
I even posted a blog entry about it: *"I'm going to start the second half of my
life with a bang!"* A bang! she wrote.

Of course, you know where this is heading.

chapter two

China

The Bitch and the Boss

It's not lost on me that it is the Chinese who coined the phrase "Be careful what you wish for."

Because I got my bang all right. And we've only been gone two days. My taxi got rear-ended on a freeway outside the San Francisco airport yesterday, leaving me with a bruised spine and mild concussion.

Today peril has found me again. Not because I'm on a freeway in Beijing, *hailing* a taxi, in the *dark*. Because it's raining and Mia paid for a blow-dry.

"I can't fucking believe I let you talk me into this!"

I hate it when she swears.

Three Days Earlier

If you have to travel with someone who's headstrong and head-injured, well . . . run.

Much like an alcoholic who refuses to stop drinking because they don't think they have a problem, my obviously concussed mother refuses to give me the reins because she doesn't think she has a problem.

She's right. She doesn't. I do.

It's been three hours since we landed in Beijing and she's already left her new (and only) jacket in the airport bathroom, withdrawn the equivalent of nine measly American dollars from the ATM because she forgot about the conversion rate, and then forgotten her card entirely in the ATM, which promptly sucked it up. So we'll be sharing my jacket, using my debit card, and, thanks to the fact that she just glugged down three glasses of water from a bathroom sink, making infinite pit stops. Because, as we just learned, tap water = traveler's diarrhea.

My mom, twenty-six other jet-lagged Americans and Canadians, and I are in our hotel lobby, getting the official rundown from the organizers of the annual event, Bill and Pamela Chalmers. Bill's impossible to miss; he's toweringly tall, with piercing blue eyes and dark hair streaked with silver. His wife, Pamela, is as gentle as he seems stern, a petite, pretty woman with delicate features, a wide smile, and gleaming hazel eyes.

The trip technically began in San Francisco, where we'd had a welcome dinner and basic overview, but today marks the official start date, and Bill's all business. As are we; there's no small talk, and expressions tend toward giddy excitement or type A laser focus. Most teams are couples aged forty to sixty, save for another mother-daughter duo and some teams there just as friends.

"Welcome, everyone," Bill says. "Hope you've settled in okay. Pamela is handing out the scavenge booklets now. You will receive a new booklet at the beginning of each leg of the trip, and they will become your bible. They have your hotel information, key phrases in each language, emergency phone numbers, and, of course, the scavenges. Do not lose these. You will not be given another.

"Have a look," he continues, gesturing for us to open the booklets Pamela's pressing into our hands. "You'll notice that Beijing has eighty-five scavenges, each worth a different amount of points. You will always have more scavenges than there is time to do, which means that there will be a lot of strategy involved. We'll tally up your points at the end of each leg."

I flip through the book, curious to finally see the scavenges. They don't disappoint: trying "delicacies" like locusts or silkworms, taking a Chinese cooking class, doing tai chi in a park, singing at a karaoke bar. Some scavenges are riddles themselves, like enjoying sam seh, *photographing a* kaidangku, *and finding out what happens at 29 Luilichang Street. I like how many of them allow for interactions with the Chinese, like flying a kite with local kids at Tiananmen Square, or attending a court session and explaining the proceedings.*

And Bill clearly has a sense of humor: Scavenge #42 requires documenting egregious commercial trademark violations, and Scavenge #66 asks us to visit an Internet café, Google the Dalai Lama, Taiwan independence, and human rights in China—and then hightail it out of there.

The scavenges range from five points to two hundred and fifty points (the more challenging or time-consuming the scavenge, the more points it's worth), and following Bill's rules is imperative. Points are deducted for using the Internet or calls home to solve scavenges, showing up late to meetings, or failing to prove we've completed scavenges by taking photos and showing ticket stubs. The boot-camp school I was in as a teen was based on a system of points and levels (gaining points = advancing levels = going home; while breaking rules = losing points = a lengthier stay in hell), so I may be the youngest person on this trip but I definitely have an advantage there.

"So," Bill concludes, "we'll meet again as a group three days from now, at ten P.M. *sharp. Remember, our motto is 'Trusting strangers in strange lands.' This trip is what you make it, you can spend as much or as little time on each scavenge as you like; you can just take a taxi or you can go to the driver's house and have dinner with his family. You'll see, even with identical instructions and scavenges, each team will go home with very different memories. Now . . . good-bye and good luck!"*

With that, everyone scurries out of the hotel, poring over the booklets as they go. My mother, however, apparently unable to walk and think at the same time, steers me to a set of chairs, pulls out the scavenge booklet and a map of Beijing, and proceeds to do . . . nothing. Thirty minutes later, there I am, sitting with my foot tapping, stomach grumbling, and teeth gritted.

"You heard him," she says, after I ask her for the tenth time if we can leave, "strategy is everything. Beijing is absolutely enormous and we'll backtrack like crazy unless we map everything out and order the scavenges."

"Yes, but we're hardly strategizing! There are eighty-five scavenges—it's idiocy to map them all out now, we're jet-lagged and haven't eaten in eight hours! Look, scavenge number ten has lots of food options and they're twenty-five points each. If we go to the Noodle Loft and order old-style Peking duck, a Chinese pancake, and Asian fondue—whatever that is—we get one hundred points and can strategize while we eat. Okay? Good, let's go."

She doesn't answer, just continues to stare at the map while making nary a notation or plan. I feel badly, because I know she's still foggy from the accident and even with enough aspirin to toxify her liver for life, her head's throbbing, but hunger's beginning to trump sympathy. She's being so illogical I'm about to walk over to the wall and bang my head against it just so we'll be on the same page.

On a trip like this you can't *plan everything, but my mom's the kind of person who actually practice-packs. We argued in the weeks before leaving, because she felt I wasn't doing enough to prepare and I thought she was going overboard. Case in point: Pamela e-mailed a list of sixty-two countries, at least ten of which we'd be visiting. I scanned the list out of curiosity and then forgot about it; my mom divided days before departure by countries and sent this e-mail:*

I've done Argentina, it's attached for you to use as a template. Under the name of each country, give the time zone and country code for phone numbers and then list . . .

1. Major airports, and distance to them
2. A bit of history of the country/city—I found I could do this while listing the places, people, or things in #3
3. Major sites—historic sites, temples, mosques, shrines, landmarks, museums, etc. Please give the address and hours open
4. Some folklore, heroes, or legends
5. The quintessential foods of the country or area
6. The quintessential clothing (i.e., the longyi in Burma, or the lei in Hawaii)

7. Any major dos or don'ts or cultural advice/customs
8. ANYTHING YOU CAN THINK OF THAT I MISSED

Need I say more?

I sit with her for another ten minutes and just as I'm about to lose it, an elegant woman in a red silk suit, with her hair twisted in a tight chignon, walks past us. She's very pregnant and very loud, hollering Chinese into her cell phone and punctuating with her one free hand. Midsentence and without breaking stride, she hacks really loudly and shoots a well-aimed stream of spit into an urn two feet away from her.

I'm shocked, mildly disgusted, and thrilled—spitting is on par with nails on a chalkboard to my mom, who, horrified, takes this as her exit cue.

Athletes spit in every country. Men spit in many countries. In Beijing, *everyone* spits. Once we hit the streets of downtown Beijing, people of every size, age, and gender are hacking and spitting left, right, and center. You could throw down a skim board and glide down entire blocks without a hitch. Or you could if any block were clear enough. Which is, of course, impossible.

Because Beijing is home to nine million bicycles, fifteen million residents, and two million tourists. *And they're all on this block.*

Maybe it's the concussion, pollution so bad it actually coats the roof of your mouth with filth, the fact that the Chinese speak very, very loudly, or that there's no such thing as personal space here, but thus far Beijing feels like an assault. We're bumped and nudged from every direction, buffeted about like corks on the open sea as we walk in search of food. Beside us, six lanes are packed with anything that will transport humans or lumber. Cars, bicycles, buses, motorcycles, trishaws (three-wheeled rickshaws), phone-booth-size aluminum boxes with a man and gas pedal attached to the front, cement trucks, backhoes, and the occasional military vehicle.

Beijing looks a cross between Orange County and *Blade Runner,* sprinkled with pagoda-style roofs. By the time we arrive at Wangfujing, a wide, pedestrian mall that is Beijing's premier shopping area, Mia and I are ready to drop. She's also very irritable. There are a lot of food scavenges from the night market's food stalls but it's too early and nothing else here beckons—Häagen-Dazs, McDonald's, and a multistory KFC the size of a Costco.

"I vote for the Colonel," Mia says, working to clear her throat of slime. She looks like a dog trying to eat peanut butter. "God, it's like having pond scum in your mouth. Come on." She pulls me toward KFC.

"I didn't come all the way to China to eat something I don't even eat in my own country."

"I didn't come all this way to starve! We've got three days to eat like natives!"

Ninety percent of the time, Mia is an absolute delight to travel with; she's energetic, curious, resilient. Ten percent of the time, however, Mia's digestive system is the bane of my existence, even when we travel a mile from home.

Given that her mood is only likely to get worse, and my head's pounding, I should be kneeling before the Colonel in gratitude, but I want to eat *real* Chinese food, Travel Channel Chinese food.

"We haven't looked that long, I'm sure we'll find something." I turn and head toward the big street. "If we don't find anything in a few minutes," I call behind me, "we'll do KFC, okay?"

I reach the sidewalk, feeling Mia's eyes burning into my back. And, as if by magic, there are the red-and-white striped awnings of food stalls across the street. I plunge into six lanes of solid traffic. Nothing's going to stand between Mia and Peking duck.

Brakes slam and tin-box-cycles swerve around us. We hit the opposite side shaken but standing.

"That wasn't so bad," I lie. "Now, let's go eat."

We snake through the crowded sidewalk toward merchants upon whose culinary delights we shall sup. I see ahead things being threaded onto skewers, I see things being dipped into big, steaming vats, I hear laughter and orders called out. I don't care what they're selling, we're eating it.

Then the stench hits us. I stop so suddenly that Mia rams into me from behind. I hear her gasp. The smell is a blend of rancid oil, ammonia, fish, the rotten sweetness of warm raw meat, and a dark tang.

Food, it seems, is a relative term in China. There are rows of meticulously aligned wet, lumpy things of various shapes, in a variety of meatlike colors and pale fishy hues. It's visually quite compelling, but a lot of it doesn't just look parasite-*inducing*, it looks like giant parasites, period. There are yellow grubs the size of my shoes (picture a big fat hot dog bun, segmented, with an identifiable butt and mouth), and it's one thing to see six-inch-long black scorpions on a skewer on the Travel Channel, another entirely to have them inches away.

One food article in particular fascinates me. It's a caterpillarish thing as long and thick as a cucumber, with a slick, pearlescent gray surface and a stylish fringe, obviously some kind of rather fashionable sea critter. I lean down to examine it, captivated in a horrified kind of way. When one suddenly JUMPS IN MY FACE!

I leap back with a shriek. Everyone around us laughs as the guy who fooled me with that thing keeps wiggling it at me.

"Centipede, lady! Centipede for you! Excellent for you lady, ha, ha, ha, ha!"

It *is* funny and I start laughing, turning to see if Mia's laughing, too. Hardly. She's leaned over the curb holding her stomach, gagging with dry heaves. I rush over.

"Mia, are you throwing up?"

"Throwing up *what*—dust?!" She straightens up. "So, let's see, now, we can have *fried chicken* or fried *scorpions*! Gee, tough choice, Mother!"

"I'm sure there's chicken-like matter here, too, honey. And pork, you love pork."

"Just give me a PowerBar before I faint."

"I don't have one."

"What are you talking about? You lined your entire suitcase with them."

"I told you I brought them for you—why didn't you put one in your backpack?"

"Because I thought I saw you put one in your purse."

"Why would I do that? I can't stand them."

"Because your daughter might want one. Because you always carry food."

"What am I, a pack mule? You're not ten years old. I bet you don't have toilet paper with you, either."

"This was so stupid," she mutters, which means she doesn't. "You had to sit and plan, plan, plan, and what good did it do, we can't find anything! We could have eaten two hours ago!"

"You know, Mia, I'm hungry, too. If I were one of your girlfriends you wouldn't be throwing a tantrum."

"Yeah, because none of my friends would have a problem eating at KFC—they're not prima donnas! Are you sure you didn't pack a Luna Bar? I swear I saw you pack one."

"Yes, I'm sure."

There's a lot to see today and it's not as if being hungry will kill her. I pause to think of how I can defuse the situation, try a more patient and loving approach. But before I can stop it, "You might consider that suffering in silence is a highly underrated skill" pops out.

Apparently, she has considered it. She's been silent to me since. We're on a trishaw on a quiet street running along the eastern wall of the Forbidden City, which is not red, as I expected, but a soft clay-rose color. The trishaw's cushy tires, along with the driver's steady, rhythmic pedaling, glide us dreamily along beneath pale clouds of cherry blossoms.

One of the hallmarks of a mother-daughter relationship is what I call the Zero to Sixty Factor. We can get *instantly* irritated at each other and just as instantly move on. As in:

"I can't believe you told a complete stranger that!"

"What, that you have prolapsed ankles? Honey, she's fitting your shoes!"

"I don't care— Oh, my God, I *love* those sandals, second shelf, bronze, are they gorgeous or what?"

"Oooh, yeah, they'd go great with our linen pants." (*Our* meaning mine, of course.)

Men don't get this. Paul will hear us going back and forth and say, "Girls, stop fussing," and we'll immediately turn to him and say in unison, *We're not arguing,* puzzled that he would even think that.

Mia's obviously not back to zero yet. As a mom, you learn to gauge how long your daughter's going to be mad, but this time I'm not sure if Mia's being quiet because she's over it, falling asleep, or bitching at me in her head. Maybe discovering that I actually *did* have a melted PowerBar in my purse helped. The one she swore I put in there and I swore I hadn't.

I have no recollection of doing it, that's how autopilot that kind of mom behavior is—always anticipate every possible need for the family. Paul makes sure the car has gas, I handle everything else; Mia's autopilot is to just assume we've done everything. My girlfriend Chris, who has a daughter Mia's age, says the same thing. God forbid you try to give them advice, they're all grown-up and know *everything,* but they still expect you to take care of them.

Travel is stressful, and it's not like renewing our relationship is going to happen in one chat over tea in China, tra-la-la. I knew at some point we'd regress to old patterns the way we're doing now, which we call our B&B—Bitchy (Mia) and Bossy (me). But I figured it would happen after we'd been gone long enough to get on each other's nerves, like after three weeks. If it's like this every time something comes up, we aren't going to make it a week, much less five months.

So important is it to the Chinese to always know which way is north that to be so swept away by something that you lose all sense is to "not even remember which way is north." Jingshan Park, once the emperor's private garden, and a twenty-five-point scavenge, sits outside the north wall of the City, where its densely forested hills can block the dark yin forces of the north—yin being the female element. You know, like dust clouds, storms, evil spirits, the murderous Mongols, and power-hungry Manchus. To further avoid these yinny female dangers, structures were always built to open to the south to take advantage of the positive, nourishing yang forces, which are male elements. Like light and nourishment. I'm not going to say *anything*.

The plaza at the bottom of the hill is filled with young couples in tight jeans holding hands and nuzzling. After all the shouting and hacking, it's pleasant to weave through them. We stop at the spot where in 1644 the last Ming emperor, Chongzhen, hung himself in shame and dishonor as peasants overran the Forbidden City. I give a capsule history to Mia, who listens even though she's still not talking.

"He made a quick stop on his way out to kill his teenage daughter, lest she suffer dishonor at the enemy's hands."

"What a guy."

Sarcasm, a good sign! Maybe she's thawing. She's already starting to hack like a native and I'm afraid she's going to start spitting like one, but I don't dare say anything.

Why is it that mothers are so willing to walk on eggshells around their daughters, far more afraid of their silence than daughters are of ours when we're upset? Why do daughters usually call the shots in the speaking-silence battle? You don't hear many daughters saying, "You never call me!" I wonder if it's how they level the playing field, finally wield some power, after eighteen years of us being able to boss them around?

After climbing steep stone stairs through dense firs, we arrive at a terrace with a circular pavilion. Fat red-lacquered columns support eaves and beams that are kaleidoscopically painted. The coffered ceilings dance with white cranes and clouds, separated by geometric bands of bright cobalt blue, red, white, greens. Repeated swirls of gold on the columns turn out to be the snaking bodies of dragons twisting and curling about themselves with bared claws and fangs.

"Hey, Mom, come here," Mia calls from the edge of the pavilion, in her normal tone of voice. I feel the muscles in my neck and shoulders relax. Discord with Mia makes me feel crappy like nothing else can. I walk to the railing and stand beside her. She gives me a gentle elbow and looks at me sideways with a grin. That look and the ensuing laughter is our standard "sorry for being a jerk" routine, no words needed.

Nestled in the misty brown air, a complex once known as the center of the universe looks like a haunting, sepia-tone photo in a history book. By obscuring almost everything to the east and west, the pollution presents us with the Forbidden City of fifteenth-century Peking that I've been studying for a month.

Because the yellow vapor also obscures the southern end, its sea of roofs seems to stretch on as endlessly as an ocean, wave after wave of russet and ochre that vanish into the false horizon. It's as if a spell was cast when the last emperor, Puyi, left, taking two thousand years of history with him.

It's pitch-black when I wake up to my mom shaking me. I bolt up and fumble for the light, thinking she must be feeling woozy or sick. Concussed people aren't supposed to sleep too much; I should have been checking up on her.

"Do you feel okay, Mom? What year is it and who's president?"

"It's 1962, JFK's in office, and I'm Marilyn Monroe. Come on, honey," she says. "I didn't hit my head that hard."

"Well, why'd you wake me up, then?" I snap, angry because she scared me, and annoyed because I'm fully awake now.

"Because I think we should get going. I was going to let you sleep more but it's five thirty, you've slept eight hours, and we've got a ton of things to do today. We're going to start at the Great Wall, then go to the Summer Palace and from th—"

"What do you mean, you were going to let *me sleep?" I interrupt, annoyed. "I set my alarm for six thirty A.M. because that's when I wanted to wake up!"*

"Fine," she sighs, wanting to placate me. "But don't sleep too much longer or by the time we get there we'll roast."

We're roasting. By the time we arrive it's almost noon and blisteringly hot. Thankfully, the Wall is breathtaking enough to eclipse physical discomfort.

The Great Wall of China dwarfs everything in sight. The taupe-hued bricks match the dry and rocky terrain so well that it almost seems the Wall naturally sprung up along with the mountains, a goliath stone serpent winding across a series of jagged mountaintops. It's such an ancient and commanding structure that standing at its base feels like being in another era.

Almost.

There's a two-story Starbucks with green lettering big enough to see from Mars, a KFC, and a swarm of street vendors rushing toward my mother and me yelling, HEEEYYY LAAADY!!!! I wasn't expecting China to be lotus blossoms and bound feet, but I didn't expect to be surrounded by people thrusting Mao wristwatches, miniature jade dragons, and "real" Chanel handbags and Rolexes in our faces. One man actually screams, PAY ATTENTION TO ME, LADY!!!!

Astonishingly, my mom does. Of all the god-awful, tourist-trap merchandise to choose from, she's buying one of those hard, conical bamboo hats worn by laborers in the rice fields.

"Don't give me that look," she says, tightening the strap under her chin. "This is the only hat for sale with a full brim."

"Mom, please, people are going to laugh at you."

"Mia, there is zero shade here. So what if I look like a rice farmer? I can take it off when we're done. You're going to leave here with a sunburn—and you can't take that off."

My mom's clearly back to normal: awake at the crack of dawn and sassy.

"Well, don't ask me to stand in any photos with you, because you look idiotic."

You look idiotic? What's wrong with me? I've never cared about what people think or how my friends appear; my friend Dave's gone out with a necktie knotted around his forehead like Rambo and sparkly gold shoes. In general, I've been bitchier than I normally am. I make a vow to start acting more myself around her, and purchase our tickets.

The Great Wall of China was an utter failure as an unbreachable defense. Sentries could be bribed, Mongols on horseback could find ways around it, and, had the Ming dynasty bought European-style artillery instead of spending a fortune to expand and maintain the Wall, they might have staved off the Brits.

Not that it didn't have its uses: in ancient times it was a fancy elevated highway of sorts, enabling the quick transport of people and supplies across normally difficult terrain, and in the absence of e-mail and cell phones, lightly dried wolf dung on fire created smoke signals that enabled watchmen to silently holler, "Hey, move your asses, Genghis is on the way!" In more recent times, the Wall became a favored stomping ground for ravers looking to party.

Up ahead I can see my mom's hat bobbing along the sea of people on the Wall, a Where's Waldo–*type decal that actually turned out to be a useful tracking device. I catch up with her and we take a break to lean our elbows on the Wall and stare out over the valley.*

"I'm glad you're feeling better today," I say.

I am glad. Not just because I love her and don't want to see her in pain, but because I love her and if we'd been standing here yesterday I would have been tempted to push her over.

Control is an issue between most mothers and daughters, and my mom will be the first to admit that she likes to be in command. Half of the time, I don't mind, because the more control she assumes the less responsibility I have, plus she usually picks things to do that I'd have chosen anyway.

But I do sometimes mind, namely when she tells me when to ask for a raise, whom to date, or what color to highlight my hair. When I was growing up, this caused arguments, but one thing I really learned from my teenage detour is that control is usually driven by fear. Understanding this allowed me to stop reacting to her and start interacting with her differently—for example, rather than snapping at her to mind her own business, I'll examine what she's really afraid of (not knowing my professional worth, marrying the wrong person), and simply talk to her about it.

Clearly, however, that wouldn't have worked yesterday, and traveling with someone as controlling as they are inept would make Mary Poppins homicidal. From the corner of my eye I notice my mom staring at me intently. I turn

toward her and, just as I think she's about to make some profound comment
about China, she leans in and lightly touches my eyebrow.

"If you plucked just these two hairs your brow line would be perfect."

She's a melancholy beauty, the Forbidden City, a giant, feminine corpse
who gave up the ghost the moment she was no longer forbidden. The
paint peels from many of the enormous red doors, which are studded
with perfectly aligned bronze half-spheres the size of softballs, most
mildly corroded. The deep green or red paint on many buildings and
corridor walls is faded or dusty. Most of the once-brilliant yellow roof
tiles are darkened and rust-colored. Still, there's a tired glory in her symmetry and stillness, her sheer size.

The Forbidden City is walled into a rectangle of a hundred and eighty
acres. The three great palaces are lined up down the middle, surrounded
by elevated pale stone walkways punctuated by gargoyle spouts. The rest
of the 9,999 structures inside the City are royal residences and buildings
used for everything from concubines, state affairs, sacrifices (that was a
surprise, animal sacrifices here), pavilions and gardens, libraries, house-
keeping, and other things—like keeping warm (Palace of the Warm
Chamber) and self-denial (Hall of Abstinence).

Deliberately built to confuse, it's a disorienting rabbit warren of red,
green, or rose-colored passages, gardens, and courtyards. Almost every
surface is painted, gilded, or ornamented. The end of every roof gable
ends with a row of yellow mythical beasts, led by a guy sitting on what
looks like a giant chicken, to ward off fire and calamity.

The five-claw dragon motif, which represents the emperor, is ubiquitous. The empress was represented by a phoenix, a creature with the
head of a swan, the chin of a swallow, the tail of a peacock and a fish, the
forehead of a crane, the back of a tortoise, and, lastly, the neck of a snake
(isn't a snake pretty much *all* neck?). Personally, I think they were going
for a one-dish meal.

The names of the buildings reflect the values and hopes of past dynasties: the Pavilion of Pleasant Sounds, Hall of Peaceful Old Age, Hall of the Blending of Great Creative Forces. Human nature being what it is, history made mockery of most names. While Chongzhen was preparing his noose out back, his wife, servants, and favorite concubines hung themselves by white silk nooses in the Hall of Earthly Tranquility. During the second Opium War, the Germans sailed through the Gate of Divine Military Genius as the U.S. forces plowed uninvited past the Gate of Correct Deportment.

We're here with another couple on the trip, Rainey and Zoey, both lawyers who are energetic and very funny. We're looking for the Hall of Clocks and the only building guarded by dragons, but I'm feeling like I want a few moments' quiet so I decide to wander ahead on my own.

"I want to go all the way to the south end first," I tell Mia. "I want to see how it feels to 'Enter the Forbidden City.'"

"How do you know which end is south?"

"Because it's late in the day. I just have to keep the sun on my right."

"Suit yourself, Girl Scout, don't get lost."

I know Mia puts little stock in my orienteering skills, but they're invaluable in places like this. It looks the same everywhere; it's *Groundhog Day* every time I turn a corner. I finally trudge into what has to be the biggest front yard on earth, the great court in front of the main palace. Built to hold over a hundred thousand people, it was meant to awe, to leave no doubt in anyone's mind that it was a *very* long way between you and the emperor.

Six centuries later, it's an eerie, windswept place, still one of the largest enclosed spaces in the world. The scale is such that a saffron-robed monk walking across it right now looks like a pumpkin seed.

After catching up to the others, we have just enough time to gawk at an anomaly here—a half-finished nineteenth-century Italianate structure with an empty moat, part of a complex that housed the emperor's concubines. With chambers for 1,420 beds, it may be the most aptly named building here—the Palace of Prolonging Happiness.

Though becoming a concubine could bring wealth and status to your family, once chosen, you were in here for life. If you bore the emperor a child, you earned some privilege. If you bore him a son, you could wield power. If you bore the emperor no kids, were no longer young, or were never selected to be stripped, shaved, powdered, perfumed, and deposited in the emperor's bed, you didn't have sex, ever. You lived out your days, chaste and bored out of your mind, in the Garden of Dispossessed Favorites.

Possibilities did exist for the creative, however. There were always a couple thousand eunuchs in the City. Hence, what were called "vegetarian affairs." This wasn't without risk. One emperor caught wind of such a dalliance and proceeded to slaughter nearly three thousand eunuchs and concubines in one night.

The last true ruling imperial, Empress Dowager Cixi, was a concubine who rose to power by retiring her sickly hubby to the Summer Palace, then hanging two princes and beheading another, all by the time she was twenty-two. She then allegedly managed, between 1861 and 1908, to end imperial rule in China. She put the "last" in the last emperor.

Which should have been good news for our gender in China. The Communist regime that followed imperial rule gave women rights and outlawed female infanticide, which had been common for centuries in a culture where daughters were seen as a double liability, first for requiring a dowry, then for leaving to care for the husband's parents. In the latter half of the twentieth century, however, a one-child policy has brought it back in the form of selective abortions; baby girls are also placed in orphanages, often in secret, especially in the countryside. There's a reason almost all the Chinese children adopted by Americans are girls.

What must it feel like to be a mother who goes through pregnancy praying she's not carrying a bitty version of herself inside? While it's true that women themselves sometimes carried out infanticide, women often fought to keep their girls. Cixi herself is said to have had a daughter clandestinely by a lover who came to her chambers through underground tunnels. She supposedly gave birth in secret and had the girl raised by his family. Not surprisingly, she indulged and treated many of her ladies-in-waiting like daughters. Cixi was vain, greedy, power-hungry, depicted as alternately unspeakably cruel or charming; nothing of her life reflects my own, but I have to think that her longing for a daughter was no different than mine.

As the seat of Beijing's governmental buildings and a place that invokes the image of a lone man facing off with a column of army tanks, I expected Tiananmen Square to have a somber atmosphere. Instead, it feels rather festive. Brightly colored kites flap against the wind, children's giggles echo through the plaza, parents and grandparents smile as they chase after waddling toddlers.

My mom immediately brightens at seeing the children playing, which is nice, because she was quiet throughout much of the Forbidden City. Her silences are tricky—sometimes she's quiet because she's upset, but sometimes she's just deep in thought, in which case it's best to leave her alone or she really will get upset, this time with you. As a writer, she often has one foot in this world and the other in a world of her own making; snapping her back to reality from turn-of-the-century Paris or a shipwrecked World War II vessel could make her lose track of the missing plot point she's finally unraveling. "I may never get that thought back!" was a common refrain I heard growing up.

We're meeting another team to have dinner at the Noodle Loft, whose menu boasts a mile-long noodle and hand-shredded ass meat, giving us about thirty minutes to figure out what the heck kaidangku *are, fly a kite with a child, and locate the forever sleeping Chairman and the Great Hall of the People.*

My mom walks to a nearby vendor and purchases a kite. I ask her just how she plans on going up to total strangers and asking to play with their kid, but she just waves her hand.

"See that little boy up ahead?" she says with a knowing smile. "Once he sees the kite he'll want to come over. His mom won't mind, honey—she'll see I'm here with my own child."

Sure enough, the kid's spellbound, eyes wide and mouth ajar as he watches it flit back and forth. He keeps looking from the kite to my mom but turns and buries his face in his mother whenever my mom gestures for him to come fly the kite. Everyone's laughing, and after enough ushering gestures and encouraging words he toddles over, and is soon shrieking with joy every time a gust of wind lifts the kite higher into the sky. While everyone's absorbed playing with him, I kneel down and snap a quick picture of his kaidangku, which turn out to be brightly colored pants split open at the crotch so when nature calls tots can squat 'n' go. It is rather cute seeing all these little kids wandering around with plump little butt cheeks peeking out.

The ease with which my mom did that amazes me. Small kids sometimes make me uncomfortable. Until they're crawling, they can't even sit up on their own. What do you do with a crying or gurgling blob that you can't leave alone for nine months? My friend Sunny put it best when she told me that if she had a kid, she'd probably water it and hope it would grow. My mom says once I have kids, knowing what to do will come naturally, but I'm not convinced. I mean, the kid's cute but Mao's Mausoleum is far more interesting to me.

One of my favorite college courses was the History of Dictatorship, and it's oddly exciting to be so near the pickled remains of a man I studied and wrote about at length. Much like when he was alive, Mao rises every morning with the sun, is available to the general public during the day, and returns to his chambers every evening. Rather than containing a bed warmed by a waiting consort, however, his chamber is now a giant refrigerator, and "rising" actually means that his prostrated corpse is elevated mechanically.

Despite the propaganda, cruelty, and mass killings, Mao is publicly venerated, and a goliath image of him looking almost grandfatherly hangs prominently in Tiananmen Square. China's official stance is that Mao was 70 percent right and 30 percent wrong. I'm not sure who came up with these numbers or how, but I'll make a quick list of Mao's "rights" and "wrongs" and you can do the math.

The Wrong: he massacred, often quite brutally, between thirty and eighty million of his comrades. Unlike the Nazis, Mao's Red Army wasn't encouraged to meticulously document the carnage, so death toll estimates vary considerably.

Either way, when he once said, "China is such a populous nation, it is not as if we cannot do without a few people," he meant it.

The Right: he ended China's "Century of Humiliation" from Western and Japanese imperialism, greatly increased literacy and life expectancy rates, outlawed foot-binding and female infanticide, and granted women the right to divorce and inherit property. He may have enlisted women solely to further his revolution, but you have to love his slogan "Break the chains, unleash the fury of women as a mighty force for revolution!"

Some things look the same in all languages. Failing at a decent drawing of the Bird's Nest for the taxi driver, I flapped my arms like a chicken and, bingo, we're deposited on a dark road full of construction equipment and debris. A patchwork barrier of battered blue metal panels disappears into the darkness in either direction. Behind it, China is building her first Olympic venue. It's close to ten and we're tired, but I persuaded Mia to come. Groups of locals peer through gaps in the metal.

Surrounded by acres of darkness, the Bird's Nest lies under the night sky like a glowing red larva safe in its blue playpen, napping after the effort of spinning half a cocoon round itself. High-rises under construction around the far edges of the barriers send spectacular showers of sparks from fifty stories up. The pollution makes everything so filmy and surreal it feels as if this whole scene is part of the giant creature's dream.

Groups of locals and a few tourists peer through gaps in the panels. After getting the driver to shoot a photo of us in front of the panels to prove the scavenge, I find a heap of stones and climb up beside an elderly Chinese woman in a dark blue Mao-style jacket and trim pants. She's not tall enough to see it even on tiptoe. She looks in the general direction of it, then turns to smile at me. Oh, my God, I'm thinking, she wants me to hold her up? My footing's unsteady as it is. I smile awkwardly.

She turns back to the Bird's Nest, then back to me, beaming. She doesn't want a lift. Pride also looks the same in every language. I smile at her and bow my head in honor and agreement, which pleases her greatly. She bows back.

"America," she says in a thick accent, "happy you come!"

Which practically puts tears in my eyes for some reason. We turn and she allows me to take her arm to steady her on the way down. She bows a thank-you and vanishes into the night.

Since we can't get any closer, I suggest we walk to the other side to see the Water Cube, the already-famous water sports venue.

"Mom, it's dark and there are holes everywhere. It's not worth breaking our necks."

"Oh, come on, what's pretty is how it's lit up at night. It's just a short walk, then we'll get a cab."

We make our way over piles of stuff that shifts and crumbles beneath us. There are almost no streetlights and China doesn't use safety barriers, no orange cones or construction tape as warning. We skirt the troughs and holes we *can* see, some of which could hold a VW, and pray we miss those we can't. I'm sure there are some folks in Beijing who simply never show up for dinner, ever again.

We follow the blue barrier wall until we hit an unlit tunnel where the walk narrows to fit one. And nearly get decapitated. Poles, pipes, and two-by-fours poke horizontally out of the wall with no flags. Cars speed by so close that they knock my purse.

"Mother, you're going to get us killed over a blue blob! Starting tomorrow I'm in charge!"

"Fine! Here, hold my hand!" I call back, reaching my hand behind me.

"No way, you're the advance warning system!"

Maybe it's wishful thinking but I think I hear a teeny hint of a chuckle in her voice. I'm also beginning to wish I'd listened to her. We finally emerge, hearts palpitating—to yet more battered blue metal fencing that just goes on and on. I keep walking optimistically, freeway on the left, Water Cube on the right. Somewhere.

She's so quiet that I know it's the lull before the storm. But I am *not* turning around and going through that tunnel again. There's a racket ahead and a steep freeway embankment appears, full of Chinese tourists clinging to it as they try to film the Water Cube.

"Look, we'll be able to see it from up there!" I gush enthusiastically.

"Now I *know* you're really desperate," she says drily. She knows I get vertigo from heights.

"Well," I sigh, "I kind of am, Mia. I know we're tired and disoriented, and all my planning turned out to be useless, and maybe this was another one of my stupid, impulsive ideas. But maybe if we accept that this trip *is* going to be chaotic and we probably *are* going to be hungry and we *will* have to squat over a lot of holes to pee, we'll see the world together in a way we'll remember the rest of our lives."

"Yeah, I know," she admits. "Sorry for snapping."

She takes the camera and climbs quickly, wedging her bottom into a cement divot to see the Water Cube. I clamber up shakily with the heavy backpack, wedging each hand and foot into a divot as if I'm scaling K-2, happy she's back in the spirit of things.

And then the rain starts.

"My hair, goddamn it. Give me the umbrella!!"

There is no umbrella in the backpack, and she paid for a blow-dry in San Francisco. It starts raining harder. The tunnel is too far. There is only the freeway. Up there. I can die by falling or by Mia.

I'm on that freeway faster than you can say Jack Robinson, pulling Mia with me with one hand, waving wildly for a cab with the other.

"I can't believe I let you talk me into this! I had a job with benefits! I had free subway fare! I had a great apartment!"

You're acting like a ten-year-old! I want to yell, but that will send her over the edge. Then a plume of filthy water hits my face and sends *me* over the edge. So what flies out of my mouth instead, paragon of restraint that I am, is—

"If you had such a great life, why did you decide so quickly to leave it?"

chapter three

Malaysia

Wallet for Elephants

*I*t was for the best that I kissed straight hair good-bye in Beijing, because a resounding boom of thunder sounds as we leave Kuala Lumpur's airport. Seconds later it's pouring, and after Beijing, this cool, damp air is wonderfully refreshing.

Beijing was trying in many ways—jet lag, a huge language barrier, pollution, figuring out how The Global Scavenger Hunt worked in practice rather than theory—and I don't think my mom and I are the only team eager to start this next leg.

As we are driving through Kuala Lumpur, the rain spreads a shiny topcoat over bright yellow, baby pink, and sea green building façades. It glazes the bushy fronds of palm trees and pours from the spiky plumes of orange birds of paradise.

Malaysians seem like a happy lot. Rickshaw drivers oblivious to the rain shout out greetings to one another and women in bright saris, resting beneath umbrellas protecting arrays of fresh fruit, laugh among themselves. My mom's relaxed as she watches the world pass by and turns to me to smile when she notices I'm watching her. There's a silent easing of the tension that followed her asking me why I left my life. I'd fumed for hours, not just because big questions should never be asked angrily while both parties are about to be hit by oncoming *traffic, but because it seemed ungrateful. The main reason I left was to spend time with her and help her through a rough period.*

Our experience in China proved the importance of a square meal after a long flight, and after Bill distributes the scavenge booklets, we beeline toward food. We pore over the scavenges while wolfing down a heaping pile of nasi goreng, *the most amazing fried rice I've ever had, at a restaurant whose menu doesn't include centipedes, scorpions, or any kind of ass meat.*

"How many points are there for each city?" my mom asks.

When the teams meet three days from now, it'll be in Singapore, and the booklets contain scavenges for five different cities; it's up to us to decide which, and how many, cities to visit. With Beijing under our belt, we're getting the hang of strategizing, and we begin by mapping out what's where, estimating travel times, and deciding roughly how long each scavenge takes.

Bill touched base with everyone while on the plane—looking at photos from the scavenges we completed and tallying points—and I told him that, after China, I understand why he said the trip is really what you make it. With so many scavenges to choose from (and now, potential cities to visit), how you strategize determines how you'll experience each country. For example, you could have a leisurely, in-depth experience by spending an entire afternoon on a single scavenge (i.e., the Great Wall of China, 250 points), or you could have a more chaotic and exhilarating afternoon racking up points by eating as many foods, finding as many mystery items in shopping bazaars, and visiting as many temples as possible.

"Six hundred fifty for Kuala Lumpur, seventy-five in Melaka, a hundred and twenty-five in Penang, fifty in Johor Bahru, and six hundred for Singapore," I reply after using our calculator-cum-translator-cum-currency-converter that, yes, I admitted, I was glad she planned far enough ahead to buy.

Looking at a map of Malaysia, we deliberate and decide to skip Penang. We'll scavenge Kuala Lumpur tonight and tomorrow, take an evening bus to Melaka, stay the night, complete the Melaka scavenges before sunrise, and catch an eight A.M. bus to Johor Bahru. There are only two scavenges to complete there, so we'll arrive in Singapore around eleven A.M. and have all day to scavenge since we don't regroup until ten P.M.

It's still pouring when we leave the restaurant, and thin ponchos and travel umbrellas do little to keep us dry while we're hailing a cab. Thankfully, soggy passengers don't faze Aza, a chipper Malaysian with an impish smile and mischievous black eyes. With casual shorts, flip-flops, and gel-spiked hair, he looks more like a grad student who puts up a taxi sign between classes than a bona fide taxi driver. While driving between scavenges, we talk about what seems to be his favorite subject: American pop culture.

"There's a Malaysian Idol?" *my mom and I ask in unison.*

"Of course-lah!" *Aza laughs.* "We watch the American shows, you know, CSI *or* 24. *But there are Malaysian versions too-lah.* Fear Factor Malaysia, Project Runway Malaysia."

Why he ends every sentence with "lah," I have no idea, maybe it's Malaysian slang.

"But what about regular Malaysian shows, you don't watch those?" *I ask.*

"We watch them, yes. But they are not always so good-lah. They are little bit . . . I think cheesy is your expression?"

By cheesy he no doubt refers to shows like I Have a Date with Spring *and* Night of Soulful Stars, *which air on the popular station NTV7—Your Feel Good Channel!*

"It's the age. To younger Malaysians, anything American is very, very cool-lah. Older people, my parents for example, really only like Malaysian music and TV."

He turns up the volume on the ABBA CD that's been playing since we got in the car and smiles.

"Me, this is what I like. Okay, ABBA is not American, but they are Western so whatever, same thing-lah. The lyrics are nice, they're happy, you know? No violence, nothing about the pimps and hos."

"You're not a fan of gangsta rap?" *I joke.*

"Some of the beats are good-lah, but I can't listen to the lyrics! So much of your music and television is violent, and with so much sexy stuff. I see your reality TV and, wow! America must be a crazy place to live!"

I cringe, although his literal interpretation of "reality" television is understandable. Some cousins of mine who were born and raised in Budapest laughed themselves silly when I told them that American teens don't get new BMWs or have outrageous parties like the kids on MTV's My Super Sweet 16. *"But those aren't actors, Mia," my cousins patiently explained, wondering how on earth I couldn't know this, did we live out in the middle of nowhere like pioneers with no TV?*

Sure, Americans understand reality TV is sensationalized and often scripted, because we live here and can put it in context; your average Joe who's never visited America likely thinks we're a nation of Real Housewives throwing Super Sweet 16 parties for kids on the Jersey Shore.

"Of course there are teenagers in gangs, or having sex, or using drugs," my mom explains to Aza, "but far more don't. Trust me, the people you see on TV, even 'reality' TV, are not indicative of most Americans."

"That makes sense-lah," he says, nodding and looking almost relieved. "Like you, the Americans I have met here in Malaysia are very nice and, well . . . not how you seem on TV!" He pauses for a minute, hesitating. "But then why are all the shows like that? I hope you don't mind that I say this, because I truly mean you no disrespect, but the problems you have with your teens are starting here, too. It is not as much because we are a Muslim country-lah and there is a strong tradition but our kids are starting with the sex, the drugs, the guns. Not respecting their parents so much now. They think it's cool because it's American. You're like the big brother, you know? They want to be like you, to do what they see you do, so it is something for your country to think about. A big brother has much responsibility."

He's right in that, like it or not, America sets the cultural pace for much of the world. I've personally done nothing wrong, but I feel almost embarrassed. I don't think anyone who travels abroad plans on being an ambassador, but you're often seen as such nonetheless. You're asked, sometimes quite angrily, why your government does certain things, or, in this case, your media. And I like that Aza has no compunction about saying so, that he's not worried about being labeled old-fashioned, conservative, or politically incorrect.

"But hey," he brightens, seeing our expression, "there is always ABBA-lah!"

I don't know which I'm more excited about, seeing Pasar Bandar Baru Sentul, one of Kuala Lumpur's premier covered markets, or getting out of the car. Aza is a great guy, but I've heard more ABBA in the last couple of hours than I heard in the entire 1970s. After the tenth looping of "couldn't escape if I wanted to," I was about to yell, "Just watch!" and throw myself from the car at the next stoplight.

Pasar Bandar Baru Sentul is a microcosm of KL's melting-pot culture: there's a Chinese shrine at one end, a mosque at the other, Indian sections in the middle, and everyone seems pretty happy to be there. Markets are my favorite place in any city. First, because they're a good way to see what women's lives are like. Second, I don't think you can really know a people until you know what they eat.

And what they eat here smells fabulous. As we pass rows of food stalls where shrimp and red chilies dance on sizzling grills and giant pots simmer, I sniff coconut, fish paste, tamarind, ginger, lemongrass, vanilla bean. The cuisine is as diverse as the population—Malay, Chinese, Portuguese-Eurasian, Indonesian, Indian.

Standing fans cool off groups of men socializing over tea or curries. Women shop in loose ankle-length dresses and headscarves, but many young women are in jeans, with no head covering. A few Indian women wear jewel-toned saris. As in the rest of KL, the young outnumber everyone.

Much is familiar: piles of cucumbers, beans, tomatoes, oranges, and, as far as I can see, nothing we hire exterminators for, but I could gawk all day at everything else.

"It's like piles of gigantic jewels," Mia observes as we pass tables laden with sleek coral ovals of dragon-fruit with their sassy little yellow flaps; big pink-and-orange rambutans covered with long, bright-green hairs; slick red fruit shaped like flattened candy-apples; a pile of durians, the King of Fruits, tan-spiked balls the size of a watermelon. They're said to taste like the most heavenly cream, but when opened, the smell is so horrible that they're banned in public places.

It's a surprise at first to see produce and merchandise in blue plastic bins just like ours, but, duh, Claire, like a huge city in one of the most prosperous countries in Southeast Asia is going to trot out its wares in palm-frond baskets. I call this Pier One syndrome.

For most of Middle America in the seventies, Pier One was our first "taste of the Orient." You could do nothing cooler than show up in my seventh-grade homeroom with a Pier One *tchotchke*.* Until we overheard Renee Cohen's mom talking with a few other greener[†] about something they bought at "Peeyer Vun," right after having "a very modern salad" at the mall, one *mit* bean *schprouts*. That was it for Pier One in my circle. Nothing un-cooled something faster than our mothers finding it cool. It was back to Pet Rocks at Spencer Gifts.

We're scavenging for jasmine garlands to give as temple offerings and could easily have found the flower section blindfolded. Piles of tuberoses beckon with their heavy vapor of roses dunked in honey, overpowering tables of orchids, fuchsia, carnations.

I've been intoxicated by scent since I was a child. When we lived in L.A., where roses grow everywhere, I taught Mia where to find white ones that smelled like lychees, fat pink blooms that smelled like Kleenex and clove, bloodred roses with the scent of a baby's powdered neck.

Mia and I sniff like drunks toward white ropes of jasmine that announce themselves with the aroma of thick summer nights. A woman about my age is bundling the strands behind a table with two young men helping her, probably her sons.

"We'd like four jasmine garlands, please," Mia asks.

She nods and as she starts to wrap them in newspaper, she begins to scowl. A beautiful young woman, a student with an armload of medical textbooks, arrives with her girlfriends. The woman stops wrapping to speak harshly to her, scolding her as if she were five, right in front of her friends, and us. Mia and I exchange a glance—what should we do, leave, or stay and pretend we don't hear it?

The young woman simply listens to her mother before replying re-

---

* A little trinket or ornament, bric-a-brac.
† Yiddishized version of "greenhorns," meaning a newcomer from the Old Country.

spectfully. Satisfied with whatever she said, they exchange a few words and a quick kiss, the woman takes our money and returns to work, and the girl returns to gabbing with her girlfriends as if nothing happened.

You can spot a mother and daughter a mile away even if you don't understand a word. They do the Zero to Sixty in every culture, though it sure looks different here. It would be rare to see this scene in the States, where parents rarely discipline even young children in public. Here, no one bats an eye with an adult kid.

Of course now I'm formulating all kinds of questions for Aza. It's as if this scene was deliberately orchestrated to illustrate the kind of deep familial connection and lifetime respect for parents he laments is disappearing owing to our culture's influence.

I don't disagree with him. American kids don't seem any better off for their mothers having lost the kind of respect and authority they once had—"once" being about a century ago, when the only experts on motherhood were the only people qualified to be: women who had successfully raised happy, healthy children. Before doctors and psychologists, all male, became the experts and "mother" became a diagnosis. And before children were seen as so fragile that potty training a moment too soon would lead to a lifetime of self-esteem issues.

I turn down a row lined with giant red and yellow heliconia stalks. Mia yanks my sleeve to switch my direction. "Wrong aisle."

"What am I, a horse? Stop pulling me."

"I'm thirsty. I want to try the Milo at the next market."

"What's that?"

"Basically, iced chocolate milk in a bag, ten points."

"That's got water in the ice cubes—are you nuts? Do you actually want gut-wrenching diarrhea?"

"Mother, they're my guts and I'm thirsty. It has, like, three ice cubes."

"Oh, that's not what you said to me in China when *I* had the water."

"You have a point there," she acknowledges.

After a pause, "But I'm still going to drink it."

The ice must be fine, because when Aza stops at the base of a series of gleaming limestone cliffs, my guts aren't wrenching. Tropical foliage cloaks the white cliffs in emerald, with fern leaves draping down like fluffy boas along the bare portions of rock. Two hundred and seventy-two steps carved right into the mountainside lead to the gaping mouth of a cavern with fang-like alabaster stalagmites hanging down from above.

This is the entrance of the Batu Caves; over four hundred million years old, they're a sacred pilgrimage site for Malaysia's Tamil Indian population. They come to celebrate Lord Murugan, the Tamil god of war, which explains the presence of the biggest, goldest statue I've ever seen; at a hundred and forty feet tall, he's nearly half the height of the mountain. In folklore, Murugan risked his life for Malaysians, including the not-so-small feat of banishing all evil, and every year a festival called Thaipusam is held to honor his bravery and willingness to sacrifice.

*The footage I'd seen from Thaipusam during college internships at Na-*tional Geographic *left my mouth hanging. A* kavadi *is a physical burden of thanks, and while most devotees carry milk jugs or fruit baskets up the temple stairs, some take it to an extreme. This ranges from shaving their heads as a sign of humility and atonement to piercing spears through their tongues or cheeks to piercing their backs with large hooks. A decorated chariot is then attached to the hooks and the poor pierced soul charges up the stairs.*

When asked if he was coming, Aza just laughed. Now I see why. I'm hooked only to a light backpack, but I'm panting by the fiftieth step and using the chattering monkeys clamoring for food as excuses to stop and catch my breath.

The first night we spent with Aza, I assumed he was in his late twenties or early thirties but I found out today he's only a year older than I am, and it's bothering me. I don't consider myself immature or childish, so why does he seem so much older? As though he's a real adult, while I feel like Tom Hanks in Big.

I used to think it was just me, that even with college under my belt I still had social skills to catch up on, thanks to two years out of the real world. But several months ago I mentioned to my friend Soraya that I'd been feeling in over my head, and I was surprised when she told me she felt the same. This was a girl who moved like lightning up the corporate ladder, attends black-tie charity galas, and understands the difference between a 401(k), an IRA, and a Roth IRA. Yet she was surprised that I didn't feel grown-up, given that I'm an author and public speaker. I started paying more attention, talking to other people my age, and it seems like more of us than not don't feel comfortable with adulthood. Once I realized I wasn't alone, I breathed a sigh of relief and hadn't questioned the feeling further.

Until now. Observing Aza and other Malaysian twentysomethings makes me think that it's only a normal part of American life (and millennial American at that; I once asked my mom if she felt like an adult by twenty-five and she looked at me like I was nuts. Of course, she said, I was married, had you, and had put myself through college). Some of it's probably economic. Many Malaysians under thirty support themselves and their parents, while increasing numbers of their American counterparts live with or are subsidized by their parents thanks to scant job openings, meager starting salaries, and exorbitant student loan payments.

But as I go back over our conversation with Aza last night about American culture, there seems to be more than economics. I've sometimes thought similarly, but it was usually in passing, the way you'd analyze a cultural phenomenon for a college paper, or dinner party discussion. Aza, on the other hand, was personally troubled and deeply concerned about Malaysian youth; he sounded like a protective older brother. You could feel the concern in his voice, the sadness at seeing them exposed to things at too young an age. He was very much aware of himself as part of a bigger picture, a member of a community in which older generations feel a duty to protect the younger ones.

It's an attitude that takes a certain amount of selflessness, some of which may come from Malaysian spirituality and strong sense of devotion. No matter if they're Hindu, Muslim, or Buddhist, most Malay grow up aware of something bigger than themselves; everyone from businessmen in suits to college students blasting Snoop Dogg pull over on their way to work or school to say a quick prayer or light a candle at a shrine or temple.

I'm not interested in badmouthing my generation, because we're already branded as entitled, thin-skinned, unrealistic, insert your favorite Gen Me adjective here. These stereotypes aren't necessarily untrue, but it's also true that we're creative, innovative, environmentally conscious, philanthropic, and great team players.

At core, however, I think one of our main goals is to be happy and fulfilled; we are very much the center of our own worlds. And I never thought there was anything wrong with that. After all, as long as you're not hurting anyone else, what's wrong with wanting to be happy? Nothing—except I'm not sure it's worked.

Because the saddest difference I've noticed since coming here was that Malaysians my age seem so much more joyful, innocent even. Not innocent in the sense of inexperience—they don't strike me as the least bit naïve—but there's far less snark, sarcasm, cynicism.

Sometimes I feel a palpable discontent when I'm around people my age at home, a nervous energy and anxiety. It's not uncommon for us to switch fields back and forth or join the Peace Corps or go to grad school. We're in and out of relationships, going from hookup to hookup. We live above our means without thinking about how we'll pay for it tomorrow. The trappings of adulthood— bills, taxes, relationships, and so on—haven't seemed to move us past feeling like overgrown teens much of the time. We joke and commiserate about feeling insecure or overwhelmed, but it's stressful and unsettling to not know your place in the world. Aza is relaxed in a way that comes from knowing who you are and where you belong. In a way, we got the short end of both sticks. We're neither innocent nor fully adult.

It's human nature not to question or try to change what we see as inevitable. Among my friends, I felt perfectly normal. Seeing a whole society that operates so differently, that's perhaps happier or more fulfilled, makes me question how I've been living, what I could or should be doing differently.

I'm not having an earth-shattering epiphany that's going to make me shave my head when I get home, tether chariots to my back, and invite my parents to move in. That's not the world I come from. But seeing the difference between Aza and me has unsettled me, and I think in a good way.

"I can't believe he didn't say anything! The neighbor's tree is pushing our house up and your dad's being *polite!*"

The first time our hundred-dollar flimsy excuse of an international cell phone works for more than two minutes and that's the news I hear from Paul.

The ficus tree is illegal to plant in Florida, because its roots don't grow down, they grow horizontally, shooting out like snakes in all directions, cracking foundations and water pipes hundreds of feet away to suck up water for its ever-expanding trunk-from-hell. The biggest ficus on record covers forty acres in India, which sounded like a big fat lie until I bought a house with the neighbor's eighty-year-old ficus on our property line.

It is not, however, illegal to have an existing ficus. Now there's some smart lawmaking. The tree next door, whose massive rippling base could house a family of hobbits, has been wiggling its sneaky little fingers under our house for decades, spawning a network of greedy tongues that suckle the water that pools at the base of our studs every time it rains, which is a lot. During the hurricanes, I swear I heard that monster cackling with glee.

I'd been politely letting our new neighbor know that he's responsible for any damage to our foundation. Being a polite person himself, he called in a tree expert for an opinion. Who's apparently just told him the tree was no threat to us.

"Of course he told him that," I tell Paul, "he was paying him! You yourself were the one who found the roots growing straight up—*straight up!*—into the base of our house like straws! It's tilting the house and cracking our walls! And you didn't tell him that? Are you crazy??"

Not only did Paul "forget" to tell him he found the roots, because he out-polites us all, he "forgot" to tell him I had four arborists come in, including one courtroom expert, who said otherwise; not to mention a contractor who's worked on houses in our neighborhood for thirty years who looked at me as if I were a knucklehead and said, "Well, sure it's picking up the house, look at the size of it, ma'am, it's picking up half the block."

That I unconsciously bought a house that was a metaphor for my psyche—a house in need of renovating, a foundation entangled in dark roots, buried and unexamined—has not escaped me. It's beginning to dawn on me that I may have also bought a metaphor for my marriage.

Remind me never, ever, even if someone's giving their house away, to move into a fixer-upper. My mom just hung up the phone and is fuming about some water-guzzling tree and its damn roots. I listen sympathetically as long as I can before blurting, "If you hate this house so much, why did you buy it?!"

"God knows," she mutters, pacing around the room. "I must have had a psychotic break."

I plop down on the bed and watch her needlessly rearrange the suitcase and move around items in the bathroom, grumbling to herself. I stop feeling frustrated over hearing her complain about the house for the umpteenth time as I realize the state of self-recrimination she must have lived in for the last four years. Living in a trap of your own making is a rotten feeling, and I think half the reason she puts so much time and energy into complaining about it is to avoid facing how and why she moved.

When she first told me about the house I actually thought it was kind of cool. She used to get annoyed at how impulsive I was, and here she was doing something big and crazy. I didn't think about the fact that it was so out of character for her, or question why she didn't tell me until, literally, the day the moving van arrived.

"Mom," I say gently when she finally flops into a chair. "Seriously, why did you move? You never told me you and Dad were even thinking about leaving L.A.—and why Florida of all places??"

"Because it made sense at the time," she says with a heavy sigh. "The house was a great investment, we'd have doubled our money if we'd sold before the market crashed. Most of Dad's clients are in South Florida and—"

"Everything's online now and he'd worked just fine from L.A. for years—"

"I had a connection with a big developer and back then the market was so hot I would have made a killing—"

"*Mom, no offense, but no matter how hot a market is, you'd make a terrible realtor! You hate small talk, you're not a schmoozer, you're honest to a fault, and, hello, you love writing—which is pretty much the polar opposite of a sales career. Why on earth would you make such a bizarre career change?*"

"*Because I can always write, but real estate would have meant a steadier income and benefits.*"

Is this what talking to me as a teenager was like? It's like pulling teeth. Her answers feel superficial; she's giving me the talking points for moving, the reasons that sounded good enough for others to support the move. But they're terrible reasons for her.

"*Fine,*" *I say.* "*Let's say that those were good reasons—which I don't think they were and, more important, I don't think* you *think they were either—why didn't you tell me? It's sort of a big thing to leave out.*"

She shrugs and looks at me, half-sheepish, half-exasperated.

"*Honey, the whole thing happened so quickly. I never thought, Hmm, I don't want to tell Mia about this. I was flying back and forth, dealing with mortgage brokers, there were just a zillion things going on.*"

"*Would it kill you to try—just a little bit—to be accountable? Buying a house isn't like impulse-buying a pair of shoes. Don't tell me you were so busy you just forgot to mention it.*"

She was avoiding me, plain and simple, just like she's doing now. Which is aggravating, because I see no point in her calling me, excited to take this trip together, to bond, yadda, yadda, yadda, if she refuses to open up or be honest with me.

My theory is this: I know her too well. If she'd told me about the move (before, you know, the day of), I would have cornered her into telling me what was really going on. Whether she admits it or not, a lot more was driving her to move than the housing market and Dad's clientele. And until she figures out what motivated her to drop everything she loved and leave, I'm not sure she'll ever be happy—and that scares me.

It also bothers me because it shows how far we've regressed. Five years ago she wouldn't have thought twice about calling me if she was feeling unsure of herself or thinking of making a big move. And, even if she hadn't told me, I would have sensed discord in her. I thought most women became closer to and better friends with their moms as they got older. We seem to be doing the opposite.

The only times we open up are when we're discussing something we've already dealt with, moved on from, and understand in full. Talking about something while in the midst of it, while thoughts and feelings are still raw and messy, just isn't part of our relationship now. So here we are on this incredible trip, having to guess what the other's thinking. Though granted, the scavenger hunt has turned out to be far too challenging and fast-paced to allow for much serious conversation.

But it's not just the trip, and it's not just her. I haven't exactly been forth-coming. I'm not sure why, but my confidence has wavered a lot this past year. I've felt dissatisfied with my professional life, increasingly critical of myself physically, and just generally less sure of myself. I didn't share any of this with her; if anything, I went out of my way to conceal it, telling her how much fun I was having, how well things were going at my job.

I think most kids feel, on some level, that our parents' happiness is contin-gent on our own, particularly if, like me, you're very aware of the sacrifices they made for you. You don't want them to feel it went to waste, or to judge themselves or feel judged by others based on how we turned out. Like they're the chef, you're dinner, and the world's the assessing customer (no pressure, right?).

You wouldn't think anyone would miss a boot-camp school, but one thing I do miss is how easy it was to open up. Even for those of us who didn't take advantage of it often, it was a comfort to know we could. I remember one time I was crying in a bathroom stall when everyone gathered outside of the door and sat there while I had a good cry. That just doesn't happen often in the real world.

Nor has it been happening between my mom and me the way it once did, even though we know that honesty and vulnerability were precisely what repaired our once-shattered relationship. Funny, I always associate the term "keeping up appearances" with neighbors or acquaintances; it's disconcerting to realize my mom and I are doing that with each other.

Keeping your passport and money on a string around your neck may prevent theft, but it invites other dangers. While waiting to ride the elephants at an elephant rescue sanctuary in the Pahang jungle, we wandered down a trail and found a baby female elephant with an injured foot. She was chained outside a big cage to keep her from wandering off but seemed otherwise happy and well-fed. She was as affectionate and playful as a puppy. She just snuffled her cute little trunkie all over us, tickling it up our arms and winding it around our necks.

Then she ate Mia's giant passport wallet. With eight hundred dollars and all her identification in it. While it was still hung around Mia's neck, yanking Mia toward her munching mouth.

"Pull it out, Mother!"

"You're closer, just reach in there!"

Which Mia tried to do but it was so slimy all she pulled out was a frothy hand.

"Eeuuww, gross!" I laughed.

"Oh, that's helpful, Mother! Do something!"

"Just shove your hand up there, if the wallet doesn't hurt her neither will your hand!"

Which she finally did, playing tug-of-war with the elephant until, grimacing, she pulled the wallet out, drool-soaked and bunched up. It didn't bother little Ellie at all, in fact it seemed to make her love us even more. She nosed all over me, which had Mia and me giggling like kids. Then the little pickpocket snatched *my* purse, which I snatched right back before she could suck it up.

I'm holding Mia's soggy wallet now as she mounts an adult elephant beside the river. Behind her, several adult elephants are housed in large cages around a small circle used for rides, an experience I found pretty depressing. Such magnificent, intelligent creatures going from a cage to circle people round and round and then back to the cage, day in and day out. The high point of their day is their scrub-down and river bath. Their trainers wade them into the water with several guests on their backs.

I know several people who've brought back parasites from exotic trips.

And I know this river probably has some of them. Which seems to trouble nobody but me. Not even the other mother on this trip, Caroline, whose daughter, Cara, is sitting with Mia atop Big Bertha as she sways her way to the river. Caroline is as carefree as a butterfly, laughing as the elephant dumps her daughter in the river.

They're about a decade older than we are and seem more like close friends than mom and daughter, either because they've had a longer time to cultivate the relationship or simply because their personalities are alike. I think much of the adult mother-daughter relationship is dependent on personality. I've always been a bit squeamish about germs and the biological. Seeing someone spit literally turns my stomach. At its most extreme, it's not something you want to pass on to your kids, and clearly I haven't, but being cautious isn't the worst thing in the world, either.

Mia and the others tread water around the big beasts as they splash and trumpet, squirting jets of water on everyone. On the one hand, it's really a joy to watch her having such a blast. I love that Mia loves life, that she welcomes challenge and adventure. I love that she's taken the parts of her personality that once brought her such suffering and danger and directed them positively. I know I have to let go of trying to control her mental and physical health, I don't want to rain on all the parades she's going to create with her life. Most of the time I'm glad she ignores me. Better broken bones than a broken spirit.

On the other hand, I have to admit some envy of that Malaysian mother's authority. I know I can be a little neurotic at times, but I also know that mothers usually know what they're talking about. We've been around the block, and we almost always have our daughter's best interest at heart, sometimes more than they themselves do. There isn't a woman I know who hasn't said they wished they'd listened to their mother when they were young on some of life's big issues. Sometimes years of our lives are lost because we don't see ourselves as clearly, or respect ourselves as much, as our moms do, and we're too cocky to acknowledge that someone *fifty*-five might know a little more about life than someone *twenty*-five, especially where the three Big Ms of women's lives are concerned: mothering, money, and men.

Perhaps in this regard, mothering from now on won't be terribly different than when she was younger—I'll have to pick my battles, find a middle ground between Caroline and the mom in the market.

If you've seen Madea's warning expression on the cover of Tyler Perry's Don't Make a Black Woman Take Off Her Earrings, *you'll know exactly the kind of look that's inspiring a Malaysian cabdriver to shrink back in his seat like a sheepish child.*

Fifteen minutes ago, I wanted to pull my hair out because after hours of careful planning, it seemed impossible to cross the Malaysia-Singapore border. After a sad good-bye to Aza last night, we boarded an evening bus to the port city of Melaka, woke up at five A.M., completed six Melaka scavenges in two hours, and sprinted to catch an eight A.M. bus to the border city of Johor Bahru. After admiring the gleaming Sultan's Palace and sparkling azure Strait of Melaka, we sped over to the Malaysia-Singapore border to find a taxi to take us across.

Who knew this would be like trying to enter North Korea. Only certain taxis can cross the border, and they can only do so a limited number of times a day. After we pleaded unsuccessfully with several drivers, meeting the other teams tonight in Singapore seemed impossible.

Enter Cheryl and Konra, a mother-daughter duo newly back from Singapore. While chatting (conversation is inevitable when two American mother-daughter duos find themselves at a Malaysian bus depot), we explain our dilemma to them. Cheryl raises a brow, and without another word she marches over to the cab she just exited. We can't hear her conversation with the driver, but we don't need to. The more firmly she plants her hands on her hips and the further she leans in toward him, the more deferential his expression becomes and the fewer protesting hand gestures he makes. Ten minutes later, we're tucked into his cab, waving Cheryl and Konra a fond good-bye.

Save the thirty minutes it takes to check into our hotel, we're running literally nonstop throughout Singapore. We've just left a Mahjong *game (another near miss given we had to first convince some very stern-faced elderly people to let us into their private club,* then *ask them to teach us how to play) but before that we'd found "hell money" in Chinatown, cruised a river in a bumboat, ate pigtail soup, and spoken to a group of young Muslim men about the call of the* muezzins *outside of Singapore's largest mosque. We're now off to try and find some parrot in Little India to tell our fortune, but I get a certain familiar feeling and tug my mother toward a bathroom.*

"Mom," I whisper from under my stall door, "I need a tampon."

"Mia, hello, I haven't gotten my period in over a year."

Oh. She'd mentioned menopause in phone conversations here and there but I guess it didn't really register.

"Sorry, I forgot. But, Mom, you seem so . . . normal."

"As opposed to what—a lunatic?" she asks, laughing. "And don't you always carry supplies on you anyway? What if I wasn't here?"

We exit the stalls and start washing our hands.

"I'm not supposed to get my period for another week so I didn't think I'd need any yet. Now stop lecturing me, and wait, I thought women got horrible hot flashes and were really cranky when they're going through menopause. Sarah told me that she called 911 because she thought she was dying and the medic told her to take a cold shower and then call them back, remember?"

"I'm not lecturing you, I just really don't like being your pack mule. Now I know how my mother felt. Last time they traveled, your aunt Vivian kept asking Bubbie to carry things for her—she hated to carry a purse—and Bub got so fed up with her that in the middle of a busy street she stopped and snapped, 'Buy your own damn purse!' So . . . carry your own damn tampons. And PowerBars. Now, about menopause, yes, I did get hot flashes, and yes, they feel like you're being burned alive. Thank God they passed after six months."

"Is it weird? I mean . . . do you feel any different?" I ask, a little shyly.

Talking to her about menopause feels strange; I think of menopausal women as a lot older than my mom is. I know she's fifty, but she doesn't feel "older." Or at least she didn't—maybe that'll be changing soon.

"Different as in have I gone through some sort of big spiritual transition? No. I know it's a lot harder for some women, emotionally and physically, but, aside from the hot flashes, it hasn't been a big deal."

"Well, you always said you didn't want more kids, and since that's the main thing that goes away with menopause I guess it wouldn't matter too much."

"Mmmhhh," she says absently, blotting her lipstick and checking in the mirror to make sure it's evenly applied. Something about her demeanor suddenly says that the conversation's over.

I'm an adrenaline junkie; it takes a *lot* to make me feel like I am truly firing on all cylinders. Today was hands-down one of the most unforgettable, exhilarating, and exhausting days of my life. Every single sense, skill, and faculty was going full-tilt, challenged under a delicious pressure. And, hey, any nation that fines you $500 for spitting or not flushing a toilet and canes you for writing graffiti is my kind of place: clean sidewalks, clean bathrooms with real toilets, and respect for architecture.

I'm recovering from our final sprint to the legendary Raffles Hotel, where everyone in the group is drinking Singapore Slings, our final food scavenge. Thank God they don't fine you for public idiocy. To avoid losing points for being late, I ran the last half-mile with a heavy backpack, wild-eyed, beet-red, and desperate. I'm in okay shape but I've never run half a mile in my life, even empty-handed.

Mia's chattering away with the other teams in the rattan chair beside me as I admire my surroundings. Dating to the late 1880s, Raffles has been restored to its original 1915 decor, which is colonial plantation with a little bit of Eiffel (cast-iron gazebo and veranda). It has a grand literary tradition, featuring guests such as Joseph Conrad, Rudyard Kipling, and Somerset Maugham (who spent his days here drinking and eavesdropping for material to put into his stories).

It's one of the few places we've been that I actually remember from my crazy-making, be-prepared-for-every-country cramming before departure. I lean toward Mia to share that the last tiger hunted in Singapore was shot under a billiard table in this hotel when I overhear her informing a teammate that it's too bad we missed the sharks because she loved swimming with the stingrays in—

"Belize?!" I stammer. "When were you in Belize?"

Mia turns to me with an "oops" look on her face. "Wellll," she says sheepishly. "During junior year spring break, with Graham. I thought you'd get mad at me for going out of the country with my boyfriend, so I never told you." She pauses. "Then I never told you because I thought you'd think I was silly for waiting so long to tell you."

I'm actually not bothered, I'm amused, which surprises her more than me.

"I wouldn't have gotten mad. Hey, Belize is a lot better than Miami Beach."

"Really?"

"You were over eighteen and you paid for it."

"Mom, come on, like that always matters."

"Yes, but even if I did get mad, isn't it better to just be honest?"

"Yeah . . . sometimes," she concurs. "I just hate getting lectured."

"Sometimes what you call a lecture is just giving my opinion, I'm entitled to it. So you listen to it and then do what you want anyway. That's at least honest. We're both big girls, we don't have to always like each other's choices. God knows you let me know when you're mad about something I do. It's just not called a lecture when a daughter does it."

She thinks about this. "That's actually a good point. Which is probably unfair."

"Probably?"

She smiles and shrugs in agreement, then returns to the group conversation.

Our conversation makes me realize that not once on this trip have I done what I always used to do: catalog my travel experiences into sound bites in my head, even as they were happening, so I could share them with my mother. Which sends my rocket ship of a day into an instant nosedive. Because my mom and I haven't communicated in two years.

It's the great unspoken on this trip, and in my life in general. My relationship with her has had its ups and downs since I was a teen, but this is the first sustained disconnect between us. Some of it is my very American expectations and approach to life clashing with her more European mind-set and habits, some of it basic personality differences; mostly it's an accumulation of hurts and misunderstandings over time that has made both of us stubborn and oversensitive.

It's extremely painful, so I avoid it. Not that I succeed at it. Your mother is in your bones. My mother's absence is a constant presence, like the dark side of the moon—cold, dark, and hidden but always there behind the bright, smiling face the world sees, the other half that's part of my whole.

In the wake of *Come Back*, I've spoken with thousands of women about their mother-daughter relationship and I've seen that wound leap into a woman's face more often than I can count, just at the mere mention of their mother. While there are certainly a lot of younger women with a broken or strained relationship with their mother, I've noticed it seems more common in my own age group, boomers.

I've talked to successful, confident women whose faces instantly downshift when I ask about their mother, reminded of the hole in their heart that nothing else can ever fill. Whatever the reason for our mother's absence, oh, how it waylays us. For me it's sweaters. My mom's a big knitter; a yarn shop can send me fetal.

"It's like the flotsam and jetsam of my life," our friend Tracey lamented over lunch in Manhattan one day. "No matter what road I'm on, something reminding me of my mother will show up out of the blue and I'll trip on it, and it just tears my heart out. It sends me whirling back to the place of when we were happy, and wondering where that went."

Even something wonderful will sucker-punch you. Tracey stood in line for hours to see Amma (an Indian woman known to have hugged millions, a powerhouse of love). The second Amma hugged Tracey, she broke down. For the same reason I start to cry at the end of a yoga class when we're lying on our backs, in the dark, eyes closed, and I feel the yoga teacher's fingers caress my forehead.

chapter four

Nepal

Kaleidoscope

I never imagined it possible for a city of eight hundred thousand to be lit almost entirely by candlelight, but downtown Kathmandu would be pitch-black if it wasn't for the flickering light emanating from smoking wicks.

My mom and I are silent as we wander through narrow and uneven streets that are half-paved and half-dirt, all of them largely empty and fairly quiet. Ancient and ornate buildings of brick and wood jut out above run-down store-fronts advertising Internet services and money exchanges on faded plastic or handwritten signs. The scattered pools of light exaggerate shadows, and it feels dreamlike. It would almost be romantic if you didn't know the candles are ne-cessitated by an extreme lack of electricity. Considering we're in Thamel, the main tourist district, I can only imagine the total darkness many Nepalese must live in once the sun sets.

We suddenly hear, "Madam, madam!" and two girls emerge from the dark and come running toward us, smiling and out of breath.

"Beautiful purses, look madam, you buy for your friends."

They're maybe nine or ten, with high cheekbones, jet-black hair, and shin-ing brown eyes, thrusting small woven purses at us. One wears a man's button-down shirt three sizes too big for her and both have ill-fitting shoes, but they are fresh-faced, their nails trimmed and clean. They speak excellent English and are surprisingly bold, though extremely polite. The girls clearly aren't homeless but it's still unsettling to see them wandering the streets alone at night.

As we continue down the road, my mom stops in front of a store displaying small paintings filled with intricate geometric patterns, vibrant colors, and figures of gods and folklore heroes. Her nose is nearly pressed against the glass as she examines the stunning detail and delights in the gold leaf glinting in the candlelight.

"These are thangka *paintings!" she says, excited. "Buddhists used these in meditation for centuries. See how they're painted on scrolls? That was so monks could roll them up and transport them. I've always wanted to see these up close—look, some of those lines are painted with a single brush hair."*

Because she was an art history major, thangkas *don't excite her for the twenty-five points they're worth as a scavenge. Much of my childhood had been spent being shuttled from one museum to another. My favorite exhibitions were ones that came with headsets, which meant I could rest while my mom received, rather than gave, history lessons.*

It's also true that when I finally took her advice and enrolled in an art history class my junior year, I loved it and took three more after that. It's probably a healthy part of individuation, but I always rebelled against my mom's suggestions of things I would or wouldn't like. I think "You just don't understand" and "You don't know me" are refrains programmed into all teenagers, and it takes time to grow out of an autopilot pattern.

My train of thought is interrupted when, out of nowhere, a group of about twenty men burst onto the street, waving their arms wildly, spinning in circles, and dancing. A cacophony of sound accompanies them, the jingling of tambourines, the banging of pots and pans.

"Is today a holiday?" my mom asks a shopkeeper, who's leaning against the doorframe of a dark and empty convenience store. "Were they at a wedding?"

"Oh, no," he laughs. "They're just happy."

My mom and I look at each other and shrug. Three more men come hollering along as we leave and then I get it.

"It's the elections, Mom, remember? The Maoists just won."

Nepalese politics in a (very tiny) nutshell: Nepal was traditionally a monarchy in which the royals kept themselves rich by starving—sometimes quite literally—their countrymen. Violent insurrection, often led by the Maoists, began in the nineties, but it wasn't until 2001 that things really escalated. That June, the prince murdered his parents and eight other family members before turning the gun on himself in a drunken rage. Years of bloody civil war between various government forces and Maoist rebels ensued, leaving thousands of people dead and the population desperate for peace. Even the people who voted against the Maoists are hopeful. Anything's better than what they had; everyone's sick of fighting.

The young men are gone as quickly as they came, and the streets are quiet when we reach Thamel House Restaurant, a landmark establishment that could have been dreamt up by Lewis Carroll after a heavy dose of laudanum. Originally a house, it is a candlelit maze of dark rooms, narrow, tilted staircases, and low ceilings. The stairs are uneven and creaky, laughter floats from various darkened rooms. We're led up a final flight of stairs to the attic, a small room with a low, vaulted ceiling, burgundy carpet, and gold and brown floor cushions.

"This place is so cool!" I whisper to my mom, who looks less than thrilled.

"It feels like an opium den."

I think it feels much like what we've seen of Nepal so far: dark and mysterious with a hint of the surreal and magical.

Last night's spell is broken the moment our taxi leaves the gates of our hotel to inch into the jammed traffic. It feels as if we've left the castle for the land where the heroine has gone off to find the magic elixir to save her kingdom and hasn't yet returned.

It's strange to be on a dirt road in the middle of a city of two million people. Either side of it is scattered with chunks of concrete, debris, piles of garbage, what looks like a sewage trench, and skinny dogs flopped on their sides in the heat.

Nepal is one of the five poorest nations on earth, with a 50 percent literacy rate, a precarious infrastructure, severe environmental issues, a fifty-eight-year average lifespan, and a large number of malnourished, homeless children.

Five of whom are out the window on our right, scavenging on top of a block-long hill of smoking garbage. They're barefoot, only partly clothed, and two of them can't be more than five. One is trying to yank something out of a dog's mouth. Two women in deep-yellow saris with water buckets walk past the children as if they're invisible.

On our left is the kind of slum I haven't seen since my family got lost on a trip to Tijuana in the sixties. Dwellings are cobbled together from corrugated metal, branches, rope, and blue tarps. A few kids tease and play; one sits listlessly beside a group of men squatting on their haunches, staring silently at passing traffic. They're called *sukumbasi*, the landless population.

But even among the heartbreak on this long road, there is beauty. Small shrines on every block are dusted by the faithful with orange and pink powders, fathers and sons stop to leave offerings of flower petals and move on. A mother and daughter in pink tunics over lavender pants emerge from the slum, stepping over trash, dogs. Women wrapped in vermilion, marigold, and peacock-blue saris weave through traffic with babies on their hips. When women proclaim their place in the world with hot-pink scarves trailing from their shoulders as they walk beside stinking garbage heaps, beauty is a weapon, a refusal.

Even here, there are signs in English for ESL, for IT training and computer classes. Schoolkids in crisp blue uniforms with neckerchiefs tied smartly under their chin bike or walk to the schools that seem to be on every corner: Little Genius English School, Bright Future High School, National Inventive English School. Some of these kids come out of slums and walk right past starving kids. I wonder how the kids are selected, who decides whose fate is sealed with a pencil case and blue blouse?

Her hair's not even dry from her shower, but already Nepal has made Mia's face unfamiliar to me. Compassion, fascination, revulsion, sadness, delight, surprise—all flash and flit as we drive. She's never seen life like this, other than in magazines or photo exhibits. I'm as compelled to watch her as what's outside.

A mother never tires of her daughter's face, at any age. One of the most rewarding and entertaining aspects of mothering is being able to witness the very moment your little girl discovers something about herself or the world. We're always with them when they're small; we have the opportunity to see subtle changes, the lightbulb moments, the shock at harder truths.

It's part of what we, and they, lose when they grow up, the world is no longer new to them in the same miraculous way; and when it is, we're rarely there to witness it. It was one of the most amazing things about writing *Come Back* with Mia, witnessing her during the creative process, seeing something emerge from her soul, still shiny and wet as a newborn.

I know Mia watches me this way, too. Sometimes I would catch my reflection in a window near my desk and see her face off to the side, watching me. Or I'd see her through a kitchen doorway when she was young, watching me cook from a distance. So much of us is unknown, and unknowable, to our daughters. We carry a whole lifetime of *before* within us. How do you express that to them?

That *before* is all the more mysterious and inscrutable for daughters of mothers from other countries and cultures. My mother is from Eastern Europe; she survived the Holocaust in hiding in Budapest. Her family did not. We share almost no social, cultural, emotional, or, save a few cousins, familial experiences or references.

When I was little, I used to love to watch her when she didn't know it. I especially loved to study her when she was knitting, sitting on the sofa after a houseful of five kids was quiet. Knitting was the first time I remember seeing my mom as someone other than my mom. It was something she did for herself, as a person, not as a mom.

Watching her puzzle out something intricate, her blue-gray eyes silently counting stitches as her fingers danced in the air with the yarn and the *tick-tick-ticking* needles, was like being privy to some secret part of her very essence.

I learned how to knit and crochet from my mother as a child; it was a bond between us that I loved. We couldn't disagree, and it was fun and creative—it allowed us to see another side of each other.

I'm not attached to things. I toss or donate as much and as often as I can. Paul and Mia live in fear that I've thrown out something valuable of theirs. But I've kept everything my mom ever knitted for Mia or me. The writing sweater she made for me is frayed, stretched out, and tattered, but if my house was on fire, it's one of the few things I'd run inside to retrieve.

I didn't expect my first encounter with death to be a public cremation at a Nepalese temple, but here I am, holding hands with my mother as we watch bodies, now reduced to ash, smolder atop sandalwood logs.

Pashupatinath is an enormous funerary complex situated on the banks of the sacred Bagmati River. Hindus consider rivers to be holy; they bring salvation from the endless cycle of death and rebirth, and many wish to take their final breaths on the banks of a river.

The main temple is an enormous pagoda dating back to the fifth century, surrounded by a crowded patchwork of rose-colored altars, white stone statues, and small bronze temples. Wide steps lead from the temple to the river below; bodies are burned on platforms at the top of the stairs.

The body on the first pyre is a white pile of ash, and the second has snippets of cloth still visible amid burning flames. Pink and orange flowers cover the ground, and small clusters of people stand beside the funeral pyres, white robes waving gently in the wind. I feel like we're intruding, Westerners snapping photos and soaking up cultural lessons while someone lays coins in the mouth of a loved one. Even among themselves, however, there is no privacy; bodies are burned in the open, funeral processions intersect, unemployed men come to watch and pass the time.

Though Nepal is now a democracy, the caste system persists; the lower castes are cremated downstream. Beneath industrial metal pylons are six slabs of concrete, and what felt ceremonious before is more perfunctory here. There aren't colorful shrines, decorative altars, or attending priests. Mainly, the river tells the difference. The water here is very shallow, with banks that are a tangle of garbage, reeds, and a thick black sludge. A layer of ash coats the water, which is rife with burned logs and garbage. Untreated sewage, waste from medical facilities, and animal carcasses are routinely dumped in the Bagmati; the water upstream was hardly pristine but it wasn't this putrid.

Two street children are bent over in the water, their hands resting on their knees as they intently scan the river. One looks to be about six, the other ten, though it's hard to tell, because their skin is tough and weathered. They're scouring for gold teeth or coins that sink to the river bottom after the ashes from the burned bodies float away.

A flash of color catches my eye. Not twenty feet from the boys a woman my age is washing her sari. She casts the bright marigold fabric into the river, a rippling square of color floating on the water's surface, before pulling it in and wringing it out. It's a beautiful image; a cascade of black hair, brass armbands on honeyed limbs, the sun behind her creating a silhouette of the female figure behind orange fabric.

My mom's listening intently to a young guide explaining the various rituals and customs. I've stopped listening; I've formed a freeze-frame of this image, this beautiful woman in the middle of a filthy and muddy river, a stone's throw from emaciated boys panning for the teeth of the dead.

It's overwhelming, this amalgamation of life and death, of beauty and filth. I'm used to contrasts being compartmentalized. A nice part of town is clean, with quaint cafés and storefronts. Bad areas contain graffiti and concrete, sleeping crowds of the homeless, stores selling cheap clothing and tacky home décor. Our personal lives are similarly divided, friends from family, birth from death, work from play. We visit our dead in cemeteries and wash our clothes in a machine. We have no concept of a single entity being used for everything, and a dangerously contaminated entity at that.

The Bagmati is the heart and soul of Kathmandu, a living embodiment of the city. It is where you drink, die, cleanse your body and the garments covering it, purify your soul. They say the river is mythological, that it flowed directly from Shiva, the god responsible for rebirth and destruction, but I think it is more

*than myth that makes this river holy. Its waters contain thousands of whispered
prayers, rippling on the surface are the hopes and fears and joys and calamities of
a nation. Perhaps part of what makes this river holy is its intimate knowledge of
the country's inhabitants and the unity that it creates among them.*

"Swimming Pool of Monkey."

Everything at Swayambhunath is of monkey. The oldest Buddhist
temple outside of Tibet sits atop a hill in a suburb of Kathmandu, where
its stone pool is alive with chattering little fawn-colored rhesus macaques.
They trundle and spring all over the three hundred and sixty-five diz-
zyingly steep stairs, squawking and scratching their hairy little behinds,
snatching food from the hands of angry Nepalese and amused tourists;
then the little rascals eat it right in front of them.

Mia's way up ahead of me. *I'm* not about to use the shiny handrail to
aid my ascent to the temple. Because the other thing the little primates
do is polish the rail to a sheen by sliding down it on their butts. Cute,
but *yech*.

I finally reach a terrace packed with human-height statues of their
gods of air, of fire, water, sky. It feels as if I'm walking on a life-size
chessboard with little monkeys eating tidbits off the heads of knights and
queens. On the ground between them, Nepalese men and their sons light
small devotional fires that we carefully skirt.

The rest of the platform is dense with temples and guesthouses where
pilgrims file in and out. It's also a hangout for teens. Roving three- and
four-year-olds beg, alone and tattered. The biggest group here are mothers and grandmothers, all holding children, moving in a slow, brightly
colored mass toward the temple of the Hindu goddess Hariti.

It's a two-story gilded pagoda-style shrine lined with butter lamps,
where they've come to ask for protection for their children from disease.
They believe that Hariti was once a mortal who sucked the life out of
other people's children to feed her own (well, she *did* have a few hundred
of them). Upon the pleas of grieving parents, Buddha stole her favorite
daughter and hid her in a bowl. When Hariti came sobbing to him for

help, he gave her a lesson in compassion and made her a goddess on the promise she'd stop. She saw the error of her ways and became forevermore the protectress of children.

Mia wanders off to check out the little tourist shops while I observe the women. Mothers and children don't yet have the pull on Mia they do on me. Mothers focus on the world differently. We're drawn to each other no matter where we are, even complete strangers. We trade stories, advice, exchange smiles as we admire each other's children, a silent acknowledgment between members of a tribe.

There's not much easy banter here. There's an almost worried intensity to many of them, even those of some means. Nearly all the children's eyes are heavily rimmed with black kohl, a custom to ward off evil. Seeing so many of them with orange streaks in their hair makes the kohl all the more heartbreaking. Orange-streaked hair here isn't a fashion statement; it's depigmentation from severe malnutrition.

Why not ring your baby's eyes black in hope of food and freedom from disease? Nothing else has worked for those on this rung of the ladder in Nepal. Every culture seems to have customs to ward off evil. Italians use the curved horn, and Eastern European Jews used to say insulting things to babies, such as "Oy, such an ugly girl!" to avoid tempting the devil. America's magic charms are private education, science camp, and SAT tutors to ward off our evil: personal failure.

Mothers are terrified of that which they can't control. In a country of wealth and choice like ours, we usually seek God only when agency has failed, when tragedy threatens or takes away our children. Nations of poverty and worship like Nepal are now seeking agency because God, and certainly their more earthly kings, have failed them.

Mothers seek anything that works. There's always an undercurrent of fear somewhere in a mother. We hope our children don't get sick, get hit by a car, go hungry, use drugs, get assaulted on the way to their dorm. It lessens only a little when they get older—*Call me when your plane lands. Don't walk in the parking garage alone at night. Did you get your mammogram?*

It occurs to me that one of the best ways of understanding the values of a nation is finding out what the mothers there are most afraid of. In Nepal it's easy to see—malnutrition, disease, lack of schooling. It's less obvious in the United States; homeless children remain largely unseen and beaten wives hide in plain sight. Having spoken to audiences across the country in some of the toniest areas really drove home for me how democratic this kind of hidden suffering is.

I've signed countless books for women in fine wool suits who tell me the only nights they're able to sleep are when their addicted adult daughters are in jail, where at least they won't be raped, die of overdose, or be killed in a drug deal gone wrong. Whenever we speak publicly, audience members, producers, makeup artists, cameramen, and security guards approach us to share about their own experience with sexual or substance abuse, or that of someone in their family. Many tell us they've never told anyone before.

No matter where you are or whom you're with, there's always another reality beneath what's visible; each of us carries countless wounds and worries inside of us. Our culture has had no shared practice to acknowledge this, like Hariti's temple or roadside shrines. We have no place for the public, shared experience of sorrow or fear, or of receiving succor and hope together, just as a matter of course in our everyday lives.

Till now, and it is women who've led the way—through blogs. Women dominate the blogosphere in general, mommy blogs in particular. It's no wonder they're so wildly popular. Motherhood is a whole new life, with a new language, new customs and complaints, new skills and sorrows, new pressures and joys. Having a zillion other moms available in real time, or close to it, every minute of the day or night has created a virtual Hariti's temple for Western mothers.

It's late afternoon and Mia and I are walking through the city's downtown, dense with fourteenth-century dwellings of dark red brick with second floors almost entirely of profusely carved wood window screens, balconies, and balustrades. A crazy quilt of small shops, hovels, shrines, and apartments has grown up around them, squeezed and stacked into whatever space was available over the centuries.

We're headed to Durbar Square to find several scavenges and see the historic heart of Kathmandu. We turn down a narrow, dusty street with deep sewage troughs running on each side. There's an occasional board lying across for those who don't want to jump.

The sidewalks are crowded with tables and blankets of salvaged items and limp vegetables for sale. Young men trudge with boxes the size of refrigerators on their backs, held on by nothing but straps on their fore-heads. Unrefrigerated meat is sold everywhere; dead chickens dangle upside down. Headless goats hang from hooks, draining blood onto the sidewalk; a few doors down their heads, in varying states of decay, are on sale.

Many tiny storefronts hold entire families in dim spaces with no elec-tricity and no candles to light as twilight falls. I cannot imagine how exhausting this kind of poverty must be.

The street continues to swell with Nepalese, mostly men, heading to the square. By the time we cross a bridge to Durbar Square, we're in a sea of people. There is a nervous energy to Nepal and it's not just the elec-tions, the potential for violence. It's hunger. Nepal feels her future at her fingertips. But they're not waiting for the government to help them ad-vance; most of the work of innovation and improvement in this country is being done by the citizens themselves. This is a nation with no boots pulling itself up by its bootstraps anyway.

In this regard Nepal feels very much like America to me. There is not the serenity despite circumstances one hears of in India or Southeast Asia, the seemingly peaceful acceptance of one's fate. The Nepalese are *not* accepting of a life they don't want and they're doing something about it, with great industry, pride, and brashness. It's the first country I've seen signs posted in English and the native tongue: PRESERVE OUR DIGNITY. DO NOT BEG.

"I just realized why it's getting so crowded," Mia says softly. "It beats sitting at home in the dark."

"I just realized we only have one phone," I respond. "Don't go wandering off; it'll be pitch-black in about twenty minutes."

Durbar Square is actually several connected squares packed with temples, statues, and shrines going back to the twelfth century, along with the king's former digs, now a museum with an entrance controlled by soldiers with machine guns, another reminder of the wary truce here. A lone white nineteenth-century British colonial-style building stands out. Durbar used to be a hippie hangout in the sixties; there are still head shops doing brisk business.

The squares are jammed with Nepalese, a few tourists, and, in the only clear spot, a lone cow sitting, pleased as punch. Women sit behind mounds of golden mums and dahlias on sale for offerings. The Nepalese lean against their Buddhas and gods here, groups of teens congregate on the platforms of their holiest shrines. In Nepal there is no separation between the people and their art, religion, and history.

There's even a goddess living in the plaza ahead of us: Kumari, a prepubescent girl the Nepalese worship as the living embodiment of the supreme goddess. Once she gets her period, her reign ends and she goes back to her family, usually, and not surprisingly, rather maladjusted and unequipped for life as a commoner. Another is chosen through a selection process that includes having thirty-two qualities, including the chest of a lion, the eyelashes of a cow, small and well-recessed sexual organs, a set of twenty teeth, and thighs like a deer.

It would be easy to judge or mock this tradition until you look at what we subject our own prepubescent girls to. And we don't just expect little girls to have "small and well-recessed sexual organs"; thanks to online porn, grown women in the West are often expected to be as hairless and recessed as little girls.

We've come too late to see everything we'd like, so we turn to head back, or try to. The crowd has grown suffocating; we have to shove and elbow to move. I'm at the head of a crowd of people going toward a tunnel at the same time, pressed into me on all sides. This much humanity doesn't seem to move so much as *vibrate*. As soon as I reach the vaulted tunnel leading out of the square to our way back, the sun disappears entirely.

A few feet into the blackness, a giant new shiny black Land Rover starts driving slowly in, filling the tunnel as it heads toward us.

"Mother, back up!" Mia calls behind me.

I can't; we're all packed in like sardines. The headlights angle into my eyes. I freeze as it advances, pulling a few inches to the left as the crowd, apparently used to this, shifts right. The Nepalese are small. I am not. I actually have to plaster myself against the wall and *duck* beneath the car's side-view mirror as it passes.

I push my way toward the pool of light on the bridge I recognize. "We should have left earlier!" I call back to Mia.

No answer. I twist back. "Mia?" It's too black to see anything. I call her name again as people bash into me on all sides. "Mia!" No response and nothing but blackness.

I turn and quickly shove the last few feet to the bridge. There's a small mound of bricks in a pool of light. My heart starts pounding as I climb up and turn around. Pretty young women do disappear in foreign countries and this part of the world is full of human trafficking, but I know I'm getting worried out of proportion to reality.

I keep calling her name. There are thousands of people around us and it's almost pitch-black. It's a long fall off the bridge and a short fall into a sewer. It's a huge city and we're a couple of miles from the hotel where we're to meet our teammates for dinner. And, stupidly, I have all the money and the phone.

"Mia!"

My jaw starts to clench, my armpits prickle, my mouth is going dry. I'm starting to get the same mushy stomach feeling I got when we were canvassing a bad neighborhood for signatures a few years ago and she disappeared between two houses for a few seconds, long enough for my lizard brain to kick in. The part of me that still remembers how it felt when she was missing as a teen, either literally or figuratively. I try to calm my breathing. I had no idea the residue of our history could stay so long in my body.

Mia's voice rings out, "Mother!" and she suddenly rushes into the light below me. I'm so relieved my knees feel soft. "Why didn't you follow me?" I snap and I'm immediately sorry.

"The car was there! Who told you to keep going without me? Stop yelling and let's go," she says sharply.

Her anger surprises me, but I'm too shaken to respond. We hold hands and don't say anything else as we retrace our steps through near-blackness through the river of humanity. Twice we almost tumble into the sewage ditch; we trip over people's wares on the ground. We pass a circus of sights popping out of the darkness: a boy under a hanging light-bulb in a tiny blue barbershop cutting an old man's hair; a man stitching by candlelight; a young man standing on another's shoulders in a sea of boxes; the red glint of a goat's eyes; a teenage boy's T-shirt that reads BOOBIES MAKE ME SMILE!

We finally reach the big main paved street, which is patchily lit. It's a slow-moving mass of vehicles bordered by bikes. My backpack strap hooks onto someone's handlebars. I'm yanked along as I try to wrestle myself free. I needn't bother; the rider actually *shoves* me free. Mia grabs my hand to balance me as we skirt a blanket full of old shriveled limes and finally make it to a store display window with three feet of open space.

Smack! Something like a rock hits my calf. I stop as another slams into my rib, *hard*. Those petrified ancient limes. The adults around the blanket are snickering. Mia and I exchange a surprised look.

I grab Mia's arm and hurry us both on. "Let's go before they throw something bigger," I mutter, disgusted and furious. Those weren't kids. It was adults that threw them. For no reason. And right now I want to throw them back.

I hate this feeling. Fury in others is scary enough to me; in myself, it feels sickening.

"That was like Cirque du Soleil in hell." I throw my pack on the hotel room floor.

"I'll take a quick shower and then run you a hot bubble bath," Mia offers. "You still look like a deer in headlights." She peels off her damp clothes as she heads for the bathroom.

I flop onto our bed and pull up my shirt. A bruise. I'm sweaty, my feet are filthy from the streets, the rotten meat smell seems to have lined my nostrils, and my head is still ringing from the noise. I reach for a pillow and the softness of it against my skin instantly almost makes me cry. Fragrance, softness, and cleanliness are suddenly, fabulously, *ridiculously* wonderful. I listen to Mia's shower, notice my folded laundry.

I like to think I don't take much for granted in life. I look around and realize that we take almost *everything* for granted. We have no *idea* how much. Oh, yes, we all appreciate our good fortune in having food, freedom, family, good health.

I look at our room and see treasures beyond the imagining of half the people in the world. Books, pillows, candy, a mirror, a camera, contact lenses, shoes, freedom from parasites, *electric lights and clean underwear,* for God's sake. I can refuse a meal simply because I don't like the taste, take a hot bath, have quiet—or entertainment—every single time I want them, and stop them when I don't. I can control the number of people I'm with, read past sundown. Leave, I can leave. Or come. I can *decide.*

"I'll never complain about my house again," I murmur.

It's cliché, we all know it in our heads, but tonight I get it in my body, my senses. It's as if the contrasts of Nepal have seeped into me: the comingling scents of fresh sheets and rotten meat, the luxury and silence of the room and the honking far below, relief for my daughter's safety and nerves still taut from that awful moment of fear.

I could not have imagined that that degree of fear could remain in one's cells so long, so pure in its remembrance! What a perfect predator fear is, all the more ruthless and clever for knowing all the soft spots, the thin scabs. What better camouflage for the memory than the body? Especially a mother's body.

So much of motherhood is tied up in our bodies. Long past pregnancy and nursing, we feel our motherhood viscerally. We wear the medals of pregnancy forever: varicose veins, C-section scars, our softer breasts and bellies. Our bodies respond to our children with a degree of courage, fear, joy, anger, or pain that only they can elicit, no matter how old they are.

My body's ability to mock time, and my own will, worries me; I don't want my memory swinging a baseball bat at me out of the blue; or affecting how I am with Mia. I have to think these subterranean sense memories have unconsciously colored my relationship with her.

I'm glad it was dark and she was far enough behind me that she couldn't see it. The main reason we're here is to see each other anew, beyond our history.

Fold-up seats on an airplane are cute at an air and space museum. Less so when you're boarding a thimble-size jet about to fly you over the jagged Himalayan Mountains to Chitwan National Park, a protected Nepalese park near the Indian border. By an air carrier that goes by the name Yeti Air, no less. Why the Nepalese chose to name their sole airline after a large, hairy, man-like creature (who, according to folklore, is quite fond of the bottle), I have no idea, but it's hardly comforting, like traveling on the Werewolf Express.

Two hours later, we've traded one iffy form of transportation for another: the back of an elephant. I assumed that riding an elephant would be akin to riding a very, very big horse but there's nothing remotely horse-like about sitting in a raja-style carrier atop the world's largest land animal. No mane to grab, no reins, and certainly no five-foot fall to the ground should something go wrong.

We're loaded onto the elephants in pairs, along with a scout standing atop Sandra the elephant's rump and a driver sitting behind her head. His sole means of steering this two-ton beast is a small stick, and his feet, which are tucked into the space behind the elephant's ears to tap her in the direction he wants her to go. My mom and I lean our backs against each other to create a mutual backrest and clasp the sides of our bassinet as Sandra lumbers across a shallow, muddy river. My mom, of course, is wearing a formidably large hat with the strap tied snug beneath her chin so that she has to tilt her head and squint in order to see anything.

Within minutes we're swallowed up in thick jungle. The dense tangle of brown, olive, beige, and black filters the incoming sunlight to a hazy glow beneath the foliage. There's a feeling of struggle in the jungle; vines cling to clusters of vegetation, weeds entangle themselves with shrubs, moss creeps along tree trunks. One form of life covers another in a slow race for light and air.

A firm swish of Sandra's trunk pulls aside a final curtain of moss and we emerge into a bright expanse of sweeping grasslands beneath a cloudless sky. The other tourist-clad elephants amble into sight, parting grasses tall enough to tickle our dangling legs.

We pass several rhinos that are so ugly they're actually cute. Like the elephants', their hide is a tough gray-brown, cracked and dusty, but from certain angles they're almost dainty, with tiny round ears that wiggle and plates of skin that come together in scalloped folds like a petal skirt.

Besides rhinos and deer, tigers reside at Chitwan, but sightings are so rare that seeing one wasn't much on my radar until our guide's eyes widen and he starts shouting out rapid-fire Nepalese to the other guides. My mom and I lurch every which way as he whirls Sandra about-face, urges her forward several paces, then pulls her to an abrupt stop, turns her to the right, moves her forward, spins her to the left. The other elephants are turning in similar circles like a clumsy troupe of whirling ballerinas.

The elephants zero in on a large clump of marshy grasses, and though the elephants outnumber—and certainly outweigh—the hiding tiger, they're nervous, pawing the ground and trumpeting. They close in tighter and tighter until flecks of orange begin to appear and stripes suddenly materialize as he walks out into plain sight.

He's majestic, long and lean, pure muscle rippling beneath a glossy coat of stripes. A tiger's only natural enemy is an elephant, but he's not that intimidated. He's reluctant to leave his territory and stays, pacing back and forth in a fifty-foot radius, expressing his annoyance with a series of long, low grunts and growls. After about five minutes, he's had enough and saunters off, the stripes from his coat slowly becoming indistinguishable from the streaks of brown and green grasses.

After a moment of awe and quiet, we all break into a chorus of amazed comments, and our driver is grinning like a small boy even though he's been working here for years now.

"Always exciting," he says.

"How often do you see tigers here, is this common?" my mom asks.

"Not for two months now. But I think this tiger same one we see before. Maybe tiger not very smart," he laughs.

The herd separates and each elephant and its entourage take off in different directions. We settle into a contented silence, taking in the changing colors of the landscape as it turns from day to dusk, listening to the shushing of grass in the wind, and inhaling the cool, damp air. The setting sun radiates soft pinks and purples and the mist rolling in has blurred the outlines of trees and mountains, making it seem as though the grasses grow straight into the sky. The whole scene is one of muted beauty. We arrive at our tents and say very little to each other as we watch the sun sink behind the mountains.

How strange to think that barely two weeks ago I was squeezing my way into subway cars and shouting above music to friends at a party. Driving into camp today we passed young men and women who will likely never travel farther than their village. I wonder what they think when we pass them, if it puzzles them that we come from so far away to see what seems mundane to them, if it makes them angry or resentful, if they find us amusing or stupid.

How radically different their notion of "life" is from that of an American teenager texting friends about the latest song from an indie band in Iceland. For each, the other's life is almost impossible to fathom. Funny, I feel that way about my own life. How I lived ten years ago is so wildly different from how I live now that when I see old photos of myself, it's like looking at a strange girl in a foreign landscape. My life then feels more like a faraway dream than an actual memory.

Much of my life has been a dichotomy: a nightmarish childhood with my biological father versus a magical one with my mom and Paul, dropping out of high school and running away versus going to Georgetown. And within the last few years, speaking one day to audiences about abuse and addiction, then changing hats the next as a publicist raving about the hottest new diet book to magazine reviewers. I sometimes think if I were cracked open I would look like an archeological dig site, different layers containing remnants of different lives.

Before it became my default mode, compartmentalizing was a conscious choice I made; it was how I helped myself move forward. Coming home at seventeen, I immediately realized that I couldn't just talk openly; references to "the program" or "Czech Republic" were followed by dropped jaws, strange looks, or fifty questions. Then I'd really be in a pickle, because the honest reasons that I was there included running away, felony charges, and—the biggie—sexual abuse. I had no qualms about sharing any of this, but people's reactions tended toward pity, discomfort, or a fascination that made me feel like a circus act. So I opened up a drawer and tucked that period of my life away.

It also made it easier to adapt. The less I thought about "the program," the easier it was to stop saying "Excuse me" to everyone I walked by, asking for things in German (which we had to learn in the Czech Republic program; it enabled us to become bilingual, and it prohibited us from making run plans given our limited vocabulary), or panicking if I found myself alone with a guy (staff had to be present or we'd get in major trouble).

When it came time for me to transfer to a university college, I chose somewhere deliberately outside of my comfort zone. People often assume that comfort eases transitions, but in my case comfort spelled boredom and boredom often spelled disaster. So I went somewhere where no one had a background even remotely like mine, somewhere where people wore monogrammed blazers, rowed boats, and interned on the Hill. I went to Georgetown.

Being around people who compared internships rather than months sober gave me a totally new frame of reference. It kept me on my toes by forcing me to look forward and dream, rather than look back and reminisce. It also created a pattern of filing away the parts of myself that weren't relevant to my present surroundings.

Compartmentalizing contrasting facets of myself became my default drive; I filed the teenage Mia in a different drawer from the college Mia, who was in a separate location from the publicist Mia, who was miles away from the author Mia.

In a weird way, I almost feel like Nepal herself is nudging me to examine how I operate by showing me a completely different way to successfully exist; nothing is compartmentalized here. You can't take note of the art without notic-

ing the misery surrounding it. You can't look at people squatting in the streets or children digging through garbage without simultaneously seeing beautiful saris or intricate carvings on ancient buildings. Fragmentation is a first-world luxury that is physically impossible here; there is no rug under which to sweep ugliness and suffering.

It's a dangerous thing, to divide yourself, to break off bits of yourself until there's no solid core. We are, after all, just the sum of our total experiences, each one lying beneath us like a brick in the foundation of a house. To be selective, to block out portions, is to destabilize the very ground on which you stand. And, indeed, I'm just now acknowledging how disjointed I feel. No wonder I was furious with my mom for asking why I left my life; it struck a nerve with the part of me that knew I didn't just come for her. For a long time I've ignored the part of myself that knew I needed some serious time for reflection and examination.

Like a horse that didn't know it was cold until someone covered it with a blanket, this spreading calm and self-awareness is like an old friend long forgotten. I can't remember the last time I felt this peaceful. In acknowledging this feeling of wholeness, I'm also forced to acknowledge that while compartmentalizing myself once helped move me forward, I'm long past that point.

One of the few things I remember from high school science was that when we see white, we aren't seeing an actual color but the reflection of all visible light in the light spectrum. In other words, if even one color from the light spectrum was missing, we would never see the color white.

In cultures throughout the world, white is symbolic of purity and peace, and what is peace but a joining of contrasting or opposing forces? For me to find inner peace I must invite and embrace the extremes and contrasts of my life. Perhaps more than anything, it is this that I have learned from the Nepalese.

Men here have their saris, too. The van-taxi taking us back to Kathmandu is, like many, entirely painted with brilliant designs and scenes. They're feminine-looking and beautifully executed, like trucks in drag.

Some are simply a riot of brilliant swirls and patterns. Others feature deities: Shiva smiling in a forest; elephant-headed Ganesh amid a sea of aqua and purple paisley. There's the occasional Communist slogan, REVOLUTION IS MY NAME! One sports the goddess Kali, with her many arms and her long red tongue stuck out. She has Shiva pinned beneath her feet, several men's heads dangling from her belt, and the words ROAD KING! painted beside her.

Even the dashboards are festooned with garlands of flowers so thick that the men drive through a daisy-bordered world—with their pals. Most taxi drivers, including our driver, have a pal or three up front.

Which is all fine and well in town, but terrifying when they horse around and slap each other while the van is careening down a teensy, twisting, badly paved road with no guardrail, suspended over thousand-foot drops. Mia's been white-knuckling my forearm for miles.

More nerve-wracking is when he screeches to a stop to pick up a friend in the middle of the road—*hey, Kapil, what luck to find you walking at the base of a mountain out here in the middle of nowhere, hop in!* Trucks behind us swerve around and hit the horn, waves are exchanged, all while nearly killing us all. Then he turns the AC from his sweating passengers to him and his pals. Who are all wearing long sleeves and vests.

Mia's *this close* to being motion-sick when the driver pulls into a kind of rest stop with picnic tables in a small wooded strip between the road and mountain. Thank God, because after he's gone to the john and eaten lunch, he drives slowly enough to allow Mia to relax her grip and go to sleep.

Rural Nepal goes by in vignettes: families working in their gardens, little girls twirling their yellow skirts with their heads thrown back in front of colored wooden houses, four women in matching turquoise saris around a sewing machine on a peach-colored porch, brown thatch-roof huts, hovels dug into the mountainside. Little girls and boys in uniforms hurry along the road to schools with names like All Heavens Girls English School plunked in the crop fields. Little boys in rags walk in the ditch between the mountains and speeding cars, or along the top of a low wall a thousand feet above a river. Women bend to bathe and fill buckets with water from a spigot poking out of the mountain.

I'm in a state of bliss. Watching an unfamiliar landscape roll by, even for a few hours, with not a thought in my head, is more restorative for me than a week at a spa. It's one of the few things that return me to the quiet, childlike state of simply *being-in-the-worldness* that I crave, but have neglected to seek in the last few years. In the early years of our relationship, I'd sometimes ask Paul to just drive me along the water for an hour or two, no talking. Which suited him just fine; he's not a talker and loves to drive.

This *being-in-the-worldness* is more than a feeling of inner peace or stillness; it's where I am most fully myself *and* most fully in the world. My very being, beneath any doing or thinking. I had my very first experience, or awareness, of this when I was around five years old.

Our family was moving from the East Coast to California, and I was asleep with my mom and siblings in a private sleeper car on the Santa Fe Railroad. I was always awake before five A.M. (to my mother's *great* dismay) and knew I had time to tiptoe out, explore, and return before anyone else woke up. The day before, I'd wandered into the kitchen car, where a porter was having his coffee and boiling eggs. He made us both a soft-boiled egg and toast. I, being an outgoing and chatty five-year-old, showed him how my mother made us eggy-in-a-cup by tearing up the bread into little pieces to soak up the yolk, which no little kid is going to eat plain and runny. I then took his bread and made him one, too. He was chuckling the whole time about my taking over his kitchen, and in my pajamas no less.

But that morning I decided to poke my head under the blackout blind beside my bunk instead. It was still dark but a thin pale line was beginning to glow in the distance. As it began to widen and turn pink I noticed something new—that the world here was flat, utterly, which I'd never seen. There were no hills or stores or neighbors' houses, which are mountainous to a kid and gave my world endpoints. I wiggled myself completely under the blind and pulled my knees up to see, for the first

time, a world that didn't end anywhere. I can still remember the sound
in my head of my own breathing along with the soft *chiketa-chiketa* of the
rails and the feel of the window made cold and wet by my breath.

I sat there for what seemed like ages, thrilled and astonished to learn
that the world *went on forever!* I watched the sunrise blanket an endless
feathery prairie in pink and peach and felt the yellow warmth reach the
glass and make me squint.

And then I had a sudden feeling of *person-ness*, of my very existence.
And it felt very *big*, as big as the world itself. I had found a space between
me and the world that I knew even then that only *I* filled up. I stayed
there, aware of being *me* for the first time until everyone woke up, when
I crawled out and went back to being a happy kid on her way to a new
home.

I found I was never able to return to that place of calm, authentic
being-ness unless I was alone and either outdoors or looking outside. Silence and solitude are as necessary to me as air. It's where anything false
about me falls away and I'm only and ever my most essential self, as true
and powerful as we all are at our core.

Nepal has two types of street kids: children on *the street, and children* of *the
street. For children on the street, it's their workplace, where they sell various
wares or beg. They may be thin and dressed in threadbare clothing, they may
live in slum housing, but they are bright-eyed with clean hair and laundered
clothing, with families to go home to. These are the two little girls we saw our
first night in Thamel.*

For children of *the street, however, the street is both home and workplace.
These are children that have been orphaned, kicked out, or ran away to escape
various forms of abuse. They roam the streets in packs, looking almost feral
beneath matted and filthy hair, runny noses, grimy clothing and faces. Many of
them are addicted to sniffing glue, which keeps them warm in the winter and
dulls the hunger pains.*

Mainly, their eyes tell the difference. The Nepalese call these children kathe,
which means "naughty," "dirty," or "failure," and treat them as subhuman.

The emotional, physical, and sexual abuse they're subjected to by their peers, the police, and the general public breaks their spirit, makes them a shadow of who they could be. When a child has never known love, when no one cares if they live or die, their eyes are bottomless.

Fortunately, there is a man who cares if they live or die, who picks them up from the gutter, brushes them off, and showers them with unconditional love. His name is Rabin, and my mom and I are at the orphanage he runs for the kathe *children. What Rabin does gives these kids more than a second chance at life; what he does is see—and help them see in themselves—the magnificent people they are. And in this he reminds me of my mother.*

My mom saved me not once, when she bundled me in her arms and took me from my father's house, but twice, when as a teenager I needed to be taken from myself. When drugs made me unrecognizable, when I was emaciated and hateful with matted and dirty hair, when I woke up on mornings and didn't even see myself, she saw me. Really saw me. The me she knew since birth, the me she brought back.

Our most meaningful scavenge here is to work at an orphanage for at least four hours. We went first to one in the countryside, a model facility where the kids were in classes. The director there felt the greatest need was at an orphanage in town, the SOS Children's Village Jorpati, a less well-funded facility that serves emotionally, physically, and mentally disabled kids.

Rabin Nepali, the director at that facility, is a soft-spoken middle-aged man with a beautiful smile. His facility takes what he calls "the most needy among the needy kids. At Jorpati I can work not just with my head but with my heart."

His organization, SOS Villages, then does what they've found creates a success rate that would put our social services system to shame. They give them mothers—for life. They are no longer orphans, they are never up for adoption. They become part of a real family of kids with a mom who raises them as her own; they go to school, do chores, grow up. Those that are able go off to college or other training, some are given seed money for a business, those who need lifelong assistance go to group living homes. The mothers remain part of the community as grandmothers once their kids are grown; the kids return to visit the rest of their lives.

Jorpati is not in a good area, but once inside the walls of the facility, we find ourselves in a sweet courtyard of flowers and vegetables the kids here have cultivated. Rabin leads us into a cottage where several squirmy, excited children sit waiting for us with big smiles. Some are physically disabled, some emotionally challenged, and *all* are having a hard time sitting still. They are just so beautiful it's all I can do not to plop down next to them and take the littler ones into my lap. I speak very slowly to them as they're introduced, assuming they're still new to English.

"I . . . am . . . very . . . exci-ted . . . to . . . meet . . . all . . . of you!"

"They understand English," Rabin reminds me gently. "They're just shy to speak at first."

I glance at the faux-pas-a-meter otherwise known as Mia's face and realize I was doing what always makes me laugh when someone else does it—if you think someone doesn't understand your language, you speak s-l-o-w and loud.

The kids trail Rabin like ducklings as he takes us through the house to meet their mother, a stunning, petite Nepali woman around forty.

"How lucky you are to have so many beautiful children," I tell her.

"Yes," she says shyly, beaming with pride. She brings us to meet another child, a tiny little girl asleep in a wheelchair. We're surprised to learn she is thirteen. Rabin explains that she has a condition that prevents her from growing. He brushes some stray hair from her forehead as the kids flock around her, whispering. She's clearly much beloved.

When I ask if there's anything that can be done for her condition he tells us that no, this is simply how she is. I realize I just did that most American of things—assume that almost everything can be fixed.

Rabin leads us out to a porch where a few kids sit in chairs along the railing. He's trying to tell us their names but a spontaneous teenage boy who has difficulty speaking keeps interrupting him. Rabin alternates between trying to answer his questions and introducing us to the other children, no easy task.

The boy finally pops up, hugs Rabin tightly, and takes Rabin's face in his hands with such enthusiastic joy I'm half-afraid he'll hurt him. The boy begins to cry as he struggles to say something.

Rabin's eyes fill with tears as takes the boy's hands from his face and begins to kiss the palms with such humility and tenderness that for an exquisite moment time stands still.

Sometimes change comes violently, as it has here politically with the Maoists. But that kind of change comes at great cost and can vanish overnight. Lasting positive change comes for nations as it does with children—with *nurturance;* with caring and growing a nation's human resources and potential. Motherhood works. Not just biologically, as a force limited to women. Rabin is a shining example of motherhood as a concept, a way of being.

chapter five

Cairo

Never Ride a One-Humped Camel

*I*f you've never seen a Bollywood film before, rent one. Hunky actors sob while professing their love to blushing coquettes, cheesy song-and-dance routines abound, and the moment two characters lock eyes and realize they're in love, they're instantly transported to magical green hillsides.

Om Shanti Om, *a Bollywood film that actually parodies the genre, played on the plane to Cairo, and since I slept through it, my mom's reenacting it in our room at the Mena Hotel. I'm laughing so hard my face hurts as she sings and dances.*

"Your limbs are like flowers, so colorful," she croons to an invisible actress. "I want to be part of that color, my sweet!"

Apparently things didn't work out; her next move is to spin to me, wailing, "She left me, and broke my heart on the twenty-sixth of last month. Now I am a wanderer and a lover of disco. As I roam through Paris and San Francisco, my heart is alive with the pain of disco, pain of disco, pain of disco!"

And with that, she stag-leaps her way to the bathroom. When I manage to stop laughing, I sprawl out on the bed to see what Bill's served up on Egypt's scavenge menu.

My first impression of Cairo is of a city trying to camouflage itself; most buildings are made of sand-colored stone or painted in fading beiges and browns that blur into the desert surrounding it. The only colors that stand out were light blue or green doors and shutters, bleached pale by the unrelenting sun.

Cairo is a modern city but you still see much of what travelers would have centuries ago. Boys and young men in long robes and fez hats lead small donkeys harnessed to wooden carts laden with melons, tomatoes, or oranges. Men gathered around tables talk animatedly and smoke cigarettes or shisha. Streets are swept with palm fronds.

"Mia, do you have my mascara?" my mom calls, poking her head out of the bathroom as she towels off her wet hair.

I walk into the bathroom and comb through my toiletries container.

"Here." I hand it over. "I used it this morning, sorry."

"And my powder?"

I look back in the bag and fish that out, too.

"And that's my black shirt you're wearing, isn't it?" she says, exasperated. "I was going to wear that tomorrow. I brought one long skirt to wear in the mosques and that's the top I brought to match it. Mia, you know I don't mind you borrowing things but you've basically commandeered half of my wardrobe and toiletries—mainly because you didn't bring nearly what you should have," she adds pointedly.

"Sorry," I say, getting annoyed. "I was a little busy with a job and getting my place ready to sublet. Besides, you weren't even wearing the shirt. It was just sitting in your suitcase."

"Of course it was 'just sitting' there. It's an inanimate object, its job is to sit where I put it so I can find it when I want it. How many times do I have to tell you to ask me first? And when you do borrow something," she says, waving the mascara I borrowed at me, "put it back where you found it. My mascara goes in my makeup bag. Everything I buy isn't communal property, and neither am I for that matter—you've fallen asleep on me on literally every single plane or train we've ridden and not once did you ask if I minded."

She starts marching around the room collecting clothes of mine strewn everywhere, the floor included. I want to tell her to stop being so dramatic (Chicken Little, the sky's falling! Anything but an unmatching shirt!), but that might prompt her to fire off every offense I've ever committed.

"And stop," she says, *dramatically dropping my clothing on my suitcase, "making every hotel room a pigsty!"*

She gives a final look around the room, and, satisfied, plops down on the bed beside me.

"Okay, I got that out of my system," she says, smiling. *"Sorry, honey, but every hotel we've stayed in I've asked you nicely to keep it neat and I can't count how many times I've told you to tell me when you borrow something. It's aggravating, being dismissed. Chris says the same thing about her daughter. You guys get mad if we don't listen to you, but you think it's optional to listen to us."*

That's true—I do often only half-hear what she says. Sometimes foolishly, like when she told me to always pay more than the monthly minimum on student loans (I called her one day, shocked that after a year and a half of payments none of it had gone toward my principal). I think, in part, she gives so much advice and commentary because she knows I'll ignore some of it, but sometimes I feel like I have to ignore it or I'd go nuts. But she's right in that it's different to dismiss advice she's giving to me versus dismissing a request she's making of me.

"I didn't really think about it that way, but you're right, it's rude. Sorry, I'll try to be better about that, okay?"

"Thank you. If you want me to treat you like an adult or a friend, you have to act a little more like one and stop assuming I'll caretake you. I know you guys see moms as The Giving Tree, *but at some point you should outgrow the need to swing from my branches and sit on my stump!"*

We laugh. She's referring to Shel Silverstein's book about a tree who gives away every last part of herself to a little boy she loves.

"Or maybe at least water me from time to time," she adds, smiling. *"Now fold up my shirt, put on something else—preferably of yours—and let's go before the market closes."*

Never ride a one-humped camel if you can help it. And if, for some reason, like you're really stupid and shortsighted, you have to ride one in a *skirt*, just hook the chain from the lead camel's nose ring into your own nose and let him drag you across the hot sand. You'll still get where you're going and it'll hurt less.

I told myself not to feel guilty about the T-shirt. I'm always giving her the clothes off my back, off my hangers, out of my drawers. She'll often wear something out before I've even worn it once. But she's twenty-five, enough already.

I hate having "options." Picking out clothes is like having to pass a test every morning. So I buy multiples and keep colors to black, white, muted blues, and lilacs, boring but easy, and they work with my light green skin (some of us really are *olive;* in a certain light I look like Margaret Hamilton's Wicked Witch). And when I travel, I pack light. Twenty-five days around the world with a single carry-on means clothes are scheduled. And today was my skirt-and-shawl day for mosques.

I *forgot* about the camel ride. A mandatory scavenge is riding around the pyramids wearing the ridiculous-looking headgear we bought last night—a huge neon-blue chiffon square with baseball-size pompoms in Day-Glo colors attached all around.

We've hired a kind driver named Imam, who's just bought his own taxi and is pretty happy that his very first customers have hired him for two entire days. He speaks some English and he's a bit shy, but one camel joke (tick off another scavenge) and a few blocks later, he has us all laughing and is as chatty and affable as everyone else here. Egyptians are thus far among the warmest, most hospitable and humorous people I've encountered traveling.

Per the hotel's advice to avoid tourist-trap rides, Imam's taking us to his own camel connection to save us being fleeced and assure us the camels don't have fleas. He drives us through the narrow streets of a working-class neighborhood toward the pyramids.

A lot of life here seems to happen on the street, either at the side of the road or outside front doors where men are ironing, fixing tires, sewing, having tea, reading the paper.

We wait by giant cement-and-chain-link camel pens as Imam negotiates with three generations for a rate. A young boy with sea-green eyes that leap out of his dark complexion seems to be driving the hardest bargain. Grandpa finally waves his hand and I'm assigned a flirty gal with a pink bridle and multicolored necklaces; Mia chooses the horse.

"You can ride a horse anytime, Mia," I suggest.

"Not around the pyramids, I can't. Besides, I'm not getting on that beast. Those things look scary."

"Not as scary as we're gonna look once we tie these things on," I mutter as I tie the Bozo scarf on. This is where you really get just how much youth is its own kind of beauty. A pretty young woman can get away with wearing this. At fifty, you could get slapped for scaring babies.

"Oh, my God." Mia cringes when she sees me. "She's gonna toss you off just on principle."

Oh, pooh, I think, my Miss Camelia here is a little buttercup. She's got the cutest nostrils and enormous bedroom eyes heavy with lashes, and her velvety lips are pluppeting all over my shirt and arms. She's either kissing me, sniffing me, or preparing to eat me.

I notice the concrete wall between us and Cheops's former digs.

"How are we going to get there?" I ask the boy, who's attaching a chain to my camel's bridle. He just throws back his head and laughs, "Don't worry, kind madam!" As God is my witness, the camel throws back her head, stretches her floppy lips wide, and laughs right along with him.

I should have seen disaster coming.

As he beckons me to mount the camel, I notice something else: Mia's got a nice, smooth leather saddle. I have what looks like two humps with a few thick, coarse wool blankets in between. And my skirt is thin.

Oh, don't be a baby, Claire, just hike the skirt a few inches, nestle in between those humps, and follow her rhythm. The boy's father comes, picks up our chain, then hooks it to the ring in the lead camel's *nose*. I cringe and my hand flies to my nose in sympathy. My sympathies are about to lie elsewhere.

Old Camelia lumbers up slowly, groaning as if I weigh five hundred pounds, and suddenly lurches off after everyone else down the alley with a terrible racket. I'm thrown straight up in the air and then, *yowza!!* slam down not *between* her *two* humps, but on top of her *one* hump and whiz down in agony.

There's only *one* hump under the upholstery! And wool blankets my ass, it's a boar's pelt! My skirt's up to my waist and I'm getting a wedgie *and* a vaggie—this camel is going where no man has gone before.

Every trot and clop sends me shooting straight up in the air . . . then slamming back down. My arms flap and flail as I try to reach for the horns.

"Hey up there!" I try to yelp but it comes out like *hay-yay-yaayy yuh-uh-pp-pp ththth—he-el-el-p-p!!* and all the clattering drowns me out anyway.

Suddenly a bolt of inspiration, yoga, and irony strikes—Camel pose! I grab the horn behind me with both hands and pelvic-tilt my rear up—yes! Ohhhh relief, relief!

Except my arms are only going to hold out so long and I look like I'm trying to give "offering myself up to God" a whole new meaning, on top of a camel. In a Muslim country.

But, look, just ahead, the sand! Yes! Sand is soft! One more alley to go! Ohhh, yes! Camelia's front hooves plunge into the hot white sand . . . and "Whooooooaaaa . . ." off I go to the left . . .

"Oooh noooo . . ." Then my torso swings waaaay over to the right. "Whoooooaaah . . ." Then oooover to the left, then I flop forward and swing right again.

She's like a drunken bucking bronco, pitching me back, forth, and sideways in slow motion, burnishing my inner thighs to a brilliant crimson sheen.

"Stoooop!! This is awful! Stoop! I want to get dooooown!"

Mia trots up beside me. "Mom, are you okay?"

"Hell no, I'm not okay!! Where have you been?! I came to *see* the pyramids, not ride one! Send that kid over!!"

The kid bounds over and trots alongside to offer a cold drink and get a better look at my naked thighs.

"Don't worry, kind madam! We take break soon! You can buy cold drink for refresh you!" he says as he ogles me.

His dad hurries over and yanks my skirt down angrily as we continue the march of death. The skirt slides up. He yanks it down. It slides up. He yanks it down.

"Can I get down, pleeease?" I whine miserably. "It'll solve both our problems!"

If I had half a brain, I'd hold the skirt *up*, that would make him stop. But, of course, if I had half a brain, Mia would be wearing this T-shirt and I'd be in pants, on a horse.

I can't decide which is more memorable: seeing the last remaining of the Seven Wonders of the World or seeing my mom bounce around it.

I feel horrible, because (a) it must hurt like hell, and (b) I can't stop laughing. She's holding her hat in place with one hand, holding on to the camel for dear life with the other, and yelping every time it lurches forward. She knows how absurd the whole thing is and is alternately laughing, wincing, and getting mad at me for laughing.

She'll never admit it, but this is so quintessentially her. My mom's a mixture of Queen Elizabeth and Lucille Ball; sometimes she's regal and cold and proper and other times she's, well . . . not. This week it's riding a camel in a skirt; last week it was drinking from a washbowl.

Our second day in China we ate at the Red Rose Restaurant, a Muslim restaurant that was one of our food scavenges. Because the menu didn't have English translations, we had no idea what to order, so we typed "soup" into our electronic translator and showed it to our waitress.

Ten minutes later, we found ourselves staring into an enormous bowl filled with a pale orange goo. It didn't taste bad, almost like watered-down Jell-O, but I had no idea what it was, a scary thought in China. Thankfully, we recognized the next dish the waitress brought, a plate of wontons, and behind her a young busboy carried a ceramic washbowl with steaming hot water and thinly sliced lemons. He placed it on the table, but before I had time to dip my fingers, my mom plopped three wontons into it. She broke one in half with her spoon, scooped it up along with some liquid, and ate it, followed by several more mouthfuls of water.

"Mom!" I whispered, mortified and noticing the busboy's bewilderment. "What are—"

"I guess it's a do-it-yourself kind of soup," she said, chewing thoughtfully.

"It's on the bland side, though. They really should have flavored it; this just tastes like lemony water."

"That's because it is lemony water, genius! It's a Muslim restaurant. That's the washbowl!"

My mom stopped midchew, looked down at the soup, and then back up to me. She swallowed hard. And then we heard a snort. The busboy was clearly puzzled when she dropped the wontons into the washbowl but he didn't say anything. Maybe he thought she was cleansing them, too. But once she started spooning water into her mouth, he lost it, and tore out of the restaurant. Two seconds later, he ran past the window and down the block, holding his sides laughing.

If he could only see her now. I kick my horse to trot on ahead because, well, somebody *should* photograph the pyramids.

The pyramids rise from the desert, giant, pale gold structures silhouetted against a cornflower-blue sky. What's really amazing is that as majestic as Giza is today, it's almost drab compared to how it once was. Originally, the sandy pyramids were encased in polished white limestone and capped with a huge, pure gold top that gleamed, literally, for miles.

Even eroded they're near perfect; the base has a mean error of fifteen millimeters and is only twelve seconds off in angle from being a perfect square. My apartment building in New York, built on a level, paved street just in the last century, is infinitely more crooked. This stunning perfection is the reason large groups of people credit aliens for constructing the pyramids. Nothing against alien-theorists, but the actual explanation is that, contrary to Hollywood lore, the pyramids weren't built just by slave gangs but by specialists eager to be a part of such a prestigious project.

My horse picks up the pace as we near the Sphinx, and my guide suddenly pulls his horse up beside me and smiles slyly.

"I see you know to ride the horses?"

"Yes."

"You like we go fast then?"

I should give a definitive "no," given that I haven't ridden fast, slow, or anything in between in a few years, but I can't help picturing the scene from my *childhood obsession,* The Black Stallion, *in which Alec finally gains the trust of a wild black stallion and rides him bareback on the beach, whooping with delight as they race through the sand.*

So what if my horse is a dull brown instead of a shining black? So what if instead of a deserted beach I'm at a tourist haven with my yelping mother in tow? I'm being offered the chance to gallop through the desert!

"Yes!"

He says something in Arabic and, whoosh, we're off! The sand is flying from my horse's hooves, my hair is whipping in the wind, it's just like I always thought it would be!

Then he grabs my horse's halter and pulls us to a dead stop.

"Okay, you like?" he smiles, out of breath.

"Yes, very much! Why did we stop?"

"Just ten dollars and we keep going," he says, smiling.

"May I be in your picture?"

We're in the Mohammed Ali mosque atop the Citadel, a fortress built into a limestone outcrop in the twelfth century during Saladin's successful campaign against the Crusaders. Over the centuries, palaces, mosques, museums, military and government buildings were added to the fortress, which is now one of Cairo's biggest tourist draws.

The mosque's interior is enormous, jammed with tourists and the faithful; its soaring domes are filled with chandeliers and thousands of tiny lights illuminating the gilded neo-baroque designs and high-relief carvings.

We made the trek up here around the massive walls at the bottom of the fortress, with me in extreme bow-legged discomfort, through crowds of schoolkids who were warm, bold, and joyful.

Girls of all ages circled round us for photographs, with their cameras and ours, chattering nonstop: "You are American! Hello!" "We are so happy you are here!" "Do you speak Arabic?" "Hello hi my name is Luli!" "What's your name?" "Welcome to Cairo!"

There isn't any teen attitude anywhere we've been. The young here, even teenage boys, are sweet and deferential to me out of respect for my age, which you often don't see in the United States. Being seen as "old" in a way I'm not used to has been interesting. Once you're past turning heads as a woman in the United States, there are no societal advantages to being an older woman other than those we decide on ourselves—feeling wiser, more confident, empowered. It seems a worthy goal to find a happy medium between multiple wives and the invisibility of women over fifty in the West.

I'm about to take Mia's photograph in the mosque when a beautiful woman about my age, in a chic suit, asks if she can be in my photo of Mia, which isn't typical.

"Of course!" Mia tells her, holding her arm out to join her.

Not much else about her turns out to be typical. Bayan's features are strong, with wide cheekbones, downturned green eyes, and olive skin framed by very thick black hair. She has a wistful, almost sad, expression and seems both curious and wary. A trained architect, as minister of construction and development, she's one of the few women in the new Iraqi government. Her close friend, a tall, heavyset woman in traditional Muslim dress, doesn't stray more than a few feet from her at any time.

A few moments and photographs later, we begin one of the most compelling and treasured conversations I've ever had. This is an unusual trip for Bayan, who normally has *a hundred and fifty* bodyguards. Seeing how watchful and protective her friend is, I'm thinking there may be more than a slip under her loose chador.

While her friend is more vocal about how we botched the war, Bayan is more measured. She agrees (who doesn't?) that the lack of postwar planning has had terrible consequences, but as a Kurd, she's grateful for Hussein's demise and that, with American dollars, she was able to build three hundred and twenty-two new schools in the last year alone.

"Once you leave, there will be very little money for me to continue to build schools or infrastructure. The money will keep coming, I just won't see it."

We discuss politics, food, fashion, our lives as mothers and as women who want to see change in our own countries and in the world. We talk about where we've traveled, life in Kabul and Baghdad before and after the war.

I cannot imagine a group of men from such different backgrounds discussing their lives in a way that included all aspects of it. Women see their lives, and the world, much more ecologically, with political, social, cultural, familial, economic elements integrated and interconnected.

I believe we also see it much more protectively. Once your baby arrives, the world is no more the same than you are. Because from our very bodies we add to the collective human destiny. Our deepest urge is always toward life, to wholeness and well-being.

When asked if wars would still exist if women ran the world, Ellen Johnson Sirleaf, president of Liberia, said, "No, it would be a better, safer, and more productive world. A woman would bring an extra dimension to that task—and that's a sensitivity to humankind. It comes from being a mother."

A dear friend, Trish, said the same thing to me several years ago. We'd both sent our daughters to a school halfway around the world to save their lives, giving them up to get them back. Which gives one a whole new take on motherhood in general, and on oneself as a mother in particular. She left banking to found Starshine Academy, a K–12 school in Phoenix whose curriculum actually includes *hope;* there are actually classes that teach *peace.* Nations around the world are now asking her to create schools and curriculums. She's in Liberia right now, training their teachers. "It's the mothers who are going to save this world, Claire. That's what you should write about," she urged me. "This is what we should be teaching our daughters."

I believe there's something else we bring to the table, in addition to nurturance. We have a peerless ability to endure—we're tenacious and determined. Who's unstoppable if not a mother? Imagine what a nation of us can do.

Alexandria feels like a fossil. Only the faintest of imprints remain of what was once a thriving city in the ancient world, crumbling amphitheaters never restored, toppled columns lying on the sandy ground, ruins that, if they were unmarked, you'd walk right by. Still, it's thrilling to be here, because as a former classics major, I can fill in the blanks in my mind's eye.

Alexandria, founded in 331 B.C., was the brainchild of Alexander the Great, but Cleopatra, the brilliant and sexy ruler who lassoed Julius Caesar and Mark Antony, was the one who turned Alexandria into a city that rivaled Rome. It was here that Euclid developed geometry, Aristarchus realized that the earth revolves around the sun, and Eratosthenes calculated the earth's circumference. Alexandria was also home of the Pharos, a legendary lighthouse that was one of the Seven Wonders of the Ancient World.

But the library that Alexandria was so renowned for and its 700,000-plus volumes were burned to the ground in 48 B.C. During the fourth century A.D. war, famine, and disease initiated a slow but sure decline, and the lighthouse toppled in 1303 A.D. after a violent earthquake. Over time, almost all of Alexandria's monuments were destroyed by wars or earthquakes.

We pass a few hours wandering around the ruins before leaving the historic inland to head for the shore. As we do, each block gets brighter and brighter, the buildings changing from caramels and honeys to shades of peach and honeydew.

A burst of intense aquamarine signals we've reached the Mediterranean Sea. Wind whips the leaves of palm trees every which way and the water breaks roughly along the walls of the Corniche, the paved walkway running parallel to the shore. Multicolored fishing boats bob along the water, and far in the distance you can see Alexandria's magnificent new library peeking above the buildings. After Imam parks the car, my mom and I walk to the edge of the Corniche's walls and rest on our elbows, looking at seagulls swooping into the water, inhaling the crisp, salty air.

A large group of schoolchildren, perhaps here on a field trip, wave as they skip by and laugh when we wave back. Four girls walk up to us, giggling and smiling brightly as they ask for our names and if we'll take their picture. These girls are so cute, and we spend several minutes chatting with them and comparing the seashells we've each bought.

Yesterday in the mosque, before we met Bayan, I wandered off on the pre-

tense of exploring so I could have a moment alone. Since arriving in Cairo, we've been met everywhere by smiling young girls, holding hands, linking arms, singing, chattering. It's been a delight to see them at every turn, but it's been difficult as well.

It surprised me, that sudden feeling of sadness and longing. I've dealt with being sexually abused as a child but that doesn't mean I never have issues come up around it; I still have triggers, movie scenes that bother me disproportionately, times when I'm inexplicably scared or randomly get that sick, frozen feeling that something bad is about to happen.

Mostly, it saddens me that I never felt completely safe growing up, that in the back of my head I knew of the potential for human cruelty and felt like there was something wrong with me at an age when most kids think they can conquer the world.

Yesterday it was all around me. Those luminous eyes that followed us wherever we went were beautiful reminders of a painful truth: I've always lived with some degree of fear and sadness. But I must have gotten that out of my system yesterday because today I'm genuinely loving being with these girls.

This is still a newer skill for me: acknowledging and letting myself feel my feelings. It took me a while to realize that the more I let myself sink into whatever's coming up, the sooner it dissipates. This is true in general, but for me it's been especially true for anything abuse-related, where I tended to trivialize and minimize.

Once I turned eight, I lost my most intense memories of the abuse, but I've always remembered remembering, the way someone with amnesia might have a déjà vu–like awareness of something, without a concrete memory. Which can make you feel crazy. I was embarrassed and aggravated to be so affected by something I barely remembered, and I thought people would tell me I was being overdramatic or to just get over it.

It really wasn't until a few years ago that I fully stopped doing this. One, writing Come Back *put me in touch with thousands of readers, scores of whom also didn't remember the events themselves but had the same long-term feelings and behaviors. Two, through speaking engagements I was lucky enough to meet neuroscientists and child-development experts, and a huge lightbulb moment for me was learning that childhood trauma (especially when it happens before*

*you learn to speak) literally changes the structure of your brain so that, physi-
ologically, you often react to events the way a traumatized child would.*

*And three, I started spending long periods of time with young children for
the first time. As an only child who never babysat, I'd rarely interacted with
two- and three-year-olds, but about a year ago I befriended a family in Brooklyn, and spending time with their two toddlers was eye-opening. I saw just
how developmentally critical an age it is; they're little people that soak up and
interpret absolutely everything around them as they unconsciously form a view
of the world. No wonder experiencing all of that through a layer of fear and
pain alters you long-term. Imagining one of them being abused made me see my
own history very differently.*

*Maybe I shouldn't need neuroscience or other people's stories to validate my
feelings, but it's helped me nonetheless. If anything, being with these girls in
Alexandria and seeing their excitement and enthusiasm for life makes me a
little nostalgic.*

*They remind me of myself, not when I was their age but when I was eigh-
teen. My first year home was mostly forward-moving but it was still rocky at
times; I was aware I could still go back to the way I was. But by the time I left
for college, that fear had left me completely, and every day I woke up feeling
much the way I imagine a child does: free and powerful and completely confident in myself and my abilities. I felt wise and childlike, a combination that left
me feeling on top of the world.*

*Most people assume you learn about the world by losing your innocence.
For those of us who lost our innocence very young, we come of age in reverse,
becoming wiser as we become* less *jaded. Some of us have to grow down to truly
grow up.*

Cairo's historic Mena Hotel is set amid jasmine-scented grounds in the
shadow of the Great Pyramid. With its Victorian maze of marbled,
scrolled, and gilded passages, it is a stark contrast to the bracing bright
feel of Alexandria. Today, with the sun and scent of the sea still with
us, and some time before visiting the ancient Coptic area of Cairo, Mia
and I meander through the nooks and crannies on the ground floor,

where plush velvet seats in golds and reds beckon the weary at every turn. The nature and pace of the scavenger hunt has meant almost no time to relax and reflect with Mia, which is, of course, fine; we'll have a whole summer for that in France. Still, it's nice to have even thirty minutes of leisure with Mia right now.

We find a quiet corner where Mia twists her hair into a knot, secures it with a ballpoint pen, sinks into a love seat, and relaxes into what looks like nap position. She gives me a knowing look and says, "Don't worry," as I sit down beside her. How well she knows how well I know her.

"Mom, this was an absolutely fabulous day," she sighs. She swings her legs up onto my lap and smiles like a well-satisfied cat. "Alexandria reminded me of how much I miss history, college, writing papers. I'm glad I had no clue what I wanted to do the first three years; I took a lot of courses I probably wouldn't have otherwise. My only regret is not having taken more writing classes."

"Why, as far as writing professionally goes, I don't think it matters what you take. I never took lit courses and the one creative writing class I took, I hated."

"Why would you? You never planned on being an author."

"Oh, yes, I did."

"No, you didn't, you went to design school, then film school."

"Are you telling me my own life? I wanted to be an author the very second I knew there was such a thing, in first grade. I taught myself to read when I was four."

"I didn't know that."

I have no idea how I learned, but one morning when I was four, the words *Chinese Butterfly* came on after a cartoon and I knew exactly what they said. I can still see the words in my mind as clear as day, because even then I knew that it was *a very big deal*. I fell in love with words right then and there. Before long I was blitzing through the Golden Books and reading everything I could get my hands on.

"Obviously my comprehension was limited to words I knew the meaning of at that age, but yeah, I did. Sometimes I'd sneak up to the attic where it was nice and quiet and read the stacks of old newspapers up there."

Which made for a bewildering ride to a four-year-old: Negroes couldn't eat at lunch counters even when they wore nice suits, hats were called pillboxes, somebody was strangling Boston, and princesses didn't rule countries but did do a lot of skiing for some reason.

Kids have such literal minds; they're all members of the Flat Earth Society. It never occurred to me that anything I read in the papers was real, that there was any other world beyond what I could actually see. All the crazy stuff I was reading was just Golden Books for grown-ups.

Till that moment on the train, when I looked out on that prairie and had the miraculous realization that there was *a world*. An endless one, where a million other people like me were doing a million things in a million places beyond what I could see. Which meant that it was someplace you could go and march your actual self around in. Which I intended to do as soon as I was old enough. If those were *real* princesses in hot pink ski pants (with stirrups!) drinking *real* hot cocoa by a toasty fire right where Heidi of the Mountains grew up, I was so there. It was like God had revealed the secret of life to me. I read even more fanatically after that, preparing myself for The World.

Of course I still didn't have a full grasp on reality. I'd always assumed books were the same as anything else in the world, just *there*, like the trees or sky, like, you know, God made them up or something. The day I found out from Mrs. Webster in first grade that an *actual person* thought up the stories and then wrote them down, I was on a cloud for weeks. I just couldn't believe my luck. Because it meant that one day *I* could be one of those people.

"Why'd you wait so long to write?"

"Well . . . because I was fed the same twentieth-century canon you got, I had it in my head that there were only two kinds of writers: men who drank and whored, and genteel older women who wrote in country manors or big-city penthouses, like Virginia Woolf and Muriel Spark, which sounded just ducky to me."

"I can totally see you with Woolf's life, minus the suicide, of course. The clothes, the house, the subservient husband."

"Very funny. So when I got to my senior year of high school, here was my plan: I was gonna become a doctor and earn enough to retire wealthy in my forties, buy a house on the moors, and write novels. Shouldn't be too hard, I thought—I was a science and math geek."

"So why didn't you?"

"I started to. I registered for anatomy my senior year of high school. I got to class, the only girl in a sea of boys. A few boys had to stand in the back of the room. Mr. Di Antonio made me stand and explained that I had to give up my seat for a boy. Girls didn't become doctors, they had families—perhaps I'd enjoy typing class or shorthand?"

"What an asshole! What did you do?"

What I did was burst into tears on the spot and go to the principal, who supported the idiot. I was so devastated that I left school. With a four-point average. I waitressed, bought a better car, then went to live with a family in the most exclusive part of town so I could go to the high school that turned out more National Merit Scholars than almost any other school in the nation.

"Then I was stupid enough to pass on a scholarship to Emory to go to college at an expensive, mediocre party school because my then-boyfriend went there."

Her jaw drops. "You followed a guy? *You?*"

"Yeah, tell me about it. I hated that school. By then, I'd forgotten who I was, what my dreams were. It was about finding work, then finding a husband. I finally went to fashion design school because it was the one other thing I did well and that paid well. Then I met your old dad, had you, and the rest is history."

She sits processing all this a moment. "Okay, so here's what I'm *really* not getting now," she says. "I was going to find a nice quiet moment to ask you why the hell you haven't written anything in the last three years. Now that I know just how *much* you always wanted to be an author—I mean, *hello*??"

"Okay, fair question. As soon as we find another nice quiet moment you can ask it again. And don't swear."

My mom and I have been in Cairo's Coptic quarters for the last couple of hours popping in and out of mosques, churches, and one synagogue, but I've paid little attention. My mom's past life seems more alien and interesting to me now than any buildings.

I thought I understood my mom better than almost anyone, in part because she's often told me I did. Now I'm questioning that; never in a million years would I have thought she'd give up being a doctor or pick a college based on her boyfriend. She's so headstrong and independent that I assumed she'd always been that way. I wonder if she evolved past that self-doubt and insecurity (encouraging, because it means I'll probably grow out of mine), or if she still feels that way but hides it really well (utterly discouraging).

And, not to overanalyze things, but why is she telling me now? Is it because I'm older and she's not worried that I'll use her mistakes to justify my own, i.e., "You did X, Y, and Z, and turned out okay"? Or is she no longer closing herself off because she trusts me not to hurt her?

It's one thing for your mom to trust you while you're growing up, that pretty much revolves around her believing that you are where you say you are, and you'll come home when you say you will. It's something else entirely for her to trust you with herself, *the way any two friends learn to.*

And if I want the latter to occur, I need to honestly examine how I've treated her for the first time in a long time. Like most daughters, I've done things to her I'd never in a million years do to a friend, most notably when I insisted on bringing my college boyfriend, Graham, home with me for Christmas break, despite the fact that my mom was still mourning the death of her father, who'd passed away a few weeks earlier.

Lest I seem like a complete jerk, I should add that I'd never met my grandfather, nor had he been much of a presence in any of his kids' lives. My mom rarely spoke of him, so when she called to tell me that she was in West Virginia taking care of her dying father I was baffled. And when he passed away, I didn't expect her to grieve much for someone she'd hardly seen in several years, and whom she didn't seem that close to. If I had been more mature I would have understood that that gave her even more to grieve about; she wasn't just mourning the loss of what was, she was mourning the loss of what wasn't and now would never be.

In the absence of understanding her feelings I still should have respected them, and she was understandably angry with me for failing to do so. If my head hadn't been filled with passing my final exams and planning where to take Graham, my first real boyfriend, when he came to visit, I would have thought more about her. Hardly behavior that would make me want to befriend someone.

It was only several months later that I realized how incredibly selfish I'd been, but I was too ashamed to apologize to her. I was afraid to find out if she was still angry with me or if she harbored resentment, and it was easier to just move on, to do nice things for her or call her more often as a silent apology.

On the flip side, I've done things for her that I'd never do for a friend. I had the opportunity to study abroad at the American University in Cairo and when I called my mom, excited to tell her I'd been accepted for the spring semester, I was crushed that she didn't want me to go. It was only a year after 9/11, and as someone both American and Jewish, she didn't understand why out of every country available to study in, I insisted on a Middle Eastern one.

She never asked me outright to decline but I could hear the nervousness in her voice when we spoke. I initially had every intention of going, but I started to really think about what those months would be like for my mom—that, regardless of whether her fears were warranted or not, she'd worry every day. After all the sleepless nights I caused her as a runaway teen (and with Graham's untimely visit still fresh), I thought putting her wants before my own would be a nice gesture, both out of a sense of filial duty and also just as a kind thing to do for someone I cared about.

It's ironic that I'm thinking about this now, not just because Cairo is where I was supposed to study but because Egyptian families are often extremely close, and putting your mother's needs before your own is a given for many girls my age here. Would they have had an easier time, or made that same decision more quickly? And would they, too, have felt a slight resentment simmering, even though a bigger part of me was glad I did that for her?

Because of how primal the mother-daughter relationship seems, I've assumed it was more or less universal, driven by biology. And it's true, no matter the language or cultural barrier in a country, you can almost always recognize a mother and daughter based on gestures, mannerisms, a certain tone of voice. But the similarities often end there.

In traditional Egyptian households, for example, most girls are extremely close with their mothers; socializing outside your family is often frowned upon and a girl's mother is her primary source of information about education, relationships, child-rearing, and so on. To my grandmother and a lot of European cultures, however, it's considered strange to be or want to be best friends with your mother, even as an adult. And the question of duty, of what and how much we "owe" our parents, is one I find particularly troubling. My friend Yoomie, whose parents fled Vietnam and settled in Iowa, said that in Vietnamese families talking back to your parents is unheard of. And judging by the interaction between the Malaysian mother and daughter we saw, Vietnam is hardly alone in this.

The world is full of instructions and advice on how to mother, in bookstores, in academia, on the playgrounds, in the media. Mothers are always examining how they treat their children, but aside from the occasional "Don't talk to your mother that way," or "You shouldn't have listened to your mother," there's not much guidance out there for daughters. Obviously, you can't quite compare good mothering to good daughtering; as the person who bears and raises you, mothers have incomparable developmental and emotional impact. But while perhaps never equal, the playing field is certainly more level once you're an adult.

When you see something as a given, it's human nature not to question or examine it. Seeing the degree to which it varies from culture to culture has made me realize that it is not a given, and that our assumption that the mother-daughter dynamic is biological and universal gives us a get-out-of-jail-free card from accountably examining how we treat our mothers.

chapter six

Greece and the Balkans

Weight, Weight, Don't Tell Me!

Returning to the West after weeks in modest Muslim and Hindu countries feels like being around a teenage boy; everything is about sex. The moment I step foot in the Athens terminal I'm greeted by a poster of a nearly naked waif of a girl writhing in the sand with a well-oiled shirtless hunk. Then a woman walks by in five-inch stilettos with nipples threatening to pop out of a low-cut tank top, followed by another Jessica Rabbit–esque lady. I've never batted an eye at tight or revealing clothing before, so I have no idea why I suddenly want to drape my pashmina over their chests.

Outside the airport, billboards with women's bodies are as much a part of the scenery as the yellow wildflowers and cypress trees lining the highway. My favorite is of a woman wearing a fishnet body stocking, her checkered cheeks in full view as she hugs a long, cylindrical object. I can't read Greek but I'm assuming the text would clarify whether it's a vibrator, a man's electric hair trimmer, or a Jedi lightsaber.

While heavily polluted, Athens is greener than I expected, and the dry Mediterranean vegetation so common in this region spills out from the buildings and homes in the rocky hillsides. We won't be here long; we have four days to get from Athens to Bucharest, and eleven cities throughout Greece, Macedo-

nia, Bulgaria, and Romania to scavenge in between. Because it'll be such a
crazy leg, Bill's given us the afternoon off, and I want nothing more than to
relax in a hot bath.

The hotel bathroom is filled with gleaming marble and a glass shower door
directly across from a huge mirror. Perfect. The first hotel where I have to stare
at myself naked comes after days of pigging out in Cairo.

I take a few moments to study myself. My cheeks are sunburned and chub-
bier, I need to bleach my mustache and condition my hair. And then I spy the
scale. Knowing it's a bad idea even as I step on, I wince as the dial continues
ten pounds past where it normally reads. Ten pounds isn't the end of the world,
though being short and small-boned means it shows more. But rather than
fattening me up proportionally, incoming calories seem to have beelined to my
belly and thighs.

Argh! Why am I suddenly thinking about this?! A few sets of boobs, some
airbrushed models, and insecurity is already setting in? What's wrong with
me? I've just come from countries with malnourished children playing in streets
filled with sewage. Now feeling fat and ungrateful, I do my best to deep-breathe
my way to a more Zen-like place while soaking.

It halfway works, and by the time we leave I'm only mildly dispirited. I
perk up as my mom and I reach the Plaka, a charming historic quarter where
narrow streets and colorful buildings clump together beneath Athens's famed
Acropolis. We stroll down Adrianou Street, named after the Emperor Hadrian,
who ruled around 117 A.D. Hadrian was a peaceful emperor, a great patron
of the arts and a lover of Greek culture. He built libraries, theaters, and aque-
ducts, and he humanized the legal code and forbade torture. He also massacred
over half a million Jews; when Jewish documents mention Hadrian, his name
is followed by "may his bones be crushed."

"You know that's one of your best colors," my mom says, pointing to an aqua
shirt in a store window.

"Mom, that shirt could be poop-colored and you'd say the same thing. You
just want me to buy it so I'll stop borrowing yours!"

"Well, yes!" she says, laughing as she steers me inside. "But it'll also flatter
you."

That shirt, five pairs of pants, and several tops later, I feel like crying. The only thing that actually flatters me is cute but looks like a maternity top, and no amount of wriggling, writhing, and hopping up and down will make me fit into the jeans I'm trying on. My mom sweetly offers to buy me the maternity top—either out of pity or self-preservation; I'm not much fun when I'm cranky.

"Are you sure you want dessert, honey?" my mom whispers quietly as I order a piece of baklava.

I repeat my order to the confused waitress, and turn to glare at my mom once she walks away. "Yes, I'm sure I want dessert," I snap. "That's why I ordered it!"

"Well, it makes no sense, you were just complaining about your weight."

"I knew I should have kept my mouth shut," I mutter.

"Honey," she says, surprised I'm angry, "I'm just trying to be helpful. You were upset earlier, and I don't want you feeling bad about yourself."

"Well, you're not being helpful, you're just making me feel worse." Of course she's right but, hello, it's not like I don't know that baklava isn't the road to weight loss. Clearly, I don't want to do anything to lose weight now, but I still reserve the right to complain about it. I'll start working out when I'm home, and I don't need her watching my weight for me until then.

Half the reason I'm cranky isn't the weight gain, it's my reaction to it. I didn't realize it until walking into that bathroom earlier today, but being in countries where most of the time I literally wasn't able to compare my body to other women's meant I didn't feel physically insecure for two glorious weeks. Sure, I knew I'd put on a few pounds, but it didn't bother or preoccupy me, and I never felt a tug to weigh myself.

Now I feel like I've just run into the mean girl from high school you thought you'd forgotten about. It's unpleasant, coming back to airbrushed, anorexic, and implant-filled standards of beauty, but what bothers me most is how instantly, and almost unconsciously, I bought into it. It took all of one hour for that upset, frustrated, and depressed feeling to come flooding back, and strongly disliking part of myself, even if it's weight I can lose, feels crummy.

Typically, I think disparagingly about my body at least once a day, and I'm not unique. My girlfriends always lament problem areas, and I almost think it's a way that women bond. What's sad, too, is that when I see college photos of myself, I think I looked really great. Yet at the time I was so self-conscious, always trying to suck in or cover my tummy on the beach or in front of my boyfriend, always worried that my chest was too small. When I see those photos, I wish I had enjoyed and felt better about my body at the time. And even though my stomach is meatier and my thighs have some cellulite now, I wonder if in ten years I'll look at photos of me now and think the same thing.

Unrealistic standards of beauty are part of our daily visual culture, but maybe I could control my visual landscape more when I'm home, read different magazines, snap a rubber band around my wrist when I think something negative about a ridiculously attractive woman.

Terms like "the body temple" always made me roll my eyes, but when you think about all of the functions it performs, the human body is an amazing thing, and I like the idea of respecting and appreciating mine more. And doing it now, *unconditionally—not after losing ten pounds and toning.*

The road leaving Athens narrows and begins to twist into the mountains of central Greece, where the drier gray-greens of the south become a lusher blue-green. Our driver, Cristoforos, is a handsome, towering man who must smoke three packs a day; I'm not sure if Mia's asleep or passed out from the smell of his suit.

We drive through mountain villages where Easter is still in full swing for the third day. Families bundled against the mountain chill gather in parking lots and plazas where the mountain meets the road, laughing and drinking. Entire baby lambs roast on huge wooden spits, half-obscuring the road with so much smoke I'm afraid we're going to arrive at our destination with a new hood ornament. Hopefully well-done enough to eat, because Mia is going to wake up hungry.

One of our must-see scavenges is the site of a James Bond movie, the astonishing monastery-topped cliffs of Meteora. The pinnacles look as if Zeus thrust his mighty hands up from beneath the green hills, poking tall, slender fingers of dark shale and sandstone up to the heavens. The honey-colored stone buildings with clay-tile roofs on their peaks are charming and familiar, but like the Grand Canyon or Yosemite, the scale of the whole view is so unlike anything we usually behold that it's hard to take in.

In the fourteenth and fifteenth centuries, fearing the increasing incursions of the Turks, local monks decided to build monasteries and churches atop the cliffs, using winches and pulleys, which seems a feat as remarkable as the pyramids. Until someone finally built stone stairs in the 1920s, the only way up was a *long* rope ladder, or being hauled up in a net sack like a bucket up a well. If you weren't a believer at the bottom, you probably were when they reeled you in up there an hour later.

Mia's standing close to the edge of a cliff, which is scaring me silly, but the sight of her profile against the sky as she stares across miles of such breathtaking beauty is as thrilling to me as the cliffs. She's standing completely still, in happy reverence, with wisps of breath white from the cold escaping her smile. She returns to my side and we hold hands, taking in this beauty together without speaking. It's one of the most glorious moments of the trip.

It's not often mothers and daughters relate in silence. We speak our whole lives long in conversations reckless, tender, thoughtless, bold, honest, funny, hypersensitive, unconscious, cutting, healing. Our daughters hear us in utero long before they see us and we hear our mothers' voices long after they're gone. "I have conversations with my mom all the time," my friend Leah recently told me. "She's been dead twenty years and I still have things to say to her."

Macedonia has beautiful vineyards in the south and a faded but determined little capital, Skopje, with very friendly folks, but is otherwise memorable primarily for four things:

1. Borders still so hotly debated that our concierge in Athens nearly hit me for saying *Macedonia* instead of FYROM (Former-Yugoslav-Republic-of Macedonia). He waved his cigarette all over the place as he set me straight: "Was Alexander the Great *Yugoslaaaavian*?? NOOO!!"
2. Mother Teresa's birthplace.
3. An astonishing little church no one's heard of with more medieval bling than I've ever seen in one place.
4. Bojan.

Our Thessaloniki cabdriver agreed to drive us across the border to his connection, a guy in Skopje that, without a doubt, will be the taxi tsar of Eastern Europe before he's thirty. Bojan's a tall, chunky *Fyrom!*-ian, very hip and fluent in English right down to the slang. He juggles his running commentary with us with animated conversations on two ringing cell phones. It's very clear that he is *in command*—he's either scolding, ordering, soothing, schmoozing, or instructing. He is what Yiddishers would call a real *macher,* a *produ*-sah.

At one point, he takes a call and his voice goes sweet and reassuring. That had to be your mom, I say when he hangs up. Of course, he smiles, she wants to know when he'll be home for dinner. As in many countries outside the United States, even men usually live at home until they're married.

Bojan asks us what we want to see, nods, takes the TAXI light off the roof of his car, and hits the gas. An Ottoman bazaar, stone bridge, mosque, monastery, cheese pie, and Turkish weenie-on-a-stick later, we're heading eastward to Bulgaria, where one of Bojan's minions awaits us outside customs in yet another Mercedes taxi, "an extremely comfortable ride I assure you and the driver Borislav is one of my best, he knows how to take care of whatever needs taking care of," which in this part of Europe can come in very handy at border crossings and such.

Borislav is adorable. He's about forty, stocky, shy, with the cutest smile and dark eyes, reminding me more of a giant teddy bear, what with his knitted vest and all that real fur on his chest poking out of his collar.

"But does he speak any English?" I ask Bojan, under my breath.

"Not to worry, he understands everything! He's the perfect driver for you! I negotiated a very good rate!"—adding, "He canceled his other rides to pick you up."

Borislav smiles as if on cue. Small wonder. A good rate for Americans at the Bulgarian border late in the day—where there is no public transportation, no lodgings, and customs is processing a busload of fifty people in front of us at a snail's pace—is ridiculously exorbitant. I bargain outside the car with Bojan, but have no wedge whatsoever. He knows that I know that once it's dark out here in the boondocks, we'll be whatever's the Balkan equivalent of SOL.

A few minutes later Bojan's waving good-bye to us. So is the customs agent.

"They're not saying good-bye," I mutter to Mia. "They're all saying *Thanks, suckers!*"

"I'll take a *rakiya* and a *mastika,* please," I say to the bartender as I join Mia at our hotel's dim, smoky bar. Bill makes the traditional libations of each country a mandatory scavenge. Mia's face is bright red. That's one half of the team down.

Because we arrived so late at the hotel in Bulgaria's capital, Sofia, I had to pry my desiccated contact lenses out of my eyes while Mia went ahead to tackle liquor scavenges.

I don't care what color it is, what country you're in, or what herb, root, or fruit is pictured on the bottle, anything 80 proof tastes like liquid hell. Period. *Poire Williams?* Not unless *Williams* means "petroleum distillate" in French. Better to just get it over with, and besides, I have good news.

"Cheers!" I raise the glass, and it's down the hatch.

Holy Mother of God. My entire head feels like it's caught fire. I gag down the other one before I change my mind. The heat spreads down my chest.

"What took you so long?" Mia asks, somewhat tipsy.

"I was on the phone with Paul," I manage, choking. "We got the studio in Avignon."

"Yaay!"

I'd asked Chrystelle, a close friend who's lived near Avignon all her life, which areas of town I should focus on for a rental in Provence. "Let me think about eet," she said—then e-mailed me a couple of days later with information and photos of five choices that she'd already looked at, in our modest price range, which is typical of her generosity and efficiency. Our first pick was a studio belonging to an older woman, Madame Oudin. I'd spoken and e-mailed with Madame Oudin before leaving but there wasn't time to finish sealing the deal.

"Where's a menu?" I ask Mia. The alcohol's making me hotter by the second.

"It's right in front of you—here." She hands it to me. "Where are your glasses?"

I use the menu to start fanning myself. "I couldn't find them."

"How'd you find your way here?" she asks, knowing I'm just about legally blind without them.

"The entire hallway is pitch-black, all I had to do was walk toward the light, like a near-death experience."

"Borislav's driving was a near-death experience," she says, imitating a gagging puke.

"You leave my Borislav alone. Why, he half-bows when he speaks to me, like men of more chivalrous times." I just want to pinch his cheeks, that Borislav, a consummate gentleman.

She gives me The Look. "God help us," she mutters. "He doesn't care if you die when he sails over the edge of a mountain. I can't believe you actually obeyed him."

Borislav looked so wounded when I reached for the seat belt, it was as if I'd insulted his very manhood. "You no need, madam—I am Borislav! I keep you safe!" He absolutely *insisted* we not wear seat belts.

"He sees a seat belt as an affront to his manly ability to keep me safe," I say languidly, because the liquor's really hitting me and I'm getting that isn't-life-just-grand feeling. "He was telling me, in his way, that he sees me as precious cargo he'd let no harm befall."

"That's more nauseating than last night's drive."

She suddenly jabs me with her elbow and whispers, "Mother, it's those two guys from the lobby, the ones that kept staring at you."

When we arrived, two tall, pale, bald guys in black jeans and tees with Armani jackets pulled tight across big chests were hanging out in the lobby. That uniform, along with their broad, stony Slavic faces *and* the pretty young prostitute at the hotel guard gate, says one thing—mafia, most likely Ukrainian. You see them in New York City, Los Angeles, Miami.

"They look the same everywhere, Mia. I think they're manufactured somewhere outside Kiev."

"Sober up, Sparky, they're still staring at you—look! Well, squint," she whispers. "They must have followed us here."

I cast my myopic eyes around for them. Sure enough, in the darkness off to the side of the bar are what looks like two giant, glowy onions about six feet in the air.

It's them. The heads of the Euro-pimps.

"Mom, they're really creeping me out," she says. "I think they want to follow you to the room and rob you. They think you're a rich old Westerner."

"Honey, it ain't me they want. This place has a little side business going, in case you didn't notice."

"No shit. But if they're looking for merchandise why are they watching *you*?"

"Because I'm the mother bear!" I whisper fiercely, because that's just how you whisper when you drink too much. "They have to get past me to get to you!"

"I'm telling you they want to rob you. I can't believe you left your glasses, come on," she says in the increasingly familiar voice that tells me exactly what my life as an aging parent is going to be like with Mia. She grabs my hand and yanks me away with her. Which ain't easy, given that my internal architecture is currently sketchy.

Sure enough, as soon as we hit the dark hallway, the onions float right out of the bar, like two moons tethered to us.

Holy cow, what if she's right? Mia squeezes my hand so hard I want to holler but don't dare, because what if they shoot me or something?

I can hear the inner thighs of their pants *wheek-wheek-wheek*-ing in on us. If she makes me run I'm gonna wet my pants.

"This is my last clean pair!" I squeak desperately into Mia's ear.

Mia gives me her WTF look, then suddenly pulls me into an elevator I didn't even see and smacks a bunch of buttons.

But do the doors close? Noooo, the doors are just taking their sweet time . . .

Their pale-domed heads come into view . . .

And then float by in the darkness . . . silent . . . thinking their Bulgarian-Ukrainian Armani-wearing pimp thoughts.

The door slides shut and I collapse into giggles. I laugh so hard I slide right down to my knees.

"Oh my God, Mom, breathe through your nose! Your breath is flammable!"

I grab the handrail and right there in my face is a giant red poster with two American mud-flap girl silhouettes as big as life, flanking a sparkly gold disco ball. Below them in words so big even I can read them: STRIPTEASE JACUZZI MASSAGE HAREM

You couldn't make this stuff up.

I am experiencing a perfect moment: I'm on a medieval cobblestone street high on a lush green hill overlooking a two-thousand-year-old Roman amphitheater, under a pale blue sky, there's a fresh green scent in the air, a young woman's ethereal voice floats out of the second floor of a buttercup-colored nineteenth-century manor. Her voice stops, another piano chord is hit, and she trills out another scale. A middle-aged woman leans out a weathered windowsill, smiling.

I wish I could freeze this moment. Her voice, the sky, the scent of spring in the air, a smile in a window. A certain softness, a sense of being out of time. Funny how some random collision of elements will suddenly anchor us so completely in the world, connect us to the absolute beauty and magnificence of life.

I'm learning to pay more attention to these moments, to notice what notes are being struck within me that make me sit up and say *Yes!* Ever since that delicious reconnection with myself on the ride back from Chitwan in Nepal, I've become very clear that finding my way forward in life isn't going to come from figuring out *what* I want to do, but by staying grounded in the person doing the wanting. The very core of my being, my essential, authentic, whatever-you-call-it self never has any trouble knowing what she wants, and certainly never worries about how she's going to get it. That's just mechanics. And she never goes away, though I've done a good job of shutting her up for a lot of my life.

The girl on the train watching a prairie sunrise never left me. She's the one who reached up from deep within when I saw the article about this trip, grabbed me, and gave me a good shake, hollering, *Hey, wake up, I'm dyin' in here!*

Without questioning or analyzing why, I'm supremely content now. I don't feel any need to say, do, or even think about anything (normally panic-inducing).

"That is probably her teacher." My reverie's interrupted by a lovely gentleman named Peter, who is pointing at the woman in the window.

If women could design the perfect college professor, it would be Peter: tall, dark, and handsome, modest, gentlemanly, tweed jacket over khakis. He was our second big surprise of the day.

The first was Plovdiv, Bulgaria's second-largest city and a World Heritage site. As an art history major, I'm familiar with the Thracians as highly skilled goldsmiths; the biggest hoard of gold jewelry from antiquity ever found was Thracian. They were also powerful warriors eventually conquered in the first century A.D. by Romans, who named the capital Philippoupolis, after Alexander the Great's papa.

But I had no idea that Bulgaria is where Thrace lay and that Plovdiv, a city I'd never heard of, *is* Philippoupolis. Which means it's older than Rome or Athens, or even Constantinople. And which explains the enor-

mous Roman amphitheater spread out below us, well enough preserved
for outdoor concerts. The city was built upon seven peaks (well, it used
to be; the Soviets knocked down one hill for the stones).

Borislav is proving less knowledgeable about Bulgarian history than
border politics. He knew how to get us to Plovdiv's historic area, but
little else. We wandered out of a dim church, blinking like moles after
admiring murals depicting the liberation of Bulgaria from the Turks by
the Russians. We were looking for a *kashta*, whatever that is, the Milyu
statue, and Sveta Nedelya church. Nothing's marked and there's almost
no one around to ask. Which meant our last scavenge wasn't likely to
happen—have someone teach us the Cyrillic alphabet over a beer at
Rehap Tepe, wherever that is.

Then up walked Peter, briefcase in hand, asking us in English (is it
that obvious?) if we needed help. He's a professor of biology at the university, on his lunch break. Like most Plovdivians, he's rightfully proud
of his city and used to Americans knowing almost nothing about it, or
Bulgaria. We gratefully accepted his offer to spend an hour showing us
around the historic area on one of the peaks.

The historic quarter is so beautifully restored that it's hard to imagine
it looked this good when it was first built in the eighteenth and nine-
teenth centuries. It's like stepping into a fairy tale. Block after steep,
twisting block of cobblestone streets are filled with fabulous and ornate
homes and manors shaded by tall fragrant pines and sycamores. Some
are built flush with the street, where their extended second stories form a
kind of archway above the lanes. Others are enclosed in courtyards with
fountains and gardens. Fruit trees drooping over the stone walls will be
heavy with figs and plums in a few months.

"Most of the homes now are museums and galleries, or used for concerts," Peter explains as we stroll. We talk about Bulgaria's economy, his
research in zoology, the tensions in the Balkans, which have largely escaped Bulgaria. He leads us down a street to the edge of the peak; there
are several huge rocks with views of the city. I must really have turned a
chronological corner, because he takes my hand to help me up and down
some of the bigger rocks the way I take the hand of someone older.

Borislav rejoins us for the required beer at a bar called, of course, Rehap Tepe. Peter writes out the alphabet for us on the back of a receipt. Unlike in most of our other cities, we've not rushed through Plovdiv, which allowed us to really savor the unique experiences Bill intended these scavenges to be.

I'm so enjoying the moment I didn't think about the fact that offering to buy Borislav a beer was probably not a good idea, given the mountain roads we're about to take across the country on the way to Romania. He's taken off his leather jacket and pushed up the sleeves of his sweater, baring the most well-carpeted arms I've ever seen.

You know how you sometimes get a feeling that someone understands English better than they let on, because there'll be that little look or unconscious gesture? Well, Borislav either understands far less English than I thought or he's a very good actor. Because when Peter laments that he and his wife can't really afford to have more kids because his monthly salary is roughly what we're paying Borislav for two days' work, Borislav's beer keeps going right down, not a burp or hiccup. I, of course, want to gag on mine.

Peter returns to work and Borislav gestures that we can take our time walking back. The sun through the tall trees creates a forest of slender sunbeams in Plovdiv's narrow lanes that makes walking back magical. I fall in behind Mia as she descends a steep, bumpy street.

I take my time, lagging behind. A yard on one side has a row of fat peonies not fully open, their petals balled up tight like purple cabbages. I run my hands lightly along a tumble of tangled morning glory and grape vines spilling over a high wall, feeling the tiny bright-green balls that will become grapes as the months pass.

All of a sudden, I'm filled with an unexpected melancholy. It feels like grief almost, my throat catches on an inhale and I have to force myself to swallow tears that seem to be coming not from my eyes but someplace much deeper.

It's bewildering and distressing. Where is this coming from? Why here? An hour ago, I felt more authentically happy than I've felt in ages. I'm glad I've stayed behind because I don't want to give in to my immediate response to shrug it off. Because I need to notice this, too. I've made far more, and bigger, mistakes in my life by ignoring the nos than the yeses.

What woman hasn't? If for no other reason than we're trained from a young age to please, to be a good girl—"Don't be so negative, smile!" After a while the hesitation, the doubt, the *I don't really wanna*s are so subtle we can miss them altogether. But there's always a moment. It may be hard to recall, but there's always an exact moment when we go underground, twist a *no* into a *yes*. And for me it usually feels like this, but I bury it so quickly I just experience it as a drop in energy, a flash of sadness in my body.

I want to pay attention to this melancholy, but not analyze it. Women can tell themselves all kinds of great stories; we'll analyze the *why* of something until we're disconnected from the raw emotion. I want to simply *name it*—I'm sad.

When I worked with families in crisis, I would cut short women's stories by asking, "If you were sobbing so hard right now that you could only get out *one word* about what's going on inside of you, what would it be?" For some women it was easy, immediate. But most would go mute for a moment, then they'd burst into tears and choke out the one word they'd avoided for a long time. The only one that would heal them if they hadn't been so terrified of it: sad, lonely, hurt, scared, worthless, unlovable, angry.

Mia stops at the bottom of the road to wait for me, which makes me instantly tense up. I realize that *this* is one of those exact moments—I'm about to bury all of this on autopilot and put on a smile for her, avoid the vulnerability that once brought us so close and that she's asked for again. I would have given her the same fake self that's been passing herself off as me for a good part of my life, especially these last few years, without blinking, probably without awareness.

And I'm aware of something else—the first *no* of that earlier sadness felt deeply right, so utterly authentic I felt my whole body relax; I feel this *no*, this shutting down, as physically unpleasant, discordant. My jaw is tighter.

"Loss" passes from my lips on an exhale. My one word.

"What?" Mia calls as she walks up to meet me.

"I don't want to leave here, Mia," I say quietly, and somewhat bewildered. "I'm sad I'm leaving, like *really* sad."

It's that simple. I don't want to leave this shade of green, the peridot-colored tendrils of the vines, or leave the way the air smells and the trees droop. I don't want to leave the peonies or the old yellow house. The boulders and lush slopes, the moss and lichens in the shadows.

"I'm sorry you're down, Mom," she says softly. "What do you think it is?"

"I'm not sure. It's a lovely, simple kind of sad, the way a child feels sad."

Her understanding smile melts my heart and makes me happy that I shared this with her.

"Maybe it's just having to leave someplace I find so beautiful," I muse. "Not Meteoros-spectacular, or the grand peaks of the Himalayas—that scale feels off. This is beauty one can live in. This is going to sound stupid, but I had the sudden feeling like I belonged here, like something matches me, my whole body seems tuned in to it. I feel like I'm being dragged away."

"Maybe it's not important to know now," Mia says as we continue down. "I'm sure it'll come to you at some point."

After a moment, she adds, "I'm glad you told me. I've hardly ever heard you acknowledge feeling sad."

"I'm almost never aware of it myself. It's sort of my no-fly zone. That's the problem with autopilot. You miss half the territory."

"What would cheer you up?"

"Cheer me up? Are you kidding? I've never been so happy to feel sad!"

After a long enough drought, you can get drunk on a thimbleful of authenticity.

The drive to Rila Monastery is beautiful. So I hear. Borislav, bound and determined to get us there by sunset, drove so wildly through twisty mountain roads that I forced myself to sleep before motion sickness had a chance to set in.

Two hours later, we stop at a monastic complex surrounded by wilderness. The setting sun has turned the snow on the mountaintops to a soft gold and cast a tawny glow over everything in the valley. Borislav grins in satisfaction when he sees the wonder on our faces, and you just know that if he spoke English he'd say, Now was this worth it or was this worth it?

From the outside, the monastery is austere, a four-sided fortress of gray stone, but when you step through the main arch and into the cobblestone courtyard, the bright and whimsical interior is a delightful surprise. Surrounding the courtyard are four tall stories of arched porticos, each painted with fat black and white stripes; the walls behind them are painted in thin red and white stripes. An ornately painted five-domed church sits in the courtyard center.

The complete lack of symmetry and dizzying stripes are zany in an almost Willy Wonka–esque way, creating a visually thrilling frame for the old-world frescoes covering the exterior church walls—azure skies filled with warring angels and demons, Old Testament kings with flowing beards and pale-peach skin, stoic-faced martyrs and apostles.

The monastery was founded, rather unintentionally, by Ivan Rilski in 927 A.D. Revered as a saint even in his own lifetime, Ivan was a bit of a loner. When the miracles he performed brought him fame throughout the country, he sought solitude by moving to a cave deep in the Rila Mountains. Solitude was short-lived; growing numbers of believers set up camps around his cave to seek his blessing, and their settlements eventually came to form Rila Monastery.

Every Bulgarian tsar made large contributions to the monastery, which turned it into an important center that kept Bulgarian culture and language alive during the five hundred years of Turkish rule. The monastery also houses the remains of the beloved Tsar Boris III, the ruler who famously defied Hitler by refusing to deport Bulgaria's fifty thousand Jews to concentration camps.

My mom's quiet as we wander through the monastery, and I wonder if she's thinking about her mother and the Holocaust or if she's simply spellbound, as I am, by the uniqueness and beauty of this place. I don't ask, because if she's not thinking about it, I don't want to bring it up and possibly ruin the moment for her, and if she is thinking about it, she might lie, not wanting to ruin the moment for me. So we walk side by side, quietly pointing out things the other might have missed.

I took this trip to figure out what's been going on with my mom, and, considering I know no more about her daily life today than I did a month ago, I'm not sure I've succeeded. But I don't much care. These past weeks have made me realize that I don't want to know about her life over the past few years, I want to know her, period. It's interesting how at some stages in life I've needed to point out our differences, to stake out a separate identity, but at others, like now, I feel like understanding her will help me understand myself.

Especially given we have more in common than I thought. Listening to her talk in Cairo about being lost and confused in her late teens and very early twenties was sad, because I think she might have been happier if she'd made different college and career choices, but part of me was pleased. I've only ever known her as determined, focused, and self-possessed, none of which I've felt much of the past few years, and therefore none of which I've wanted to talk to her about.

"I'm glad I decided to go with you to France, Mom," I say suddenly.

She turns from the fresco she'd been studying to look at me.

"Me too, monkey," she says with a smile, using my childhood nickname.

It's silent for a minute until I realize I've been waiting for her to ask why, and that she's not going to.

"Well, you know I wanted to go to France to spend time together and all that—which I definitely do—but remember when you asked me in China why I left my life?"

"Yes."

"Yeah, well, aside from feeling like you were being ungrateful, it pissed me off because it was the first time I was confronted with the fact that I came just as much to get away from my life. I'd never say I was unhappy—I was having a lot of fun, I love New York and being with my friends—but I wasn't at the best place with myself. I was aware of elements that really weren't working for me, but I couldn't put my finger on it so I sort of shelved that feeling of . . . I don't know, maybe a nagging discomfort would be the right term?"

Partially because it's getting late and partially because I just don't feel like *it, I don't go into the specifics, the part that I can put my finger on now—not feeling grown-up, not liking my body, not liking my job but not knowing what to do instead.*

"Generally, I didn't know what I was doing and just felt kind of lost. Which is why I loved listening to you in Cairo—I totally related to it, and had no clue you ever felt like that. Yes, sometimes I don't like telling you things because it's like opening the advice floodgates, but sometimes I don't talk to you about feeling insecure or confused because it's kind of embarrassing. My whole life you've known what you wanted to do, you're extremely self-possessed, and don't even get me started on body issues, because you've never had to deprive yourself of baklava!"

My mom's five foot seven and thin, despite eating like a horse and rarely exercising. I'm five foot three and, even when exercising, am of average weight.

She shakes her head and looks at me, a little surprised.

"Mia, just because I didn't have to watch my weight doesn't mean I didn't feel insecure. Looking 'ethnic' is exotic now, but when I was growing up, Bo Derek and Farrah Fawcett were in vogue—and I had black hair, olive skin, and big lips. And the confidence I felt when I was twenty-five was only because I was doing what I thought I should be doing. If I'd been truly confident, I'd have gone to medical school. Your questioning yourself and what you really want, even if it creates anxiety for you, also means you're more likely to consciously choose your life. Assuming you pay attention, that is, rather than continue shelving it," she adds pointedly.

"I know; that's why I said I was glad I'm going to France. If I went back to New York right now I think I'd be more aware for a few weeks but I'd go back to business as usual pretty soon."

"I'm glad you realize that. And I hope you also realize that unless you regularly allow time for solitude and reflection, you'll probably go back to business as usual once you're home, even after a whole summer away. Think about it, Mia, you're basically always available, by text, tweet, e-mail, Facebook; you guys even sleep with your cell phones. You're never truly alone in the way that matters most—in your own mind; part of it's always on alert, listening to see

how much you matter to everyone else. All of my formative years, unless I was in school or happened to be home when that plastic box on our kitchen wall rang, most the time my mind was mine, walking, driving, studying, doing chores. Being by yourself is a big part of how you get a sense of self. I think you're all scared to death to unplug and find out how much you really matter. It doesn't seem to be enough for you to matter just to you."

She's just given me a lot to think about but it's well past dark and Borislav is waiting, leaning against the courtyard wall and staring up at the half-moon gleaming silver. Something else occurs to me.

"You know what's funny, Mom?" I ask, laughing a little. "Right now, at fifty, your life is more similar to mine than if we'd both been in our twenties."

She thinks a minute, smiles, and nods in agreement. How could she not? The sudden and dramatic change of careers and locations, the feeling out-of-control and unsure of your future. She's a quintessential quarter-lifer.

I'm glad I never brought up my question to her in China again. Which is a major shift for me. In the past I would have wanted an answer, to explore it. I would have seen this as supportive, as being about the issues or problems, the circumstances of her life; but the deeper message would likely have been that I don't trust her ability to explore her own life, without my intervention—i.e., that *she's* the problem. If a daughter, of any age, senses her own mother doesn't trust her, how can she truly trust herself? I think a mother's silence at times like this creates a space for that to happen.

Which may be why she hasn't said anything to me in the past two years about being unhappy in any way. My loving advice and "voice of experience" filled all the space. But as we crawl into bed after the long drive back from Rila, I'm thinking about a more troubling possibility— that I modeled it.

Vulnerability has never been my strong suit. All those years I staffed personal-growth seminars with families in crisis, I saw myself again and again in parents who were fearless in their career or on the battlefield but were often terrified of opening up emotionally to their own kids, or to themselves. But once I understood how I modeled that for Mia and the dreadful cost—a daughter who abused drugs and ran away to mask pain—I worked through it, because the stakes were too high. I guess when my own road got too bumpy, I didn't bother to do it for myself. And, again, maybe it came with a cost for Mia, and our relationship. Just as in the past, she hid her thoughts and feelings to protect me. But I didn't think she had been burying them from herself.

"Hey, Mia," I say quietly, once we're back at the hotel and in our beds.

"Yeah?" she says as she pulls the covers all the way up to her eyes as she always does.

"Thank you for opening up to me the way you did at Rila."

"You don't have to thank me."

"Sure I do—some daughters wouldn't. I feel honored. And I'm really glad you're starting to ponder your life in a bigger way. Even if it is scary."

"It's scarier to think about not doing it."

"It sure is, monkey, because the time goes by faster than you think. My twenties seem like a blink away." I reach over and turn off the nightstand light. "That's why it's so important to pay attention, not just to when you feel badly, but also when something comes alive inside of you. Even if you don't know why, the way it happened to me in Plovdiv. We tend to sneak up on ourselves in life, even with things that make us happy. Which makes it especially important for you."

"Why do you say that?"

"Because you're one of those people who gets moving when they're excited about something."

"What's the other kind?"

"They're more motivated to avoid what they don't like, the negative."

"Huh, I never thought about it that way. Doesn't seem like a fun way to live."

"It has its advantages; you have to be balanced. When you're mostly future-focused you avoid the negative stuff. So you don't learn from your past and tend to repeat your mistakes—or not see them at all."

"I do that sometimes. Not so often as you do, to be honest."

"That's true. It's one thing about me you should *not* emulate."

She yawns. "I think you're not even aware how much you do it, Mom. It's why you've started saying *should* all the time again. I should have done this or shouldn't have done that. Used to drive Dad and me crazy."

"It used to drive *me* crazy."

So crazy, in fact, that I decided to count every time I said *should* or *shouldn't* in one day, as a way to stop doing it. By noon I'd hit forty-seven, which was pretty sobering.

I lean toward her bed to make sure she hears me before drifting off. "Mia, I'm really, really sorry if I didn't seem like someone you could talk to the last couple of years. You don't need to protect me or worry about me. Or worry that I'll judge you."

It's silent for a moment and I'm afraid she's asleep, but then she says quietly, "I know. I think it was both of us. I'm really glad you had the crazy idea to take this trip. And I'm glad I'm coming to France with you." She pauses and I hear her breath slowing.

"Sweet dreams, Mia," I murmur. I get out of bed quietly and, just as I used to do when she'd fallen asleep after our bedtime chats when she was little, I bend over and kiss her forehead softly.

No matter how old you are, or what kind of relationship you have with your mother, she is the most significant woman in your life. We matter to our daughters more than we can imagine, whether or not they, or we, admit it or like it. As different as our personalities are, as open as I am in so many ways, I'm just like my mother in guarding my feelings. Mia doesn't do it to the extent that I do, but she clearly does it, apparently sometimes without realizing it. Who we are as women finds its way into our daughters.

Once they're grown and we can't tell them what to do, the only way we can influence them is by inspiring them. Which is also a part of why I didn't share aspects of my life with her. Just as I wanted to continue to see her as the golden girl, my hero and inspiration, I wanted her to continue to see me that way, too. I don't want Mia to see me and think *I don't want that to be me later in life,* and then maybe go on to create what she fears. It's what fears tend to do—they give you an unconscious blueprint to follow. What a burden to place on a daughter, what a sad legacy.

I want her to see me the way I want to see myself again—as powerful and authentic, as a woman living by design instead of default. As willing to fight for myself the way I did for her when the going got rough. My sage pal Leah said it well shortly before we left: "Isn't that what all women want, Claire? To be brave in their own lives?" We do, and as a mother I want it even more. So my life can be not a burden but a beacon for my daughter.

After Romania, we had one exhausting but extremely interesting day in Amsterdam (like twenty-five points for asking a prostitute her rates interesting) and a final day in Toronto where we just did the scavenges we liked, which included the Shoe Museum and taking a misty ferry ride to one of the islands, at a normal pace. Our score didn't land us in the top three, but we've raised several thousand dollars for charity and experienced the world and the people we share it with in ways we could never have imagined. We were welcomed everywhere we went, invited into homes and hearts, and have a more meaningful understanding of our nation's impact on the world.

We've also experienced ourselves and each other in ways we could never have imagined. Till now, Mia and I have been coasting on the closeness we had in the past, when we saw each other, and our roles, in a way we've both outgrown. This trip has shaken all of that loose, forced us to see and be with each other in new and unexpected ways. We've seen each other call upon inner resources neither of us knew we had, and we've had our nerves, wits, and stamina tested.

I've had the priceless opportunity to observe Mia interacting with strangers without the benefit of language, to see what fascinates or repels her, what delights or frightens her, to see how she takes in the world, turns it over in her mind, and integrates it into her spirit.

We experienced old patterns, new insights, and saw what was and wasn't working in our relationship, even if we didn't have the time to explore what would work better. Mostly, we learned to trust each other.

Tomorrow the most amazing journey of our lives will come to an end. Thirteen teams played hard, creatively, and well, sometimes disagreed heartily, and always laughed heartily. Mia and I would do it again in a minute, but we're ready to head home, where we'll no doubt sleep for two days straight. Then we pack up again and head to Avignon, where we'll have time to relax and reflect, to learn, grow, and to chart a new course for our lives and our relationship.

Part II

GATHERING

chapter seven

Avignon

French Lessons

*T*he name *Avignon comes from the word* avenio, *which means "town of violent winds." This city in the south of France is marked by a western wind, known locally as* le mistral, *that can reach sixty miles an hour. In winter, the wind is often biting and cold, and year-round it whistles and roars so loudly and unrelentingly that it was successfully used as an insanity defense in a murder trial.*

Le mistral is why the Provençal farmhouses that people love to renovate usually face south and have small windows, and why bell towers in villages throughout the countryside have open iron frameworks that allow the wind to blow through. It is also why, if you look at Van Gogh's paintings of olive groves, the trees all bend to the same side, having grown in the wind's direction.

For centuries, artists flocked to Provence because the light there is literally unlike anywhere else in the world. When le mistral blows through, it takes with it the dust and particles normally found in the atmosphere, more deeply saturating colors and adding nuance.

Most skies have a sense of depth—you're aware of staring through air and clouds—but Avignon's sky is such an intense cobalt that it feels opaque. It caps the region's quaint villages and sunflower fields much the way the indigo-painted church domes of Provence cover the worshippers within.

And Avignon is no stranger to worshippers; for most of the thirteenth cen-
tury, the papacy resided there. As Christendom's epicenter, Avignon ruled the
medieval world, and the city's wealth attracted pesky bands of troublemakers.
The popes ordered the total fortification of the city and the creation of what
remains Europe's largest Gothic palace: the impenetrable Palais des Papes (the
Popes' Palace).

Centuries later, it's a sight virtually unchanged: a small city tightly en-
circled by a protective Dungeons and Dragons–esque stone wall, complete with
watchtowers, crenulated battlements, and slits for archer's arrows. True, honk-
ing cars are now heard instead of clopping horses, and a modern city with a
hundred thousand people now surrounds the walled area. But intramuros
(literally, "inside the walls") little has changed since medieval times, and the
population is a mere fifteen thousand.

It is, however, about to increase by two.

What we call a mother when we're little—someone who knows everything, loves you unconditionally, banishes boo-boos and bad guys, enter-
tains, educates, and scolds you—is called an angel once you're grown-up.
Everyone should have one. Ours is named Chrystelle.

She even comes with a medieval town, a chic wardrobe in our same
size, a chef, and a new swimming pool. And she's waiting for us at the
Avignon train station, waving from *le parking,* wearing big Jackie O sunglasses, an olive linen military-style jacket, skinny jeans, and the Converse sneakers Frenchwomen love. The last time I saw her at this station,
my train was pulling out and she was crying as she waved good-bye.

Chrystelle has the carriage and style of any well-bred Frenchwoman
but doesn't look typically French, or typical anything. At almost six feet
tall, she's both commanding and delicate, with the perfect ivory skin,
wide brow, and big hazel eyes of a Botticelli. She's really quite beautiful, with the kind of fresh, open face artists treasure for its expressive
qualities: she can ask entire questions with just a glance; when she smiles,
which is often, her whole face smiles; and when her face clouds, you hope
that whatever it is, you didn't do it.

Most of the time, however, she seems to channel Audrey Hepburn—fun-loving, witty, inquisitive, charming. She has that rare gift of making those she cares for feel not just loved but *treasured*. When Chrystelle says, *I weel arrange somesing,* you're in like Flynn. I met her ten years ago while staying with friends, and we've remained close.

Chrystelle adores Avignon; she's lived in and around here all her life. "When you arrive een the airport of Paris, you see nussing, just a lot of corn. New York ees also not so pretty to arrive, just some buildings and messy things. Avignon, you arrive to find a queen. The thing of eet is this," which is how she prefaces Somesing Important, "you don't put a diamond just like that, pffft, on a desk, eet doesn't look like anysing. *Non,* you must put eet in a beautiful box, with, 'ow you call that material, soft, like an aneemal?"

"Velvet."

"*Oui.* And suddenly eet ees somesing very special. Every morning I drive over the bridge and there she ees, a jewel in her special container, with a gold reebbon on top."

The container being the fortified walls and the "gold reebbon on top" being the Popes' Palace towering over the heart of the city. Chrystelle drives through a wall portal onto the main drag of Avignon, Rue de la République, Napoleon III's sole raze-and-rebuild contribution here. Once medieval, it's now a broad avenue of ornate, nineteenth-century buildings with wrought-iron balconies. It's very Parisian-looking, down to the big fin de siècle brasseries shaded by the massive plane trees so beloved by the French.

Chrystelle wedges into a minuscule parking space and we unload our luggage.

"First I make you see some very nice things," she announces, "and then I take you to the studio. Eet will be very easy to find your way, you weel see."

She weaves us through sidewalk tables full of tourists eating platters of oysters and *anchoïade,* an oily, garlicky dip for vegetables that's very popular in the south. She and Mia chatter away in French, which has become incomprehensible to my jet-lagged self. Another ten minutes and English will be just as confusing.

She then turns off the main drag into another world. A densely packed maze of tiny streets, filled with medieval churches, cathedrals, and mostly unpartitioned buildings, all of beige-gray stone. There are cafés, patisseries, galleries, shops, kebab *"sandwicheries"* with Algerians smoking and talking outside, gay bars, expensive restaurants. The first impression is of equal parts Portland grunge, West Hollywood eclectic, and *un peu de* Paris, plunked in a medieval stage set.

The streets buzz with chic hipsters, working-class folks, well-dressed couples gay and straight, college kids in jeans with iPods, the requisite Frenchman with beret, cigarette, and baguette on a bicycle. A girl with matted dreadlocks leads a troop of mutts past a *boulangerie* whose storefront probably hasn't changed in a hundred years: crusty, golden loaves framed by a dusty blue façade and window boxes overflowing with purple blooms. The façades mimic the people, alternately grimy or pristine. If Paris is the well-bred and manicured Lady, Avignon is the scrappy but endearing Tramp.

Mia and I have assumed what will come to be called "the position": two ducklings waddling single-file as fast as we can through the ridiculously narrow cobbled lanes (calling these "streets" is like naming your Chihuahua Hulk), praying not to become human graffiti. Sidewalks have become nonexistent or a mere ribbon of stone we'd call a *curb*, and cars seem to be the exact same width as the lanes; cars are actually touching my person. Being thin here isn't a matter of vanity; it's survival of the flattest.

"You weel really like your area," Chrystelle assures us cheerily. "You 'ave all you need right 'ere and the people are not snob. There are a lot of artists and eet ees *très branché* ("plugged in," i.e., hip) at night."

She continues giving what is no doubt fascinating commentary about everything we're passing, none of which registers, because more dangerous than the cars and walls are the cobbles. What in God's name—and just about everything here was built in God's name—would have them paving streets with stones the shape and size of a domed lunchbox?

Chrystelle eventually stops before the cutest, cobbliest alley I've ever seen. I look around for a landmark, and I am not disappointed. Just behind her is a gigantic white metal box mounted on the corner of the building—a condom dispenser.

"'Ere we are—you see, eet was very easy to find."

I'll say. Nothing says "easy" like *Feeling Extra!* or *Pleasure Max.*

We follow her into the L-shaped alley where Madame Oudin will meet us with the key. On the left is a row of attached seventeenth-century four-story stone buildings that curve around with the alley to where it opens onto another street. On the right is what makes Americans such cheap dates in these parts: a twenty-foot craggy medieval stone wall we'd take a dozen photos of. Behind it are towering plane trees that shade the entire alley.

"This is such a great wall!" I say.

"Yes, eet is a wall." She shrugs. "You can look at eet all you like," she points to the huge fourth-floor windows facing the wall. "The thing of eet ees this," she says authoritatively, which is how the French say most things, by the way, "you will be away from the beeg street, so eet will be peaceful. And whenever you want to come 'ome, you just need to tell me. You 'ave a garden to relax, you can 'ave a swim, eet will be like a vacation for you."

'Ome being her 'ouse, which I find just so touching.

"After I take 'ome Antoine from school, I will be back to be sure you are *bien installées* (settled-in)."

"You don't have to do that, we'll be fine," Mia protests, because she doesn't know Chrystelle well enough.

The French love to raise the index finger when admonishing or advising and wag it in time to *Non, non, non,* said through lips pushed into a very Gallic pout. You know those beautiful fingers and toes in Michelangelo's paintings? Long, slender, perfectly formed, turned up at the tip, the kind almost no one has in real life? Well, Chrystelle does, and when that lovely conductor's baton of a finger snaps to, so do you.

"*Non, non, non,*" *le* finger scolds, "I don't just leave you on the street like this. I 'ave to be sure you 'ave all what you are supposed to up there."

Yeah, like sheets and towels, which I forgot to bring, and no place will be open to buy them. Even furnished places don't always come with them here; they're considered strictly personal items.

"Are you going to remember the way here, Mia?" I ask after she leaves.

"Bah-*wee!*" Mia assures me with a very Provençal-accented *mais oui* (but of course!).

What that really meant, and she thinks I don't know, is a carefree *hell no!* Before I can say anything, a motorcycle whips into the alley and parks. A *très* petite young woman in pointy-toed black boots and a tightly belted riding jacket hops off, takes off her helmet, and shakes her straight blond bob loose. I half-expect James Bond to show up next.

"*Vous êtes Madame et Mademoiselle Fontaine?*" she asks. She has a bronze tan, a very pretty, heart-shaped face, and a smile that crinkles her green-gold eyes.

"*Oui?*" we say, uncertain. "Madame Oudin was not able to come?"

She looks at us funny. "*I* am Madame Oudin."

We're so shocked that it takes a few seconds to respond. She was so formal in all our e-mails and calls, using *Madame Oudin* and *Madame Fontaine* for weeks, never a first name. Of course we assumed she was elderly.

She's just as shocked that we'd be expecting a prim senior. I explained that in America, it would have been first names, and no one young expects to be called *madame,* especially by someone old enough to be her mother, which I am.

Madame Oudin does the Gallic lip pouf and brow raise. "Ooohlala, c'est beezarre, to use ze first name so queeck! Of course I am *madame.* One cannot say me *mademoiselle* at sirty!"

I know I've found a kindred spirit, because we then launch into an academic discussion on language and social structure that would bore anyone else to death. She studied literature and is a language fanatic. We exchange mutual permission to use first names (hers is Isabelle) and agree to *tutoyer* with each other, which means using the informal *tu* for "you" instead of *vous.*

We don't know it yet, but we've gotten our first taste of the magic of Avignon—young, edgy, artsy, earthy—yet as full of history and formality as Versailles, with more than a soupçon of mystery and surprise.

❦

When in France, it's imperative to understand the expression comme il faut. *This translates loosely to "how it's done," and in France, there is a proper way to do everything. When to wear what, how to greet whom, what to say when, these all fall under the category of* comme il faut. *And because the French alone happen to know just what that way is, they see it as their sacred duty to civilize the rest of the world.*

True, for centuries France was the authority on fashion, food, art, and literature, and until 1918 French was the international language of diplomacy. Which explains why Victor Hugo wrote, "France, France, the world would be alone without you"; President Charles de Gaulle called France "the light of the world, its destiny to illuminate the universe"; and President François Mitterrand vowed that France will "light the path of mankind."

I believe my mother sees herself similarly, at least when it comes to me.

We flew here separately and agreed to meet at the airport Sheraton Hotel lobby at noon. I waited for her but after an hour jet lag kicked in, so I propped my head up with my backpack and dozed off until I heard my name harshly whispered. I looked up to see my mom standing with perfect posture, a blue silk scarf tied around her neck just so, and visible disapproval at seeing a situation that was "pas (not) comme il faut." *She informed me that this wasn't a hostel and not only was I asleep in a nice hotel lobby, but asleep in sweatpants and flip-flops (that's what grungy teenagers wear, Mia—do you know how many people find jobs or meet spouses on planes?).*

My mother has always been very French in her ways; she just never knew it until the first time she visited and found sixty million other people "Just like me!" A whole population in love with ideas, who find politics and religion perfect dinner topics, who love to fuss over food and correct others.

Having a cultural guide to ward off potential faux pas is terrific, but we're unpacking now and I see her eyeing what I've brought. I'd bet money that if she wasn't so jet-lagged she'd already have commented on what I packed, didn't pack, should have packed, and shouldn't expect to borrow from her. I'm surprised it never occurred to me that rooming together (in a studio, no less) gives the most critical person in my life a front-row seat to the action. The amount of junk food I eat, how late I'm sleeping in, if I'm slouching, if my nails are neatly trimmed—without things like jet lag, skewered scorpions, and one-humped camels to distract her, this might be like living under a microscope.

The fact that it's a spacious studio should help; it's open and airy with high ceilings, a separate bathroom, a full kitchen, and two enormous windows that open into the robust cluster of trees growing from behind the alley's stone wall. Isabelle has simply but tastefully decorated it with two white desks, a circular glass coffee table, and matching black leather chairs. It looks minimalist and modern, although decidedly un-modern is the complete absence of anything electronic; no TV, no telephone, no Internet connection.

My mom sees this as a good thing, happily noting how this will force us to unplug and be present for each other and ourselves. I wait for Isabelle and her boyfriend Anthony to leave before telling my mom that just because Avignon looks medieval doesn't mean we need to live like we're in the Dark Ages, but she just shrugs me off.

I've just opened my groggy, half-blind eyes to find my darling daughter's face bent right over mine, framed by the bright morning sun. She leans in and pulls out my earplugs.

"Hey!" I protest.

"Mother, you can *never* plop into this bed again, do you hear me, ne-VER," she barks. "This thing will swallow us up like a Venus fly trap! One minute you're mumbling by the bed and the next—BAM!" she smacks her hands, "you pass out! You're lucky I grabbed the other end of it."

It being *le Click-Clack,* the big hybrid futon/hide-a-bed/sofa Isabelle introduced with a Vanna White sweep of the arm, just after she introduced her boyfriend, Anthony. He's as tall and gregarious as she is tiny and quiet, with big blue eyes and curly blond hair. They launched into an enthusiastic demo of *le Click-Clack,* which involved a symphony of maneuvering and grimaces, during which we were instructed to listen for the distinct *CLICK!* Aaaaand, voilà, ze bed!

And indeed, it looked kind of flat. Then Anthony touched something that made it snap shut like a mousetrap. There was some fast prying and pushing (and I'm sure I heard a *merde* or two) and finally, voilà, le sofa! Perspiring, Anthony praised it as a feat of engineering, all ze mechanicals inside ze bed, where you cannot even see eet!

Apparently I fell asleep before *le clack* fully *CLICKED*, because I'm in the gully of a V—not that it kept *me* awake. When Mia doesn't sleep, your best hope is to mollify, mitigate, and make every kind of nice you know. Which will be easy now that (a) I've had ten uninterrupted hours of sleep and (b) I'm in France. There's a lovely cacophony of birds coming in the windows along with a cool breeze.

"Isn't this place lovely?" I sigh. "Let's—"

"Listen up!" She crawls over me to get to her side. "I'm gonna rig this thing into place and then we're not going to touch it, got it? We're going to leave it open for the rest of the time we're here."

"Okay. Can I go to the bathroom first?"

"No! Just go to the foot of your side, *slowly*," she orders.

I move by inches, not because I'm afraid of getting jackknifed between *click* and *clack*, but because I'm scared I'll be clacked inside with *her*.

She curls her top half under the bed and starts futzing around down there. Muttering is occurring and *merde* has already become her expletive of choice.

"And you failed to notice how nicely your messy daughter unpacked and organized everything!" she calls out. "I had to do *something* while you slept for ten hours!"

"Welcome to my world! I'm always waiting for you to wake up. How long will this take? I have to go to the bathroom."

"Well, you'll just have to wait! My God, you're like a baby!"

And I actually turned down long-term care insurance last month.

"No problem, honey! Just tell me what to do next."

"Feed me!"

Lesson One: The French generally think they know everything. The good news is they usually do and they want you to as well (I just love this in a person). Along with any request, and sometimes without it, they may correct, instruct, or advise you. Take it as the kindness it is intended to be and be grateful you're not a child-size French person, in which case the lesson is sometimes reinforced with a smack, sometimes upside the head. Like American parents of yesteryear, the French have no taboo against disciplining children strictly, loudly, and publicly when deserved, in ways most Americans today would find shocking and disturbing. Consider yourself warned and try not to stare. French parents are keenly aware that they're raising citizens of France. They see allowing poor manners as abuse, handicapping a child's ability to become part of civilized society. You needn't worry about *les enfants*. Clearly, it has *not* caused any loss of self-esteem.

Lesson Two: The only thing the French like better than knowing everything and *gastronomie* is solving problems. It allows them to engage in logic and discourse (they're taught dialectics in grade school: thesis + antithesis = synthesis) all while helping their fellow man, something also very important to them. If it's a group effort, all the better.

Case in point: I once went into a shop in Chartres for directions to a monastery. Now, a monastery is a big thing and Chartres is a tiny town in the middle of cornfields. The shop owner couldn't believe she didn't know it.

She called in a neighbor to help, a big woman with a ruffled dress, plenty of rouge, and fabulous, aqua, side-button kidskin shoes that looked as if they came right off Jean Harlow. The sky darkened and it started to rain as they pondered and debated. Arms waved, shoulders shrugged, lips pouffed. In another country, they would have apologized, made suggestions, and moved on.

Madame Ruffles took my arm and walked me around several blocks, in the rain (*nous ne sommes pas faites de sucre, après tout!;* after all, we're not made of sugar!), looking high and low, as if a giant Romanesque structure might have somehow escaped her notice all these years. We returned to find the shop owner joined by two men. *Incroyable! Il n'existe pas!* I assured them it existed, showing them a card with the address, which, like most big buildings in small towns, has no number or street, just Maison St. Yves, Chartres, France.

They puzzled for twenty minutes. It was getting late and I was going to miss check-in, but I felt worse for *them*. They were trying so hard. They finally sent me off with great regret, free candy, and hotel phone numbers (turned out they had no idea the monastery had become a hostel with a new name). I've found this kind of effort fairly typical.

Till today. I've stopped into a gourmet shop to ask the salesclerk where I could find the tourist bureau.

"Oh là là," she says, with a doubtful expression. *"C'est près d'une église, je crois."* She thinks it's near a church, which describes half of Avignon.

A policewoman with a blond chignon perusing mustards overhears and says, *Non, non, non, madame, c'est* somewhere else I can't understand. Then a gorgeous, rail-thin woman in all white chimes in with her *non, non, non.* After some friendly "discussion" between them (in the United States it would be called *un petit* argument), the woman in white cedes, and they turn to me and announce with great regret:

"Desolée, madame, mais je ne pourrais pas vous l'éxpliquer. C'est tout simplement pas possible."

Not possible to explain? Say *quoi?* The women do the shoulder-shrug-lip-pouf thing.

Basically, Avignon 'ave too many leetle *rues* (streets) going zis way and zat. All they could offer was that it's near a church that actually may not be a church anymore.

No problem, I'm thinking, the entire *intramuros* oval is one mile wide and less than a mile across. If I can find a giant fish head served on a banana leaf in Singapore while under-slept, underfed, and under-pressure, I can find the tourist bureau in Avignon. And find our way home, too, because we found a second landmark. Painted on a window on the other corner of our building is a life-size pair of woman's legs, naked and spread-eagled, with *Royal Tattoo* on a fat red heart over the crotch. Right at eye level. If for some reason we miss this gem, fifty yards away is her pal *Pleasure Max.*

"Okay, Mia," I announce as I join her at Bar les Célestins, a charming bar/café near our studio. "Avignon awaits us and today I shall be our guide. Let us away!"

BASIC RECIPE FOR A FRENCH BLOCK

2 hair salons

2 *bar-tabacs* (cigarettes, maps, lottery tickets, soda, espresso, wine)

3 bar/cafés

2 bistros

2 restaurants (there are laws about what constitutes a café, bistro, brasserie, and restaurant)

2 patisseries (pastries, desserts, sometimes bread)

1 *boulangerie* (breads, croissants, sometimes quiche)

1 *traiteur* (deli/ready-made food, wine)

2 *sandwicheries* (a sliver of space with a deli case of sandwiches, pizza, drinks)

1 or more of the following shops: *boucher* (meat), *poissonnier* (fish), produce

2 pharmacies

4 *immobiliers* (real estate offices with photos posted on the windows)

1 *librairie* (bookstore, often used or antiquarian)

1 optometry shop

5 piles of dog *merde*

Five hours later, I realize zey weren't kidding. While it may be handy to be able to get a pastry, haircut, eyeglasses, and baguette all on one block, it's completely disorienting when you can do it on almost *every* block.

Add to that the fact that, designed to baffle both the powerful winds and an invading cavalry, almost every street of Avignon is either curved or deliberately zigzagged; often even the connected buildings on a single street zig and zag at the seams, as if early city planners took pinking shears to their blueprints. Meaning you can rarely see farther than a single block, or even half of one. Oh, and the same street usually changes names each block. And except for tall church steeples and the occasional tower, the buildings are almost all the same height, the same sandy-gray stone, with the same dusty blue, or occasionally jade, shutters. Wherever you are looks like wherever you just were and wherever you're headed.

No matter, we've spent a lovely day wandering into antique and clothing shops, sampling patisseries galore, and *peuple*-watching over *limonades*. The most delightful discovery was a row of huge ground-level windows that were bricked in and painted with life-size trompe l'oeil scenes from plays performed during Avignon's famous yearly Festival of Art. It's arriving here in a month, along with an extra hundred thousand people.

By sundown, I'm just looking for the way home. We duck into a dark, vaulted passageway that spits us out onto yet another unfamiliar plaza. I suggest we rest while I figure out how to get back. It's growing cool and Mia's shoulders are bare so I pull out my blue pashmina and hand it to her as we sit in one of the cafés in the square. She sinks into the chair, orders for us, yawns, and leans back to rest.

The waiter brings a rosy *kir* in a tall flute for Mia, house red for me. Even with the euro, wine here is cheaper and included in all fixed-price meals, including lunch. I got free champagne, wine, and a sweet after-dinner drink on the plane, in economy. If you white-knuckle your way up the narrow, twisting road to the peak of Mont Ventoux, the highest in France, what's waiting to fortify you on the equally dangerous and terrifying way down? A long table of cookies, sausages—and wine.

French wines are "lighter" and sharper than what they call American-style wines, which are oaky and dense, "friendlier" as the French say. When a French vintner who was trying to make an American-style wine finally succeeded, he named it Fat Bastard.

"Sorry I've walked us so far away. But I know it has to be that way from where the sun's setting." I point south, though I know Mia puts no stock in my orienteering skills.

"Mother."

Uh-oh, I know that tone.

"Do you recognize the glass phone booths behind me?"

"No, there are glass phone booths all over the place."

"Well, do you see that stone madonna up there?" She turns and points.

"Don't you love that the madonnas are everywhere here? I imagine each has its own story. I bet we can Google—"

"Well, she's *red,*" she interrupts pointedly.

As a matter of fact, she is. High on the corner of a building is a carved stone madonna with a toddler Jesus on her hip. She's perched on a half-sphere of curling leaves and has a little weathered dome above her head. She's a little chipped and faded, but definitely red.

"She was red the first three times I saw her. We've circled the same area all day, Mom. That's the madonna over the *boucherie.* Where we got our twenty-dollar stuffed tomato. Our studio is just past it," she turns and points, "one long, curved block from the Royal Red Crotch."

Now that she mentions it, I do remember seeing the red madonna, vaguely, *once.* Okay, and maybe Betty Boop's hearted-over nether parts, *once.* Nothing else looked at all familiar.

"Well, if that block is curved, Magellan, how can you be so sure the tattoo parlor is there? You're just guessing and hope I'll fall for it."

"Oh, Mom," she sighs, shaking her head ruefully. "See, here's how it works." She leans in, quoting Jon Lovitz in *A League of Their Own,* "The *train* moves, *not* the station." Gesturing for the slow students, she adds, "*Buildings* are stationary. The *sun* is not."

"Well, I think you're wrong," I retort. Actually, I kind of don't, because the scavenger hunt made clear that I somehow gave birth to a homing pigeon. "And that way *is* south, so we'd have run right into it."

"Mother, the only thing you'd have run into would have been Le Petit House of Condoms, and that's because it's sticking out a foot."

"Well, I don't know how you can tell any of these streets from the other, they all look the same!"

"I know," she says sweetly. "That's why you do this little thing called *pay attention,* where you notice things, you know, *on purpose."* She smiles, raises her glass. "Guess who's navigating from now on."

"Bonjour, mes filles," *Chrystelle calls to my mom and me, waving as she walks toward us in a chic little black dress and big, dark sunglasses.*

As we exchange kisses and hellos, she winks at me and casually slips a black sweater into my purse. I smile. She must have heard my mom chiding me earlier this week for not bringing a sweater.

"Now, girls, I 'ope you come 'ongry because today I take you to my favorite lunch place."

We follow her toward Place des Pénitents Blancs, a small plaza near our apartment.

"So, girls," Chrystelle says, gesturing up toward the tall buildings encircling the plaza. "Can you guess why eet is my favorite place?"

"It's the light!" my mom immediately exclaims. "It's different from anywhere else in the city!"

"Like you can touch the air eetself, non?" Chrystelle finishes for her with a smile.

No wonder they're such good friends. I was busy squinting up at a gargoyle spout, clueless about what Chrystelle might be referring to, while my mom instantly noticed some infinitesimal change in atmospheric conditions. They move into a conversation about some French photographer as we walk into a funky little café. It reminds me of Matisse, a similarly eclectic restaurant in the plaza just outside our apartment, Place des Corps Saints.

The name literally means Plaza of the Bodies of the Saints, named after Pierre de Luxembourg, a young cardinal who insisted on being buried in the cemetery for the poor despite his noble status. The cemetery has since been paved, and a bustling little plaza sprung up in its place, complete with several eateries, a burbling fountain, and a fourteenth-century Célestin monastery whose chapel now houses art exhibitions.

Our neighborhood's very hip, with a blend of artists, university students, longtime residents, and a thriving gay community. The side streets are filled with small shops selling artisanal products, books, antiques, and cell phones, and designer and consignment shops. There's a smattering of street art and clever graffiti. During the day it's rather quaint, but at night Place des Saints Corps is a real hot spot (though not as hot as it used to be; according to Chrystelle, our neighborhood used to be plagued with crime, drugs, and—on the appropriately named Rue de Coq—"'Ow you call them, peemps?").

Because the area within Avignon's fortress walls is so small, "neighborhoods" often consist of only a few blocks, and just two blocks away is Place St. Didier, the former executioner's block. A prominently placed plaque details the plaza's bloody history, including the time when the tables were turned and the executioner was executed. He'd been doing an exceptionally poor job decapitating one fellow (their instruments were often dull) and, fed up with his excessive hacking, the crowd turned on him and set the intended victim free.

The French aren't known for their patience.

"Nothing?"

My mom's decided she wants to take down what few paintings and decorations our studio has.

"Nothing," she confirms, this time with more certainty.

She carefully tucks a framed print of a sunflower field under one arm, gathers the vase with sixties-style straw flowers in the other, and walks them to the closet.

"These too," she adds, reaching for the Chinese calligraphic paintings on the wall. "Let's make the walls disappear."

I'd been thinking of how to make it cozier, because it felt sparse to begin with, maybe buy a bright throw blanket for the Click-Clack, *some pretty French posters for the wall. She's so certain about wanting this, though— uncharacteristically certain—that I don't say anything but just watch her move deliberately from one object to the next.*

It reminds me a little of how she behaved in Plovdiv, when she got suddenly sad but just let herself feel sad without feeling the need to explain herself. And I like that even though she clearly has no idea why she wants blank walls, she's acting on her impulse. I'm beginning to suspect that more times than not, she's ignored, or felt the need to justify, wanting certain things for herself.

Maybe it's a good sign; wanting a house and things to fill it with didn't exactly work for her before. Perhaps like the wind that blows Avignon's skies clear, emptying the apartment of all things will create a tabula rasa for my mom to reinvent herself at midlife.

A few minutes later the room is nearly bare, just white walls, a white floor, a white desk, and black leather chairs. She strides to the middle of the room, laces her hands behind her head, and stares out the giant windows. The walls have seemed to disappear, as though our apartment is nothing more than a platform elevating us skyward and putting us eye-level with the birds squawking in the trees.

"It feels like we're living outdoors," she says happily. "I've always wanted a house of mostly windows."

I'm glad she's pleased, so I don't add that (a) we're not wood nymphs and (b) when we close the shutters it'll look like a mental ward's isolation room.

While she's looking out the window I dump out the brochures and pamphlets we picked up at the tourist bureau and spread them out on the bed. An incredible number of museums, churches, and monuments are stuffed within Avignon's rampart walls, and within an hour's drive there are well over a dozen of the quaint Provençal villages and small cities that this area is so famous for. There are museums for absolutely everything: bicycles, lavender, wine, perfume, fruits and vegetables. Even garlic gets its own exhibit.

"Ooh, look!" my mom says excitedly, showing me a brochure featuring a gathered silver brocade ball gown. "There's going to be a special Christian Lacroix fashion exhibition in Arles. And check these out."

I take the matte, eggshell-colored cardboard brochure from her and examine the gorgeous, dramatic, larger-than-life sketches of nude or partially clothed women with the word "Extases" written below. Ecstasies.

The local cell phone we bought suddenly rings from my mom's purse. She looks quizzically at me.

"Mom, pick it up before it stops ringing."

She hesitates one more second before answering haltingly, "Bonjour?"

She looks at me like a deer in headlights, so I nod encouragingly at her like a toddler. Telling my mom not to bring her electronic translator was incredibly dumb of me; I've taken its place.

"Un moment, Isabelle, s'il vous plaît. *Oh, yes, sorry,* tutoyer, s'il te plaît *and I don't understand anything else,* un moment."

She then thrusts the phone at me like a hot potato.

Lesson Three: The French love their language in a way that's impossible for an American to understand; it's central to their identity. The French are verbally clever and quick, they assess and opine strongly and well and adore spirited conversation. Patrice Leconte's Oscar-winning *Ridicule* depicts brilliantly how a particularly clever turn of phrase, preferably one with cruel wit, could in a single instant win or lose you favor with the king, something that determined your entire fortune, if not your very life. There's even a government body, l'Académie française, that protects, with force of law, the purity of the language by dictating grammar, pronunciation, and vocabulary.

The French can also sometimes be a nervous people; in Paris, often impatient. Doing anything slowly can be a trial for them; *speaking* slowly feels like slow death. However, if they speak no English and you're both stuck with your mediocre French, all is not lost—

Lesson Four: The French are like magpies, they love the new, the stylish, the interesting, they love panache, *l'esprit.* You are automatically new to them, and if you are also intelligent, lively, and dressed with even a modicum of style, *quelle différence.* If you speak away fearlessly, as if you love the language as much as they do, they'll overlook every mistake, or if they do correct you, they'll come hurrying back down the block or store aisle to apologize for correcting you (this has happened to me in real life, three times).

If you also happen to be young and attractive, as Mia is, you'll be invited into people's lives, and waiters will remember every little thing about you. We haven't even left our little area and already Mia's a big hit. She navigates both the streets and the language with me happily, if cluelessly, in tow.

Our approach to French highlights a very fundamental difference between us that shows up in a lot of areas of our lives. I have to understand *everything* to understand *anything.* No continuing ed classes for me. At forty-three, I registered for college French, took four semesters, studied like mad, and made straight As. I've even brought a textbook with me here to study each day. I'm constitutionally unable to spit out the wrong words while looking for the right ones. Which means that I'm not only slow to understand, owing to nerve deafness and tinnitus in one ear, but even slower to speak, owing to, I don't know, my brain, I guess.

Mia glides through French as cavalierly as she does life, happy to be on a need-to-know basis. She's had five years in school; her vocabulary's great and her accent perfect. Her tenses and grammar, however, *oy*. But she breezes right along not caring about mistakes, telling folks that her mother will be going to Gordes ten years ago or that she'll be sure to went tomorrow. They don't care about her mistakes, either, because she makes them *quickly* and with *l'esprit*.

Next to her, I'm a lumbering, linguistic dinosaur. However, in Provence, where life is slow and sweet, I'm treated, or tolerated, with patience and downright sweetness. They are *not*, however, so patient with one another when it comes to their language. Which can make for a very memorable evening.

"Ooo care what ze academy say! *'Nique ta mère'* ees also correct *grammaire*,[†]!" Isabelle snaps angrily with an aggravated flick of the hand.

Dear God, please don't let her smack the maître d', I'm too hungry to be thrown out of here. Here being a lovely restaurant in the quaint town of St. Remy de Provence. Anthony and Isabelle have brought us here after showing us the spectacular limestone cliffs of Les Baux. As classy and delicate as she is, you don't mess with the language in Isabelle's world.

I look to Anthony but he's gone from being shocked at her uncharacteristic profanity to interested in how much more entertaining this can get, because waiters are clustering around us, adding their *deux centimes*.

---

[*] Fuck your mother.
[†] Grammar.

Fingers are wagging, lips are pouffing, and words are flying around our heads. All because of green beans; rather, the pronunciation of them.

Les haricots verts (green beans) was always properly pronounced with the *h* silent, *lay 'areeco verrr;* until an English queen who was unable to say it correctly said *layzarico verr,* running it together. Rather than correct a queen, the academy made a new rule allowing that pronunciation. A hundred years later, purists like Isabelle and Chrystelle still consider it a bastardization and say it the proper French way.

That the waiters have joined in the fray is typical. Here, everyone's qualified and eager to "discuss" their language. This kind of heated argument simply wouldn't happen in public in America without someone calling the manager or possibly the police. Here it's part of everyday life. Store clerks snap, heated discussion ensues, agreement reached (usually), everyone's happy and on their way. Friends will have awful fights and see each other the next day as if nothing happened. A couple who never fights? We see a stable marriage, they see two boring people who have no opinions of their own or enough passion to even muster a good fight. Kind of like Paul and me. In the beginning, he thought it was walking papers every time we had a "passionate disagreement." I called it clearing the air.

Almost every waiter in the place has weighed in, Isabelle's flushed with aggravation, the maître d' keeps rolling his eyes. Things reach a crescendo, shoulders are shrugged, wineglasses refilled, and it's once more a quiet restaurant. Mia and Isabelle continue whatever conversation they were having before and Anthony and I continue analyzing the complex mushroom bisque served in tiny little teacups.

"*Non,* I don't fink vey* are smoked, *les champignons* (mushrooms)," Anthony says.

"Maybe they brown the butter," I suggest. I hear the word *douche* and Mia trying to explain to Isabelle why it's hard to get used to saying their word for "shower."

Mia to Isabelle: In English, it's a much more private kind of washing.

---

* *Think* they. In France, almost anything will do for a "th," the letters *f, v, s,* or *z.*

Isabelle to Mia: You mean ze shower?

Anthony to me, about the teacup: Why do zey use zis fing, I cannot make my fingers like zis." He tries to hold it like a teacup, but his man-fingers can't manage it.

Mia: Well . . . kind of, but a bath only for (she points down into her lap).

Isabelle, puzzled: Mia, I 'ave no idea what you are saying.

Me to Isabelle, leaning toward her for discretion, pleased I actually can say it in French: *C'est un bain spécialement pour les femmes.* (It's a special kind of washing just for women.)

Anthony, nonchalantly, to anyone: Oh, I know zis fing what you say.

Isabelle to me: *Ahhh, le bidet?*

Mia to Isabelle: Well, not exactly.

Anthony to anyone: But I know vis fing.

Me to Isabelle: *Non, c'est seulement pour des femmes* (no, it's only for women), *typiquement après sexe* (typically after sex).

Isabelle, still puzzled: Do you 'ave a dictionary?

Anthony to anyone, insistent: I tell you I know vis fing what you say!

Me, abruptly, to Anthony: How on earth could you possibly know what we're talking about?

Anthony, relieved to be finally heard, proudly: Eets for ze vajeene!

A waiter's face registers this as he passes, Isabelle and Mia stop talking, I cock my head.

Anthony, pleased and quite serious: *Oui, pour la balance!* (alternating his hands up and down) you know, ze equilibrium, een ze vajeene!

Mia and I burst out laughing and immediately clap our hands over our mouths. Isabelle's jaw falls in mortification.

"Oui, chérie," he says to Isabelle, *"c'est pour le vagin, ce truc* (it's for the vagina, this thing). You tell me zis."

She smacks him, blushing. "I never say you anysing about zat!"

"Oui, chérie, you did."

"I don't use such a sing, eet's not *naturel*!"

We're laughing so hard I have to turn my face to the wall and Mia buries her face in my back.

Anthony shrugs, then suddenly says earnestly and completely out of the blue, "Do you know zat seventy-five percent of all women do zis?" He holds up a piece of bread and dunks it in his broth. "But only twenty-five percent of ze men do. Zey don't know why."

This makes Mia laugh even harder. "My God, you're as ADD as my mother!"

Laughing till no sound comes out is typical of our outings with Isabelle and Anthony. It's a combination of wine, complementary personalities, and the fact that none of us is fully bilingual but we have grand ideas and odd fascinations that we simply *must* discuss.

One of them is language. We all spent an hour in stitches at Célestins the other night just trying to get them to pronounce the initial "th" sound, which the French tongue finds near impossible. The only reason Chrystelle can is because she was an au pair in London for a year and, well, she's Chrystelle.

chapter eight

Avignon

We Are *Living Like This!*

*T*here may be a Starbucks at the Great Wall of China but no one in Avignon's heard of it. Instead, people hang out in quaint bar-cafés; our favorite is Bar les Célestins. Marked with a neon-pink sign and smack in the middle of Place des Corps Saints (the plaza a stone's throw from our studio), it's a long and narrow café with an old wooden bar, bright crimson walls, black trim, and a warm, humorous staff.

Despite making a detailed list of things to do in and around Avignon, ten minutes into our daily coffee at Bar les Célestins, we forget all about our plans. In a country where smoking and talking is a national pastime, being productive can begin to seem rather passé. Some restaurants and shops are rarely open, because whoever owns or runs them is on one of their six weeks of annual vacation, or smoking and talking at a table nearby.

Stephan is my favorite waiter, a student around my age with a sharp wit and deadpan humor. He's boyishly handsome, with pouty, Cupid's bow lips, wispy chestnut hair, big, brown eyes, and a daily uniform of faded plaid shirts and well-worn jeans. Then there's Christine, a gentle and soft-spoken single mother with peaches-and-cream skin, and Edith, who has a bitsy hourglass figure, mischievous black eyes, and short, spiky red hair. She reminds me of a middle-aged Tinkerbell, flitting about the café as she washes dishes and mixes *drinks with dizzying speed. This is all watched with amusement by Roman, a breezy, affable eighteen-year-old who looks like Ashton Kutcher, but with a French accent and more sensuous lips.*

During the hours we're there, the bar fills and empties with a colorful mélange of local artists, shabby-chic dressed twentysomethings, neighborhood residents reading books or newspapers, men in business suits (a definite minority), and high school students who smoke, talk softly, and sip espressos with remarkable maturity.

Like any proper French establishment, Célestins warmly welcomes dogs, and an immaculately groomed white Scotty named Bijoux and a floppy-eared brown mutt named Charlie trot freely from table to table. The only time I've ever seen Edith still is when she's kneeling down to coo and feed them long strips of prosciutto.

My mom and I have come to recognize Bijoux's owner, a spry woman who's the quintessential professor, complete with a thick plaid scarf, nerdy-chic glasses, and artfully disheveled gray hair. Charlie's owner is a bald British expat with a round belly stretched tight as a drum and steel-rimmed glasses that continually slide down his nose while he reads the morning paper and chain-smokes.

Entire mornings are easily whittled away, people watching, reading, talking. When Stephan's not helping customers, he'll join my mom and me in conversation, and we never seem to run out of things to discuss: people, art, politics, fashion, religion, books, men, history. And what better environment to discuss history than Avignon, a city with such a rich and colorful one; the papacy resided in Avignon for less than a century but it influenced the history, feel, and architecture for centuries to come.

The kings of Europe had vied for power with the popes for decades but there'd never been quite so grand a pissing contest as the one between the French king Philip IV and Pope Boniface VIII (pronounced, as I was corrected, bonAfachay—not bonyface). At stake was the issue of a king taxing clergy members without the pope's consent, and if we think the smear tactics used by politicians now are bad, try the accusations Philip leveled at Boniface: sodomy, sorcery, blasphemy, murder, and, my personal favorite, the keeping of a small black demon as a pet (which people actually testified to having seen running around Rome). Boniface ultimately excommunicated Philip, who in turn had Boniface captured and beaten, arguably to death.

In came Boniface's replacement, Clement V, a weak-willed pope who was crowned in Lyon and proceeded to appoint French cardinals to please the thuggish Philip. On his way back to Rome from Lyon, Clement stopped in Avignon and, though intending to stay briefly, never left. Rome was a dangerous city with an unruly population and murderous mercenaries. Avignon was peaceful, central to the powerful realms of France and England, perched above a scenic river, and had famous wines. Where would you rather be? It was like a seventy-year papal spring break, with so much greed and corruption that the Italian poet Petrarch dubbed it "Babylon of the West, the sink of vice and corruption."

Granted, papal corruption was hardly new; many popes had mistresses, and the sale of indulgences (buying forgiveness for various sins) helped finance Rome's St. Peter's Basilica. During the Avignon Papacy, however, it reached an all-time high, particularly under Clement VI, a pope who stocked his closet with a hundred and thirty-eight ermine robes, threw lavish—and quite lascivious—parties, and created a zoo for his pet lion and bear.

Much like the Forbidden City was built to express power and glory, the colossal stone walls of the Palais des Papes clearly convey the papacy's dominion and infallibility. But adjacent to the palace is an area with quite a different feel. My mom and I have dubbed it "the bluff," and while we spend our mornings in Bar les Célestins, the bluff is where we invariably spend our evenings.

The bluff isn't a heath-covered, Wuthering Heights*–esque mountain lookout; rather it's the elevated stone terrace of Notre-Dame-des-Dômes, a twelfth-century cathedral sitting on the hilltop adjacent to the second story of the palais. Like all Romanesque cathedrals, it's sturdy and strong, with thick walls, round arches, and a huge tower shooting up from its brawny base. At the very top of the tower, rising even higher than the palace itself, is a tall, gilded statue of the Virgin Mary.*

I increasingly look forward to the time when the buzz of the city calms and the streets empty, and my mother and I climb the stairs to the bluff to watch the sunset. Sitting quietly, each of us lost in our own thoughts, feels like the right way to end our chatty days.

At least it did. Until about a week ago, once the sun had set, we'd leave the bluff and stroll leisurely home to read, head out for a glass of wine, or meet Chrystelle for dinner at her house or in town. When you live somewhere, however, the nights you stay in outnumber those you go out, and I was getting mighty tired of reading every night in the absence of TV, radio, or the Internet. Most shockingly, so was my mom, who offhandedly mentioned missing TV to me last week on the bluff.

Now, my mom went eight years without even owning a TV (if she hadn't married Paul, I doubt she ever would have bought one), and they didn't get cable until my senior year of college.

"Mia!" she called me one day, "there are channels just for travel or gardening! There's an entire channel just for military history! And French! And book TV!"

"Ma, it's called cable, it's been around since the eighties."

"What about 'unplugging'?" I tease her now. "What happened to our summer sans Internet, TV, or connection to the world outside of Avignon?"

What happened was the accidental discovery of a video rental store and a new routine of utter nighttime debauchery. Now, the second the sun sets, we race from the bluff to get to Video Futur before it closes, swing by Marché Plus for avocados and lemon sorbet, scurry home, throw on jammies, mash up avocadoes, garlic, lime, and salt for guacamole (this has become our favorite dinner, which is kind of odd, but my mom, who normally enjoys cooking elaborate meals, seems to be on strike), pour two glasses of white wine, fire up the computer, and arrange everything carefully on the Click-Clack. *We've gotten this down to twenty minutes, which includes taking turns showering.*

Period pieces are the best rentals; it's a trip to fall asleep with images from Medieval, Renaissance, or Imperial Europe in our minds, and then eat breakfast the next morning while looking out at a thirteenth-century defensive wall and eighteenth-century townhouses. We quickly advanced from renting movies once a week to three nights a week, but it was The Tudors *that did us in.*

My mom had never followed a television show before, yet now we're up till one in the morning watching back-to-back episodes. The theme song alone is rousing, with trumpets playing over clips of galloping steeds, swinging hatchets, and naked, writhing limbs. She's as much fun to watch as the show itself—"Look at the embroidery on that codpiece! Wouldn't you love to have those goblets!" When I tripped on the computer cord last night and the screen went black I thought she was going to stab me with her fork.

I've never indulged so completely with my mom before; every night it's like two schoolgirls playing hooky. My mom and I are different in many ways and it's kind of thrilling to discover that, while I obviously love her, I really like her, too. If we'd been little at the same time I bet we would have been friends, and it's fun to picture us giggling under the covers in pigtails and pajamas. Though we'd probably have drifted apart when I discovered punk rock and started cutting class while she remained an A student, still in the Girl Scouts until the ripe old age of sixteen. And to think she missed the early signs of my drug use.

"Can you believe this?" she said to me the other night. "We've spent the last five hours wandering around a beautiful city, eating tarts, looking at art and a gorgeous sunset and we're about to eat guacamole, drink some wine, and watch The Tudors. *You know, Mia, I could really live like this."*

"Mom," I shouted. "We are *living like this!"*

Mia thinks I cook well because I love to, but I have a love/hate relationship with the culinary. Oh, I still love to invent tarts and ice creams. Before we left I created a creamy basil pear sorbet I could kick myself for not writing down.

But getting meals on the table every day? Or even most days? Just the *thinking,* day in, day out, of what to make, ech. When I was holed up alone in a little cabin writing part of *Come Back,* I got to cook and eat what, when, and where I wanted. Not having to think about anyone else's stomach after two decades of doing it daily was incredibly liberating.

I taught myself to cook in my twenties because I was into nutritious food for Mia and me. After years of making healthy versions of everything, in my forties I got into gourmet. I explored exotic cuisine, sugar and butter were back, and I began to drink espresso and wine for the first time in my life.

Now that I'm fifty-one, I savor *time* a lot more than *shiso* or pink Himalayan salt. If they stopped selling salad in a bag, I'd weep. My pal Leah nailed it: "So I'm standing in this long, slow-moving line yesterday, and I'm looking at my watch, and I just want to yell, 'Couldja hurry up already, I'm *aging*!'"

And that's just the cooking part of my association with kitchens. There's also the personal history part, which includes great memories: it's where I bathed Mia in the sink when she was tiny, where we banged pots and pans to songs and made play-dough, where she realized that you could spit peas farther than any other vegetable and that corn was just the right size for an earplug.

It was also where she tried to stab me with a screwdriver when she was on drugs and Paul wrestled her to the floor. Where he slammed his fist into a cupboard when he learned she'd taken off, *again*. It was where I was washing dishes when she was missing and I first heard Emmylou Harris's "My Baby Needs an Angel." When she sang the line about her baby *swimming with the sharks, out where none could save her,* I slid to the black-and-white tiles and buried my face in soapy yellow rubber gloves. Took me years before I could cross a black-and-white checker tile floor without a Pavlovian sinking-gut response.

I was actually relieved that there's not even an oven here, just a sliver of a kitchen with a stove-top, teeny fridge, and ten inches of counter space. Yet one of the first things I did was start a list of what to stock it with, on autopilot. We assumed our historic roles: I cook, she eats.

Mia's always been a sensuous person. She'll jump in the ocean just to feel the waves in the dead of winter, she'd cuddle every pet she passes if she could, she loves sculpting because she likes the squish of the clay between her fingers. And she loves food. Even as a kid she remembered scents and flavors like a chef. Not that she's big on *cooking* food, but she adores smelling, savoring, and talking about it.

She's not alone. I'm not sure why, but younger women have embraced food in a way my generation never did. For boomers, getting out of the kitchen was part of being liberated. Our kids dined out more in one year than most of us ever did in the entire 1960s.

Young women seem to have skipped a generation in their embrace of cooking, crafts, and gardening—they're more like their *grandmothers,* only online and on speed. Even some of the cuisine is a throwback, much of it a return to the red meat and martinis of the *Mad Men* era.

"The last thing we wanted to do when we left home was cook or do housey things; it was all about career," I mentioned to a friend, Elise, the grande dame of food bloggers, in a recent call. She began simplyrecipes .com in 2003 because she found herself back in her parents' home and realized that at forty-one, as a Silicon Valley MBA, she had no idea how to make even a roast. What had started as a way to share family recipes has become one of the most visited blogs on the planet. Which I doubt would have happened when either of us was in our twenties.

I suggested it might be because cooking something great or knitting a beret and then blogging about it provides instant gratification for a generation with a short attention span. She thinks a lot of it is because the Internet is such a perfect medium for women. When BlogHer was created to give women a stronger voice on the Internet, she assured them that in a few years, that wouldn't be an issue.

"I knew we'd dominate the Web—women are verbal! We love to share what we know. And food's so much more interesting and global now. There's just been so much more attention, there's the green movement, farmers' markets, first there was Food Network, then came blogs. Cooking has become a *want to* rather than being the *have to* it was for our moms. Food became cool."

But for a lot of women, she added, it's still about getting food on the table economically; in other words, cooking will always be a *have to* for many of us. Including Mia, who'd eat out every night if she could, or at my house if she lived close enough. She attempts to cook to save money, though she's as clueless in the kitchen as Elise used to be.

I'm watching her stack big basil leaves to make chiffonade for a pasta, clumsily, under my direction, because I never taught her to cook, and realize that, in yet another way, I'm becoming my mom. Because she never taught me, either.

The answer to "what's for dinner" in our house was always "Food." To her, cooking was a mother's job. Our job as kids was to play, do well in school, and avoid killing our siblings. The kitchen was her world and she didn't want us underfoot. And I'm willing to bet that for all the moms who love cooking with their little girls, just as many treasure the kitchen as a refuge, as one of the few places they can have two minutes to themselves, where they can be alone with their thoughts and feelings.

Since we've come here to spend time together, I offered to teach Mia how to cook some of her favorite foods (those that don't need an oven). Today we shopped for ingredients for a pasta with fresh tomatoes, herbs, garlic, mushrooms, spicy sausage, and Parmesan. We've washed everything, laid it out, and chopped the sausage and garlic to sauté.

We've spent half the day on this project already, and it's gorgeous outside. Mia carefully (read *s-l-o-w-l-y*) rolls the basil leaves to chiffonade them.

"Now," I hand her the knife. "Thin ribbons like I showed you."

She cuts slowly, bruising the basil leaves instead of cutting cleanly through them.

"Cut with authority, Mia. Keep your fingers clear and just"—I put my hands over hers on the knife and make one staccato downward push—"cut it."

"Hey, be careful!" she says nervously.

"You gotta cut boldly, Mia. A dull knife or a weak wrist is dangerous."

What I really want to do is take the knife and tell her to go dust or something while I whip through this so we can eat and go for a hike. Actually, I'd rather just chop the tomatoes, garlic, and herbs, throw on olive oil, salt, and lemon, toss, eat, done in ten minutes. But, you know, this trip being about bonding and all.

"Hey, Mia, do you think you never cared about cooking because you thought I didn't want you in the kitchen?"

"Why? Feeling guilty?"

"It just would have taken too long to show you what to do."

"*Would have?* I know you're dying to tell me to hurry up right now."

"Well, yeah . . . When you were growing up, I just wanted to get it on the table, not give lessons. It's not like you ever really expressed any interest in cooking."

"I also never expressed interest in piano or Kumon math, but you had me take lessons. Here"—she hands me the plate of basil—"what's next?"

"Do the same with the mint."

I hand her the bushy mint plant on our windowsill.

"I never wanted you to focus on the domestic. I wanted you to focus on a career, to be out slaying dragons and seeing the world. I still do. You have plenty of time to learn cooking."

She laughs as she plucks mint. "Sounds like you're describing yourself. Mom, it's totally fine if you don't want to teach me to cook this summer."

"It is? You won't be bothered or hurt?"

"Of course not. I don't want to stay indoors while we're here either. Let's just eat simply and buy more ready-made stuff." She pauses. "But, you know, it would be nice to have *some* cooked dinners. I mean we're in France, Mom."

"I agree. But I'm not doing them by myself. You have to be the kitchen elf, no convenient absences like you do."

"Pas de problème."

"Great. Now, strip a stalk of rosemary and chop it fine, and I'll do the tomatoes."

I'm thrilled. I don't have to think about feeding two, and when we do cook, we get to keep doing what's always worked: I give orders and the kitchen elf obeys. Nobody walks on eggshells, no arguments, no teaching. Which is definitely not typical. If you want a ringside seat to a mother and her adult daughter's relationship, watch them cook together when there's pressure on, like guests coming in an hour.

For most moms and daughters, it usually remains one place the old rules and roles don't change. Elise thinks the sun rises and sets behind her mother, who is a remarkable woman; they have a wonderful relationship. Because she's always mining her mom for old family recipes and the blog includes both of her parents, I assumed all three did the cooking.

"Oh, no," she corrected me, "it's just me and Dad. I never cook with my mom. She tells me what to do."

When it comes to mothers and daughters, there is the issue of weight—a subject often fraught with hurt and anxiety—and then there is food, perhaps one of the most important ways in which we bond. It is, quite literally, our first bond; we come into being nourished in and by their bodies, and they then spend the next eighteen years feeding us.

Food is its own language. During the times when my mom and I couldn't go two minutes without yelling or crying, it was how we said I may not like you very much right now, but I still love you.

And my mom's a great person to be in a culinary conversation with. Lamb tagine with apricots and almonds, chicken with preserved lemons and paprika, chocolate bread pudding with brandy-soaked cherries—living at home was like bunking at Chez Panisse.

My version of cooking involves combining cereal, milk, and sliced bananas or strawberries if I'm feeling ambitious. Her failing to teach me wasn't necessarily a bad thing; patience in the kitchen isn't my mom's forte, and if she'd taught me everything she knew, one of us wouldn't have made it out alive.

I remember listening with a combination of shock and awe to our friend Kelly talk about her mother teaching her to cook. Kelly Sterling, a talented chef who's worked for the likes of the Border Girls and Matsuhisa Nobu, is extremely gentle and soft-spoken. That she's spent her days among swearing and tattooed men is a testament to her love of food and cooking, which she credits her mother for.

Growing up, Kelly and her four siblings had their own plots in the vegetable garden, where they grew their own Halloween pumpkins and watched zucchinis turn from floral blooms to vegetables. Her mom taught her to make dough from scratch and cook a roast. She was patient and kind with her kids in the kitchen, gathering them around the oven to watch as the bread turned a golden brown.

This floored me. The only thing I ever saw turn golden brown in the oven was my stuffed animal Little Ann after my mom read an article about how heat kills dust mites. To my mom, being loving and patient in the kitchen meant ignoring me rather than telling me to scram. But that was always because I thought she enjoyed cooking. Come to find out she only enjoyed it part of the time, and, more recently, not at all.

It's been interesting to notice my mom as she gains and loses interest in things. Watching her evaluate everything in her life from the minutia to the big picture makes me aware that I've avoided thinking about my day-to-day New York life since coming to France, probably because it's somewhat embarrassing. I've always thought of myself as very active: volunteering, learning languages, sculpting, taking photos, playing soccer. What an outdated perception! I haven't consistently done any of those things since college. If anything, I've become rather lazy and have a painfully predictable schedule.

My late teens and very early twenties were some of the most exciting times in my life. I was finally free after two years of being locked away, and instead of destroying myself and avoiding life, I was eager to live as fully as possible. I sampled all sorts of activities. I had no idea I could sculpt, for example, until I randomly enrolled in a class. I loved everything about it, molding the dense, cold clay, re-creating the beauty of the human form.

I didn't realize how much it bothered me that I hadn't enrolled in an art class since moving to New York, or never researched mentoring programs, since I love working with teens. Sure, I meant to take up sculpting, dancing, reading more books, and volunteering—I was always about to start something. What I actually did, however, was fall into a rut of working at an easy-enough job with steady pay and good benefits but that I wasn't really happy at, going to the gym after work, and then, depending on how much energy I had left, going to a friend's party or plunking down on the couch with my roommates to watch reality TV shows that I'm too embarrassed to name here.

Because I wasn't doing anything different from most of my friends, I didn't see this as a problem. How could anyone think I wasn't doing well? I graduated from college and wrote a book! So what if I do nothing with my free time? I have a great job title and apartment, I have successful friends!

But if I was doing so well I wouldn't have been subtly disappointed in myself; I wouldn't have had to talk myself out of feeling guilty for (again) reaching for junk food and the remote. My life wouldn't have started feeling repetitive, predictable, and rather uninspiring. I wanted more, which is why I'd start feeling restless, and, like a lot of people I know, thinking about moving or changing jobs. Sometimes I wonder if we make big moves because we underestimate the importance of smaller ones. Years are just an accumulation of thousands of hours, and what we choose to do with each of them matters.

Maybe this is part of life's learning curve, learning how to structure your time and which people and activities to fill it with. I'm part of a generation whose schedules were usually structured and determined for us. When they were children, my parents never had arranged playdates, they weren't taken to soccer, piano, and art classes; they took off on their bikes and as long as they came home for lunch or dinner they were left to their own devices. I can't imagine that kind of freedom and control of my time as a kid. Granted, adult supervision is more of a factor in a city as big as L.A., but, nonetheless, I think as a whole my generation is more deficient when it comes to negotiating our time and activities.

Part of the "quarter-life crisis"—this feeling that our lives have no meaning—probably comes from not participating in the kinds of meaningful activities we were often spoon-fed growing up, and then had at our fingertips in college. Living on our own, many of us seem to have opted for what's easiest to access: the Internet, parties, the gym, TV, and dating (or, rather, hooking up).

Alanna, my former roommate and partner in couch-potato crime, put it well when she said early adulthood isn't just about adjusting to fiscal responsibility but social responsibility as well, establishing the difference between relaxation and having fun and being plain lazy. Free time is just that, activities that make you feel free, as opposed to guilty, lazy, and mildly useless.

Sometimes lessons I learned in that school as a teen are like time-release medications; I'll forget all about something I learned until it's suddenly staring me in the eyes. In this case, the lesson is twofold; one, there's almost always a discrepancy between how you view yourself and how you actually are, and, two, to stay on track it's imperative to regularly check in with, and evaluate, yourself—as long as you do it neutrally and without judgment, which is where a lot of us get stuck.

We're hard-wired to avoid pain; if you beat yourself up every time you evaluate or examine yourself and your life, it makes you less likely to do it at all, which means you'll probably keep doing more of the same.

It's more crowded than usual today on the bluff and my mom and I squish together into an open space, resting our elbows on the ledge overlooking the plaza below. Her hand touches mine lightly and I look at it. She's always joked about having old lady hands even as a kid, which I can believe because even though she's always had very firm, smooth olive skin, the veins have always been extremely prominent. I used to play with them when I was little, pressing on a big blue wiggly one and then watching it puff back up when I let go. Looking at her hands now, she has no age spots, but the smooth olive skin is thinner, with fine wrinkles in places. It seems like her hands and arms are beginning to catch up with her veins. It's one more thing that makes me realize that I'm not just beginning *to see the passage of time on my mother's body, I'm going to continue to from now on. The days of her looking pretty much the same to me are no more.*

Earlier this week, my mom and I were at Chrystelle's house for dinner when I saw a photo from Chrystelle's wedding with my mom in it. She was tan from walking outdoors all summer, her black hair just beginning to grow out of the pixie cut she always wore. She still has that dress, a long black shift with spaghetti straps and embroidered gold accents that looks almost Egyptian. It's one of the few things I've never been able to talk her into giving me.

I looked up from the photo at my mom and Chrystelle talking in the kitchen, and was startled by the difference. She hasn't looked as she did in that photo for several years now, but for some reason I still picture her that way. When I hear the word "mother," what first comes to mind is an energetic woman with short hair, a mostly black wardrobe, and signature red lipstick. I don't picture my mom as she is today, calmer, more self-possessed, a softened facial expression, and shoulder-length hair that's jet-black except for two thick gray stripes at her forehead she's let grow in because she got sick of touching up the roots every few days. "I never thought I'd end up looking like Cruella De Vil," she lamented. She looks young for her age but (and she'll probably kill me for saying this) the skin under her neck is softer.

What startled me even more, though, was that as I looked at her I was suddenly able to picture how she'll look when she's old. I saw her with her hair fully gray, her eyes a tapestry of wrinkles, her hands freckled with age spots. Knowing in a back-of-your-mind sort of way that your mother isn't so young anymore is quite different from knowing in a way that hits you in your gut that she's actually aging.

And right there, with music playing, and Antoine laughing, and my mother and Chrystelle talking in the kitchen, tears welled up because I suddenly knew how I'd feel when she's gone. I understood that when she goes my world will never be the same. Because even if I have ten children, even if I'm wildly in love with my husband and surrounded by friends, there will never be someone who understands or loves me quite like my mother, or that I love like her.

Something changed for me after that. I've been nicer to her, and more patient. I've wanted to be physically near her, rest my head on her shoulder or hold her hand. I feel more love toward her, and I wish it hadn't taken imagining my life without her to coax that from me.

The small town of Apt is home to a candy shop called La Bonbonnière, and this morning my mom and I rented a car for the express purpose of buying one particular candy sold strictly there: la Gourmandize, a glowing orange half-dome consisting of a candied clementine, marzipan, honey, and dark chocolate.

We park and, without consulting the position of the sun, the direction of the wind, the side of the tree moss grows on, or any other of her famed orienteering skills, my mom beelines toward Mecca. We stock up on les Gourmandizes, and then buy some gelato to enjoy now.

"I did this exact same thing with Jordana my first time here," my mom says contentedly, remembering a trip she took with a girlfriend some years back. "We bought those same orange candies, sat on this same bench, and I had the same flavor of gelato."

"Chestnut?"

"Yes. Here," she says, scooping some onto a spoon and handing it to me. "What does that taste like to you?"

"Why do you always say things like that? I just want to enjoy it, not rack my brain for adjectives!"

"That's the whole point, you're not supposed to rack your brain! Your best metaphors come from feelings, not thoughts. Don't think in terms of sweet or bitter—what do you see and feel when you put it in your mouth? To me, chestnuts are like clouds and honey."

It's a good description, light, sweet, fluffy. But who thinks of metaphors in the middle of eating ice cream? This drives me crazy sometimes, but it's what makes her her. I love the writing process, I enjoy crafting prose and researching and editing. But it's something I do. Being a writer is who she is.

And I like that she's sharing it with me. It's small, mentioning her first trip here or telling me what chestnut reminds her of, but it's the kind of thought she usually keeps to herself. Yesterday while we were at the bus stop she said out of the blue that she always loved the song "Bus Stop" by the Hollies because that's what she thought love would be like when she was a young teen. I knew the song, it's about a man who covers a woman with his umbrella after seeing her in the rain at a bus stop. They met at the bus stop each day after that, and by the end of the summer they were together.

I smiled, picturing her with naïve notions of love, with naïve notions of anything for that matter. She's always been drawn toward darker and more complex characters and stories, and it was such a sweet, simple image.

I've tended to view myself as the ever-changing variable, and my mother as the more stable constant, perhaps because there are few women we make as many assumptions about than our mothers. But she's continually surprising me now, from once-naïve romantic notions to almost becoming a doctor to having a conversation with a man, in German (which I had no idea she spoke), to a possible singing career.

A remix of Joan Baez's "The Ballad of Sacco and Vanzetti" started playing at Bar les Célestins the other day, and my mom asked if I recognized it, because she used to sing it to me as a lullaby. I didn't, but it prompted me to ask her if she ever took singing lessons, because she has an operatic voice. As it turns out, she did, from the man who sometimes coached Barbra Streisand, no less—and who wanted her to pursue it professionally.

"And you said no?! Why? People would kill for that opportunity, Mom."

"I thought about it, but I was so shy back then," she answered, shrugging. "And I certainly wasn't cut out for the lifestyle. I'm usually asleep by the time most performances begin."

"How come you never told me this before?" I asked. "I love hearing about this!"

"I don't know, the subject never came up, and it's not something I really ever think about—it was so long ago. Besides, you never ask, why would I think you'd want to know?"

Well, I do want to know, and told her so. Even as she's increasingly forth-coming, however, things remain unspoken, and I still often stop myself from asking her what she's thinking. Yesterday she stopped suddenly outside of a knit shop and lightly smacked herself on the forehead.

"Mia, we missed it—the knitting festival was last weekend. How could I let myself forget that?" she added, almost more to herself than to me.

It was written all over her face how disappointed and angry she was with herself. I felt terrible. She loves anything to do with yarn or knitting, because it makes her feel close with Bubbie; I know how much she misses her. She thinks I don't notice but there are times she'll stop midsentence because she knows if she keeps talking she'll start crying.

"I'm sorry, Mom, maybe we can—" I started to tell her.

"Oh, look at those shoes!" she interrupted me brightly, and marched into a store with a big soldes *(sale) sign on the window. I felt exasperated that she just completely changed subjects but maybe that had nothing to do with a level of trust between us and more to do with her having a good day and not want-ing to think about something that made her sad.*

I've always felt bad about my mother and grandmother's rocky relationship, especially because Bubbie and I have always gotten along. She's whip-smart, loves desserts and sweets as much as I do, and has a wicked sense of humor. Bub can also be feisty and tends toward blunt honesty—something I find amusing

*and endearing. I dislike emotional guesswork, and you'd have to be blind, deaf,
or dumb not to know how Bubbie feels about something. My mom finds this
aspect of her mother's personality far less amusing; it's been a source of much
tension between them.*

*Conversely, Bubbie finds elements of my mother's personality nerve-
wracking, like the fact that she's always on the go, and looking for ways to
change or improve herself. I have a little bit of both of them in me. I love to
travel and hike alongside my mom, and I like that she often pushes me. I also
love sitting with my grandmother, eating her poppy-seed pastries while playing Chinese checkers, watching TV, or talking about what's wrong with the
government. None of which my mom could sit through for ten minutes.*

I don't know why I should be surprised at how interested Mia is in something that seems insignificant to me. What daughter doesn't love learning just about anything about her mother's past? For many of us, it's a
curiosity that's never sated.

Some mothers are happy to share, and some don't like talking about
their youth, for a variety of reasons. On the one hand, a woman has the
right to keep her past private, even from her kids. On the other, as her
kid, you feel territorial, as if it's your *right* to know.

My sisters and I were always dying to know about my mom's life in
"the Old Country," but she wasn't often forthcoming about her past. Like
many Europeans, she's not in the American habit of going on about herself. Part of it is no doubt also because her past was such a painful one.
So few in her family survived the Holocaust, a few cousins. Asking her
about her childhood was like playing the lottery; you never knew when
you'd hit the jackpot and get an answer, or more than one or two.

We were greedy for any bit of history, an anecdote, a fact or memory.
When one of us would find something out, we'd share it like a golden
nugget. Photos were like hitting pay dirt, not that there were many. Over
the years, we've fought over them like they were diamonds.

Sometimes my mom would offer up something out of the blue. Several years ago, she was shopping with my youngest sister and pointed to a man's blue-and-white pinstriped shirt and said her father used to wear those. Even something like that is dear to us, it fills in blanks, helps us complete the image of the man in the sepia photo with the aquiline nose, gaunt Lincoln-esque cheeks, and big, haunted-looking pale eyes. Our grandfather.

He was smart, and usually won at cards, which he played more often than his wife liked. He was often gone, taking work as a carpenter and had the long beard typical of Eastern European Jewish men, though they weren't what you'd call committed orthodox. My grandmother wore a bob and a short flapper dress when they married. We have one photo of her as a three-year-old, standing on a stool in a photo studio, holding my great-grandmother's hand. We would have given anything to see a photo of her grown up. Close to six feet tall, with black hair and violet eyes, she was such a great beauty that people would come from other villages to watch her walk from the synagogue.

She died at thirty-two, it's believed of kidney failure, before the Nazis got to their small town in Czechoslovakia. It was a comfort to me that the school I sent Mia to for healing and safety halfway round the world just happened to be a day's drive from my mother's village. I mean, what are the odds? It was as if the spirit of the women in my family there wanted to watch over her.

I know what it is to long to know more about your mother, and her mother before her. I never wanted my daughter to feel that way about me. And yet she *does* feel this way. She says I've brushed her off, but I don't remember not answering questions or being evasive. It's possible all daughters feel this way to a degree. Or maybe I'm projecting, or repeating, my own experience. One that I paid a dear price to learn is not uncommon.

It was a blog post on that subject that created the break between my mother and me. I wrote that I was going to Budapest to see the places my mother lived or hid in, as a way to connect emotionally to her. Growing up, my mother wasn't as demonstrative as my friends' American moth-ers were, she didn't say "I love you" and hug me all the time the way I saw them do. "She loved me, took excellent care of us, she was dutiful but emotionally unavailable," was what I wrote, in the therapeutic jargon that's become part of boomers' vernacular. Like babies in a nursery, when one cries, they all chime in. Encouraged by Alice Miller, Freud, Philip Roth, Woody Allen, and so on, "emotionally unavailable mother" became the collective battle cry of millions of baby boomers looking to blame someone for their unhappiness, warranted or not.

Of course I see now what I didn't then—that my mother's background made her doubly unable to do that; she was not only of a generation that valued more hands-off mothering, she was from a culture with fundamentally different values and approaches to parenting.

What I saw as expressing how much I loved my mother, as evidenced by my traveling so far to feel closer to her, she saw as a critique of her as a mother. Which is, of course, understandable. I was so focused on expressing myself, I hadn't considered how she might take what I wrote, how it could be misread. If I'm fully accountable, I did wish she had been more physically demonstrative. So what? Who says it's a daughter's job to insist a mother be exactly the way she wants her to be? Who gets to decide? I'm sure she wishes I'd been or done things differently. And now that I've cleaned house for a family of three, I'd say you can't get much more physically demonstrative than cleaning house for a family of seven.

For immigrant mothers, it's even harder. The very things that Americans see as good mothering in the last forty years—lots of attention, praise, and self-esteem boosting, constant verbal validation—is what moms from Eastern Europe see as raising kids who will be insecure and self-absorbed. Self-esteem isn't externally generated in my mother's world, you earn it *internally*, by your own actions. I can't say that our way has been better, to be honest.

It's disturbing to me that I may have missed signals from Mia, or dismissed her desire to know me better. I know she can ask obliquely sometimes when it comes to something she feels I may be sensitive to, but if I'd been truly listening to her, I would have heard her yearning.

I know I'm not listening to Mia as deeply as I used to, at least if I want to strengthen our relationship. I was so pleased that she shared with me why she left New York, and I listened closely. I was also aware of when to be quiet, to allow her to express herself without my input. But looking back I can see that as she was talking, part of my mind was working out how best to respond. I told her why I thought she felt that way rather than let her continue to explore it on her own. I answered instead of asked. What else might I have learned in listening and questioning for *her* experience, and more important, what else might *she* have learned?

Listening was an important factor in bringing us back together and keeping us close when she first came home. In the year before she went off to college, our ability to hear each other was critical—apart from the past, apart from doubt, filters, fear, hurt, anger, worldview, expectation, all things inevitably bound up in all mother-daughter relationships. It's a skill and an art, one that requires genuine commitment and a lot of practice.

I learned active listening from Barbara Fagan, a master coach who facilitated a leadership workshop in which I took a vow of silence several years ago. As part of it, we were to take on our biggest challenge. Mine was authenticity, doing whatever it took to get my head connected with my heart. I knew there was no way I'd ever deeply connect with Mia until I did. So, while my peers were jumping out of airplanes, losing fifty pounds, or starting businesses, I took a vow of silence. Not in some monastery or quiet retreat center, in my own home during a regular work-week. None of my other ideas scared me as much as that did, always a good sign in the personal development arena if you ask me.

The first day was disorienting and unpleasant. I was home working on a script; Paul was also working at home. He found it disconcerting—for about two hours. After that it was pretty peaceful in his world. Not in mine, because I had a running commentary going on in my head all day long. I suddenly knew exactly how Mia must have felt at Morava, where kids weren't allowed to speak until they got to a certain level. My dreams that night were so noisy I woke up all night long. I talked out of the mouths of everyone in my dreams, even our cat Fluffy.

I lived my life as usual, running errands and so on. If someone spoke to me, I just tapped my throat and they immediately assumed I had laryngitis and stopped talking to me. Probably without realizing it, they also stopped acknowledging my presence. I learned fast that the inability to speak renders one invisible and irrelevant in our culture.

I'm a verbal person in a verbal profession. Being unable to talk was frustrating, but feeling invisible was dreadful. By the end of the day I felt invisible to myself, which was worse; I wondered if that was what insanity felt like.

But halfway through the second day, my mind, and nerves, quieted down. There was just silence, and an awareness of my own awareness. By evening I began to feel *more* visible than I'd ever felt before. I didn't have to "access" any part of myself, or my "true" feelings, as if they resided in some special file in the Department of Me. There was a harmony to my actions, feelings, thoughts, and an inner contentment I'd never felt before.

But the most valuable part of the experience by far was that everyone *else* became more visible. My silence allowed other people to fill up all the space in the room. They became so dimensional and rich it was almost *cubist;* like aspects of them kept unfolding and opening out and I could experience every angle of them without moving an inch.

And one very big part of Mia that is unfolding right now before me is the part of her that has nothing to do with our relationship, the part of her that belongs only to herself, and to the world. That's a part of her I want to tune in to and experience. I want her to feel comfortable being all of who she is when she's with me. I suppose all daughters censor parts of themselves around their mothers, but it should be a *want* to for her, not a *have* to, because of some way that I'm being.

If our daughters aren't open with us, we have to be accountable.

How am I being with Mia such that she hasn't opened up to me? If she feels she may not be fully heard, or heard as a prelude to advise, control, or judge, even if well-intentioned, why would she, why would any daughter?

They don't want us to co-opt their dilemma—it steals their power. Or they do, which is worse, because it means they hear our voice over their own, that they've learned from us not to trust themselves. Either way, she'll be distorting herself somehow. As mothers we have the power to stunt our daughters' authenticity in deep, often hidden, ways that the culture or men can never do.

"Ten stamps, please," I ask the post office clerk in French.

My mom waits for me off to the side, gazing at a poster. I pay and walk toward the door.

"You ready?"

"One sec," she murmurs.

I turn to see what she's studying so intently and my heart sinks when I see it's pictures of missing children. She spends several seconds on each face, committing them to memory as she undoubtedly hoped people would when it was my missing face on posters all over Los Angeles.

"I'll meet you outside," I mumble, and walk out in a daze.

She still does that. She still studies missing posters.

I remember her taking time to read them when I lived at home during community college. But everything was much fresher then; I was only seventeen. I had no idea she still did this.

"It's beautiful out!" my mom exclaims, smiling brightly as she steps out into the sun. "Should we head over to the Musée Calvet?"

I nod a yes but it's all I can do not to cry. Most people take a quick glance at those posters or deliberately avoid looking at them because it's so sad. Ten years after I ran away, she's still on autopilot to pay attention to other mothers' missing children. Such a nonchalant act on her part—she's hardly upset right now—is such a powerful message of the ways in which I permanently changed her life.

I opened her eyes to a side of life she was happily oblivious to before, and on some level, some part of her is still the mother of a missing child.

The last several weeks we spent like two girlfriends, overdosing on chocolate and marveling at medieval wonders. But in seconds we're back to being mother and daughter and the thought of being friends like any two women is laughable. History sometimes feels like a vain and spiteful God, lashing out if you go too long without stopping at memory's altar.

I spend the rest of the day irritable and do my best to talk as little as possible. Times like this I don't want to be around her; I feel guilty and agitated and I know if she says something kind or does anything nice for me I'll snap at her, which is the last thing I want to do. I'm glad for the chance to stay in tonight when Chrystelle calls for an impromptu get–together, which my mom accepts and I decline.

As I walk home, it's as though Avignon's sensed my mood. The skies are darkening early and the wind has begun to blow. The buildings here are neutral in tone, they change color depending on the sky; tonight the whole city feels dark and brooding.

My mind is a split screen. On one side is my mother in profile, hands behind her back as she bends slightly to study the missing poster. On the other side she's in Kathmandu, eyes wide and terrified as she scans for me amid a moving sea of people.

I never told her that I saw her the night we got separated in Durbar Square. When that black Land Rover pulled out between us, she didn't see that I got stuck behind it so that when it finally passed we were completely separated. Given she was the one with the phone, money, and hotel information, I was worried but not panicked. I would have figured out a way back to the hotel and I assumed my mom would figure similarly. Until I saw her.

She had scrambled up a mound of rubble and garbage, and I waved and waved at her but she didn't see me. She was so disproportionately panicked, her eyes wide, the muscles in her jaw and forehead tensed, her fear made all the more dramatic by the garish yellow light.

I'd never seen her face like this but I'd imagined it countless times falling asleep during the nights I ran away or in my more sober moments. I know my mom thinks that I never thought about her or Paul when I ran away or when I was living with my aunt several states away, because I so rarely called them. She once told me they were worried that I had lost all ability to have empathy or remorse, which scared them more than the drug use.

They didn't know I only acted like that because I felt those things too acutely. I was too far gone to stop what I was doing, but I was always painfully aware of the effect it had on my parents. That's why I hated talking to them; the longer we spoke, the longer the guilt would linger after hanging up. That night in Durbar it was like putting a missing piece of my past under UV light, an image of my mother's face showing up like invisible ink. It was an image I'd never had to see or face.

When I think about things like this, part of me wants to comfort her and part of me can't stand the sight of her, I'm so ashamed. I know what's done is done, I know I was young and having issues coming up from being abused, but I still wish I could take it all back sometimes. Everyone is always so positive— look at how well things turned out in the end, look at how much was ultimately gained! People always say to live without regrets, but I have enormous regret and not everything "turned out for the best." My parents never bought a house in L.A. and had more children. My mom still looks at posters of missing children and panics disproportionately because of what I did.

I don't want to put a positive spin on things. It's not a "yes it was horrible but look at all the good that ultimately resulted," it's a "yes it was horrible and good also came from it." One doesn't negate the other, and believing it does can alleviate the kind of guilt or regret that's healthy to feel.

I don't want to tell her any of this because she'll end up comforting me, and that feels wrong because the whole point is the pain I caused her. I want her to say Yes, you shattered my life. I'm fixing it now but you definitely screwed it up. At least that's honest. You can't move on from a lie, or heal from something you refuse to even acknowledge exists.

As a writer, my mother weaves plots and creates intrigue and develops characters. In her own life, though, she seems more player than playwright;

in some ways I feel like the one who wrote the story line and dictated the plot. What happened to her always had to do with me, directly or indirectly. When I was abused, her life was shattered, and when I was a dumb teen without a clue or a care, it got turned upside down again.

We so rarely think about the true, long-term impact we have on other people. Some of it's self-worth, how easy it is to underestimate yourself and your ability to affect other people. But I think there's another, more selfish, aspect to it. I think if we were to stay aware of it we would have to act more accountably, more thoughtfully. Forgetting our potential impact enables us to feel guiltless. But to a great degree it's gutless, too.

When I reach our apartment I curl into a ball on the bed and cry until a bone-deep physical exhaustion sinks in and I fall asleep. I don't know how much time has passed when I wake, but my mom's still gone. I feel calmer now, but in the drained way that follows sadness. The wind is still blowing outside, banging shutters against building walls, causing the trees outside our window to sway slowly back and forth, their leaves shivering as the wind whips through them.

I get up and walk to the window, catching the reflection of a puffy-eyed young woman before swinging the shutters open. Wind and cold rush into the apartment, and I'm chilled but I feel very present and alive. I feel cleansed. I stand there a few more minutes, inhaling deeply, and then tightly close them shut. I need to talk to my mom about this. I want to let this go.

The only thing scarier than French drivers on country roads in a thunderstorm is circling with fifty of them in a huge two-lane roundabout—with seven exits. One of them is ours.

"What do you mean you don't know which one? You're the navigator!"

"I told you to just go straight," Mia yells back.

"There is no straight, are you blind!?"

We're whizzing around and around the outside lane in the pouring rain. The inside lane is honking and yelling as they shoot right across me to exit.

"Mom, you're going to get us killed!"

"I'm supposed to be exiting, that's why! You were supposed to know which exit! I bet you don't even know the name of the road we were on, or which direction we're heading, do you?"

"It doesn't matter, stop yelling!"

"Oh, my God, you don't, you forgot to mark the route, didn't you?"

No answer. I whip into the inner lane. "I can't believe it. Get out the map!"

"I'll get carsick, no!"

"You'll get a lot sicker if we circle here for an hour! Or if I make you walk!"

"I forgot, okay! I'm sorry! You forget things, too, all the time!"

"Not when it's directions in the boondocks in a thunderstorm!"

"Oh, no, you're perfect! Pocahontas can't even find her way to the apartment after five weeks!"

"Great, I'm going to have to cut through the line of death over and over until we find a human being stupid enough to be out in this rain, Godbloodydammit!"

Silence.

"Where's the sun when you need it?" comes a little squeak.

We've been driving in a huffy silence for a while when my mom suddenly bursts out laughing.

"Do you remember Horti?"

"The road trip with her daughter!" I answer.

Horti is a beautiful and feisty Cuban woman in her nineties that we met one day at the beach in Florida. Sharks had been seen and whistles were blown but she kept swimming laps nonstop so we had to literally block her path to get her attention. Up popped a raisin of a woman in giant goggles, and when we told her about the sharks she just laughed.

"They don want notheen with an old woman like me. Keep blowing the whistles, I no gonna leave."

We'd have felt terrible leaving her, so we stayed and made a new friend. Horti had gone to Chile to meet her daughter, with whom she's very close, for a road trip through the vineyards there. The trip was going fantaaasteeco *until the second they got in the car, put the top down, and started driving.*

"I don know how we didn't keel each other . . . never again . . . I'd rather go to Baghdad."

After a good laugh, my mom and I relax into a contented silence as we drive into the Provençal countryside, a landscape that's a patchwork of rolling hills, fields of crops, green pastures, olive groves, and lavender fields.

Unless you're at just the right angle, lavender fields are pretty but unimpressive, a smattering of violet amid green. But when you continue driving and see them from another angle, it's as though the plants leaped to attention and scurried into perfect formation, forming row after row of what look like fat, happy purple caterpillars. Something about them feels childlike, they're so unabashedly vibrant and puffed with pride.

We drive deeper into the mountains, passing only the occasional farmhouse surrounded by well-tended fields, or herds of sheep and goats grazing beside a stone cottage. Before long we crest a hill and in a diamond-shaped valley below is the Sénanque Abbey in full panorama.

Like two halves of an oyster opening to reveal a pearl, this small, spare abbey is nestled between two olive-colored mountains. The valley floor around it's a sea of purple, row after row of lavender in full bloom. From above it looks like the amethyst center of a geode.

Sénanque is a Cistercian monastery, a Catholic order that emphasizes manual labor and self-sufficiency, and the monks here grow lavender and keep honeybees to support themselves. We spend an hour or so touring the monastery, which dates back to 1148 and is beautiful in its simplicity and austerity.

I've wanted to talk to my mom about what came up for me that day at the post office, but there never seemed to be a good time. Now may not be either; we've finally stopped arguing and I'm not sure if bringing this up would darken our day. We've got a great day planned out and Provence is one of her favorite places in the world. But now I understand why *this area means so much to her; the parts of me that feel nurtured and stimulated here were the parts of her needing to be brought back to life after what I put her through. I understand her more fully now and I want her to know that.*

"Mom," *I blurt out before I have a chance to change my mind.* "Can I talk to you for a minute?"

She looks at me, sees I'm serious, and points to a stone bench off to the side of the lavender fields behind the monastery.

"I'm no good at this kind of thing and if you don't want to talk about it now we don't have to but I've been feeling really bad since—"

"Oh, don't worry about it," *she says, laughing.* "Just read the map before we get in the car next time!"

"Not this morning, Mom, I'm talking about feeling bad about everything, like my whole teenage fiasco and everything. I never expected it to come up, but first there was Durbar and then the post office and—"

"Durbar and the post office? Do you mean Durbar Square in Kathmandu?"

I take a deep breath, think about what I'm trying to say and how to phrase it. I don't necessarily want to apologize; we're past apologies and this is so much bigger than that. It's more of an acknowledgment. Apologizing or asking for forgiveness inserts yourself in there, your own ego is catered to as well.

"Let me just start at the beginning. My understanding of what I put you through as a teen sort of came in stages. I apologized to you in the program— and I genuinely meant it—but my understanding of my actions was pretty limited then. It wasn't really until I read your parts in* Come Back *that I got on a broader, deeper scale what I put you through. And what you went through with my dad, too."*

"I wondered about that," *she says, nodding.* "I'd never told you face-to-face a lot of what I wrote. After you read it you never brought it up, other than editing, of course. I didn't want to press you. I figured you'd bring it up when you were ready to. After all this time, I just assumed you processed it and moved on."

She knows well that until I process things I'm usually uncomfortable talking to anyone about them.

"Yeah, well, some things happened on this trip that made me realize I'd never processed it, period. That I still hold on to a lot of guilt and regret."

I recount how I saw her on that pile of garbage, totally panicked, and I watch as the understanding of how I found her that night sinks in. I wonder if she wishes I hadn't seen her in so vulnerable a state.

"The other day at the post office, something just clicked when I saw you looking at those missing posters. I got on such a deep level what I did to you. It didn't just change your life, it changed your whole identity as a mom, as a woman, and I am so, so sorry."

"That's why you wanted to stay home that night, isn't it?"

I nod.

She takes my hand but doesn't say anything further. I wonder what she's thinking but in a way I'm glad she's quiet. The sun is behind the clouds now and the lavender has turned a silvery periwinkle, a more hushed version of what was just seconds ago a brilliant violet glow.

I'm often asked if writing Come Back gave me closure. It did, but mostly in terms of myself as I put my history with my dad to rest. It generated a new set of issues with my mother, however, and that's something I haven't felt closure about until now. Side by side, sitting in a silent understanding, it feels like this last piece of the puzzle that is my past is slowly, gracefully clicking into place.

Mia doesn't cry easily. Tears aren't falling now, but her eyes are shiny with them. Such vulnerability, and accountability, takes courage, even between mother and daughter, perhaps especially between them. I turn to face her as she worries a thread on the hem of her sundress.

"Thank you for being big enough to say that, Mia, I'm sure it wasn't easy. I don't want to tell you not to feel guilty or downplay the impact to make you feel better. That would deny what's true for you, and make it about me, my need to 'mother,' to protect you from your own feelings, or mine. I don't think you need protecting. I don't see you as fragile. You're one of the most powerful women I know."

I turn to face her.

"What's most meaningful to me is more than the acknowledgment of the events, it's your acknowledgment of *me*. I feel as if you're really seeing me, not just as your mom, as a person. That *did* happen to me. I *did* get derailed. And rewired. And as Barbara would say, rocks are hard, water is wet—it was what it was, and it was bad."

I smile at her and she nods and then rests her head on my shoulder. My old choice would have been to say something now that starts with a "but": but don't feel so bad, but look at all the good that came, but look how close we are now. That would be my old pattern of coming from fear, of saying I'm afraid you're too weak to feel bad or handle any pain, so let's just give it a drive-by.

We tell our daughters we don't trust them in a thousand ways. We don't consciously mean to, but we steal their confidence in their own strength by stealing their pain. And their confidence in our strength by saying *we* aren't strong enough to see them struggle.

We sit a while longer, on a cool stone bench where monks have sat in quiet reflection for hundreds of years, gazing out on these same fields of lilac-blue. This is new for both of us, not to comfort or avoid what needs to be felt and spoken.

Time is rarely enough to clean up a painful history in any relationship, especially between moms and daughters. It's often easier to keep fighting—it's familiar, and you each get to be right—or to keep silent and let sleeping dogs lie. But why have a dead dog in your relationship?

chapter nine

Avignon

Pentimento

Def: A visible trace of earlier painting beneath a layer, or
layers, of paint on a canvas. From Italian, literally "repentant."

If happiness were a landscape, it would have corridors of Italian cypress, lanes of potted lemons, purple tunnels of wisteria, hillsides lush
with roses. It would look like the seemingly endless gardens of the Fort
Saint André Abbey, which tumble into one another as lyrically and naturally as if they'd been there since time began, rather than having been
lovingly cultivated over several centuries. Who would have guessed that
all this was behind the towering walls of the giant fort we could see from
our bluff across the river?

We wander through one little paradise after another: hidden bowers
with bees and flowers; a sun-bleached crest with the crumbling remains
of a chapel; a grove of ancient, twisting olive trees. Outside, the fort is a
solid, cold, masculine enclosure of stone that soars into the blue. Inside,
however, like Avignon, it's a lush, feminine embrace.

I was almost speechless the first time we came (yes, it's *that* amazing).
It was like finding someplace I never knew I'd been dreaming of all my
life: the hilltop silence, the metallic scent of chalky stone, the soft shush

of wind through tall, pale reeds, long views through arch after arch of stone, the cool of an ancient grotto. I could set up a desk, chair, and bed and live here for the rest of my life. Everything about this place delights my physical senses.

My heart and soul, however, came alive in Plovdiv, the verdant, historic hilltop town in Bulgaria. Till now, I wasn't sure why. As Mia and I sit for lunch against a low stone wall and a cascade of ivy tendrils and the wind blows the little green corkscrews across my cheek, I suddenly understand.

I close my eyes and I'm three and sitting inside a pergola dripping with grapevines at my *tante* (great-aunt) Fox's backyard. In the sweet, heavy heat of August, I squeeze the hard little baby grapes and then tickle the curls of the young vines against my cheek. My mother and *tante*'s voices float out the kitchen window, speaking Yiddish, rising and falling as they move to and from the windows while they make dinner. Fifty years later I can still feel the happiness of that time, viscerally. I can still hear my mother's laughter and the buzz of glossy, black-bottomed bees, still see the giant heads of pink peonies lolling on the wet grass, having fallen of their own weight, drunk with morning rain.

No wonder I responded to Plovdiv as I did. It lies on the same latitude, exactly, as Cleveland Heights, where I was born and spent much of my childhood. It has the same plants and flowers, the same trees, insects, climates and constellations, the same fragrance, light, and colors. One, I hadn't been surrounded by in decades.

The landscape of our childhood imprints itself into our very being at the same time and in the same way—primal, umbilical—as our relationship with our mother; they're inextricably bound. And I think we're drawn to nature, to the land, so much because it gives us something only our mother does: unconditional love. It's the only thing in life that gives as much as a mother—sustenance, shelter, delight, solace, wisdom, challenge, company—without asking anything in return. Everyone and everything else needs, expects, or wants something of us, even if it's just our attention. Also like a mother, however, she can be terrifyingly powerful in an instant.

I share my thoughts on Plovdiv with Mia as we unpack our lunch and balance it on our laps.

"I thought it hit you so hard because it reminded you of your mom, because she's from around there."

"Well, there is that," I agree, because there is *always* that. "But Plovdiv was also *my* landscape, identical to the places where I had all my first landmarks. My first kiss in a forest while holding sweaty palms at camp, summers canoeing rivers and chasing blue dragonflies. My body remembers Ohio in a way my mind never will, picking and eating green apples still warm from the sun, or eating my way to school through a ravine of blackberries."

Nature made life feel soft and miraculous. I hated to be inside. I still do. If I was anything in a prior life, I'm sure I had leaves, fur, or feathers. I can still barely pass by a lush hedge without itching to crawl inside and sit awhile. The only other person I know who didn't laugh when I shared this is my friend Maureen, an analyst and author whose passion is nature photography. Her connection to nature is also visceral, tied to motherhood.

"Nature has held me far more than my own physical mother," she told me while describing a recent trip to Point Reyes, a national forest in northern California, a place so deeply green and damp it feels primeval. It's fog-laced and full of fallen trees teeming with life that hums and buzzes as they melt back into the loamy dark soil.

She was photographing a herd of white deer last week when they began to run. "Claire, I was running with them and feeling so much joy! To be connected to the earth and to these exquisite beings—it made me feel so alive!"

I could feel Maureen's joy as she spoke, picturing her beautiful wide smile and big hazel eyes all lit up as she ran across the forest floor behind the herd.

"You know how I always dream about houses?" I ask Mia. "Well, they're never complete or regular houses. Never. There are always walls missing, or there's no ceiling. Nothing separates it from outside—a lot of times they're tree houses, or a meadow cuts right through it."

"The abode of a restless claustrophobic."

"I prefer to say environmentally integrated."

Mia unwraps the moist chestnut leaf with the cheese, thoughtful. "You know how you always tell me to be careful what I wish for, because a vision is such a powerful thing?"

"Yeah," I reply, digging a piece of crust into the warm, soft cheese.

"Well, you got the house of your dreams."

"Like hell I did—what are you talking about?"

"A huge, bushy green tree is growing right up into it. Hello? And don't swear."

My jaw stops midchew. We look at each other. We both know she's right. I can't think of a single thing to say. And she takes full advantage of the silence.

"All these years you've been bitching about that ficus tree, you never saw it as anything but negative, you've been a total victim. I mean sometimes it wasn't even rational. You've even said you had nightmares about it."

I start to say something in my defense, but she's on a roll.

"Did it ever occur to you to see it as something positive? Like nature calling you back, or trying to set you right. If you had seen it in a bigger way, the way you usually do, as a sign from the universe or something woo-woo, you might have sold it before the market tanked."

Round two hits just as hard. And there's a slight irritation in her voice that isn't helping. It's certainly warranted, but it feels off, there's something else. My instinct was correct because she turns to me and asks, pointedly—

"Mom, are you ever going to tell me about why you really moved to Florida? Why you left L.A. so quickly without saying anything to me?"

My mom doesn't respond immediately to my question, just takes a breath and looks to her right at the valley stretched out below.

"I got scared," she says simply, still looking out.

"Of what?"

She sighs, then spits out, "Well, the proposal for Come Back *was rejected fifty-six times and I thought I better come up w—"*

"Wait, wait, back up—the proposal was what?!*"*

"Rejected fifty-six times," she says, avoiding my eyes as she reaches for the baguette. "I never told you."

"No shit you never told me! I knew of about twenty rejections, what, you just forgot to mention the other thirty-six? And don't you dare start eating now."

"Honey, you were already so pessimistic and I didn't see the point in telling you every single time it happened. You'd have been totally depressed."

"But every time we talked, you were so certain. Why did you lie to me?"

"I didn't exactly lie, Mia, I just . . . withheld some things. Fine, I guess that's lying. From the moment we started this project I knew in my heart of hearts it'd get published . . . but by the fiftieth rejection, I got nervous. Even our agent said it was a record!"

"But even then you never said anything to me," I say, annoyed. "That was really wrong of you, I would've had hardly any time to start job hunting if the book didn't sell. And what, you thought enough of me to want to be colleagues, but it was okay for you to treat me like a kid by keeping me in the dark?"

"I know, believe me, you're absolutely right. It was wrong of me, and I was, and am, really sorry."

"Okay, fine, but forget about me for now, what does not telling me about the rejections have to do with you moving?"

"Well, here I was in my late forties, still renting in an apartment. Literally a few hours after Stacey called about our fifty-first rejection, our friends Tom and Kelly called raving about the phenomenal home deals in Florida. We went online, found articles from the New York Times *saying our historic area was the hottest in the country. Coincidentally, Paul had just gotten some really big, long-term clients in Florida, it was like the universe was saying, Claire! Move to Florida!"*

"Well, I don't know what universe that might be," I tell her, "because the Claire I know lives in a universe in which Florida's so hot half the year you can hardly leave your house. And you despise being cooped up. And what about

screenwriting? If the book didn't sell, why wouldn't you have just stayed in L.A. and gone back to film?"

"What can I say? I panicked, I lost faith in myself as a writer and thought maybe it was time to make a big change. Real estate in Florida was booming, Dad had great connections with some of the biggest developers; I thought, It'll be great! We'll move! I'll change careers!"

"Mom," I groan. "Thank God the proposal sold—you'd have been miserable. If someone cooked up every single thing you hate—small talk, all things domestic, stretching the truth—and stirred it into a job, voilà, a real estate agent! Can you picture yourself discussing flower beds and paint trim?"

"You should have seen me in the licensing course trying to do the math—I was hopeless, even with a calculator. Can we eat now, please? I'm starving."

I nod, reach into our bag for the baguette with the neat little chunk chewed out of it, and hand my mom the goat's-milk Brie and an apricot to slice up. I'm still processing all of this, because it's the polar opposite of what I had imagined; I saw the move as a healthy, positive decision, not the insecurity-driven result of a panic attack. I guess I should have seen the fixer-upper that never got fixed as a red flag, an indication of my mom's lack of self-care. And self-awareness. But if I can see how obviously wrong this was, surely Dad and her closest friends must have?

"What about Dad," I ask, "or Sarah or Karin? Didn't they try to talk you out of it?"

"Maybe they did, I don't remember," she sighs, pushing away a clump of hair the wind blew into her face. "It was such a whirlwind of house-hunting and packing and researching real estate courses. And if they did, well, you know how I can be."

I know very well. Once my mom gets something in her head, talking sense to her is an exercise in frustration; intelligence and energy make her extremely convincing, to herself especially.

"And do you think that maybe, just maaaybe, you were avoiding me so you could bypass the whole what-the-hell-are-you-thinking conversation you know damn well we would have had?"

"Maaaybe," she says, then sheepishly smiles and offers me the bite of bread, cheese, and fruit she nicely prepared.

I laugh as I take it from her, though I also can't help but smile a little rue-fully. To think that a woman twice my age—my mother, no less—got scared and ran away. It's such a simple thing, feeling scared. It's so human. I guess somewhere in me is still the childhood notion that my mom is superhuman, that nothing truly awful can happen when she's there because she can do or fix any-thing. Maybe somewhere in her is that same notion. Maybe most mothers never stop wanting to be our heroes and infallible guides, maybe no matter what age their kids are, they like us to feel that the world's safe as long as they're with us.

"The thing ees this," Chrystelle says, frowning. "Eet must be kept very specifically."

Chrystelle is politely putting in her fridge the artisanal tapenades we bought at the outdoor market and bringing out store-bought replace-ments. She's still in office clothes, a sable-brown linen shift, pretty flats, and a chunky wooden necklace. Chrystelle's style is somewhere between Milan and New York. A single signature ring or necklace and well-cut, classic clothes; she never wears makeup and her honey-colored hair is usually pulled back into a ponytail. She's the only person I'd happily hand over my wallet to buy me a wardrobe and know I'd send nothing back.

When I met Chrystelle ten years ago, she had long red hair and a bohemian flair. She had just met Jean-Christophe (JC), a chef at the Palais des Papes. She'd studied business and Chinese in college and was marketing wines to China.

Now she's happily married to JC and has a son and beautiful step-daughter, two cats, a tranquil home, and a 9–5. JC is quintessentially French. Dark hair and olive skin, huge brown eyes that turn down at the corners, accomplished in many areas. I had no idea that he'd done the excellent nude charcoal in their bedroom. Or that the languid subject with her back to the viewer was Chrystelle.

"JC made that for me just after we get married," she said proudly on my last visit. "Eet made me very 'appy, this. Eet will be nice to 'ave when I don't look like that anymore!"

For a long time they lived in an artsy medieval village nearby until they bought this home in a hilly, verdant town across the river from Avignon. The house is typically Provençal, with a terra-cotta roof and big French doors in every room opening to the terrace, which is shaded in vines with tiny white flowers and edged with big pots of rosemary, thyme, and lemon verbena. The yard is bordered with cypress and cedars, with a pool and deck to the side.

She's bustling about the kitchen now making a salad while JC grills steaks on the terrace. "They were on ice, Chrystelle," I say of our tapenades. "They should be fine."

Le finger doesn't care. "Non," she says, annoyed. "Eet does not matter, you cannot leave eet in the sun like 'e do." She obviously knows the merchant. "You can get very sick. That man know this. And 'e knows you do *not* know. I don't like 'e do that to you."

Mr. Tapenade will definitely be getting a scolding come market day.

"When I get some days off," she says, "you weel come 'ome and I make you see my secret places where I get this sort of thing. I show you my *Système D*."

Système D is slang for a Frenchwoman's system of where to buy what at the best prices. She pours me a glass of wine. "Once I make you see where to go, you can shop like a Frenchwoman. I take you to our friend Ed. 'E 'ave the interesting prices."

I love that they call bargains *interesting prices*. She can't show us her pal "Ed" (a grocery chain) and her secret weapons fast enough. The market's a three-mile walk one way, and Les Halles, the covered market in town, is charming but expensive.

"Now, you sit 'ere and relax," she says as she sets out a small dish of olives. The French serve very few hors d'oeuvres; it makes no sense to them to eat before dinner. She loads a tray with dishes and walks out to the terrace, framed by a beautiful sunset.

She leans back inside to call out, *"Antoine, montre aux Américaines ton numéro de danse!"* winking my way at Antoine's habit of referring to me and Mia as *"les Américaines."*

Six-year-old Antoine's a live wire with sun-bronzed skin, big hazel eyes, and a dark blond Julius Caesar haircut. It's been a joy watching Chrystelle with him. She's very proud of her son—that he's assertive, athletic, tough, in a good way, yet tender in an instant. One minute he's yelling and horsing around on their deck with his friend, the next he's cooing sadly over an injured insect.

He leaps off the sofa to get into position to show us his dance number in his school's upcoming end-of-year performance (or *spectacle,* as it's called here). He was practicing with the precision and focus of a soldier when we arrived. Chrystelle's upset that neither she nor JC can get off work early enough that day to see him perform, so they've asked us to attend and film it for them.

Chrystelle's always had something of the wide, calm sea to her—the quality of movement and stillness at once. Now that she's a mother I notice a deeper, more observant quality to her. I also notice that she gets harried at times, something I never saw before. Motherhood, a full-time job, being a wife, and running a home is harrying, no matter how well you manage it. Especially so if you're a bit of a perfectionist, something else she and I have in common (and husbands who are frustratingly not so inclined). We also share a love of history, literature, and walking in cemeteries. But our lives as mothers differ in significant ways.

Partly because women fought for it, but mostly in response to the declining birth rate after World War II, the French government supports mothers in a way we can only dream of. Four months' paid leave and job protection, and the state pays for someone to come in to do laundry and assist you after childbirth. Child care is subsidized and you get a few hundred dollars a month for each kid, till they're in their teens. If you choose to stay home the amount can be higher.

The program paid off. France is one of the only first-world countries that doesn't have a declining birth rate, especially among educated women. It's quite common for a high-powered career woman to have four kids, which is rare in the States.

How is it we don't demand some version of what every other wealthy nation gives its mothers? Why don't we withhold votes from candidates who won't legislate to make it easier for women to manufacture and develop the single most important product of any nation—the citizens? There is no corporation, company, or entity on earth more important than we are: we make *the people*. And business and government make it *hard* for us?

We don't need any more articles or studies or reports on our dissatisfaction. We hold the purse strings and we have the Internet—all we have to do is decide to do it, *in unison*. When Mia was a child, moms got every apple grown with the pesticide Alar off of every grocery store shelf in the country in very short order. With no Internet, we got giant agribusiness and food conglomerates to do what we wanted. Just by saying *We won't buy*. Just as we can with the media, mothers could improve our mental and physical health, our families' lives, and our careers *right now*.

"It's so frustrating," I told her. "You guys go on strike for an extra *workday* a year and get it. We haven't even succeeded in getting paid leave for a *baby*."

"Yes, eet's true, but we 'ave a long history of *la grève* (strike). We 'ave the weel to fight for as long as eet must take, and we are very united, including mothers. We don't 'ave this mommy war like you. We don't say what ees right for another woman, and nobody waste time doing things that are the teacher's job or making cakes. Why, when the patisserie ees down the street? We don't make such beeg pressure on ourselves for such things. The thing of eet ees this: for us what ees important ees that a woman should enjoy 'er life and 'er fameely. Eet's one reason I never go to leeve in Paris, where eet ees all about business and 'hoo 'ave what."

The French don't expect mothers to sacrifice as much for their children as we do. Women don't neglect social life, career, and physical and emotional self-care over kids. There's simply not the guilt that's become one of the hallmarks of motherhood in the United States. Women here generally assume they'll be fine mothers, without reading a slew of books and listening to experts' every word. They also don't usually put kids before their marriage or sex life. Chrystelle sometimes refers to JC as her lover in conversation.

There is a trade-off for such balance, however. When you're expected, and expect yourself, to excel in *all* things—looking chic, being a good mother, a sexy wife, having a beautiful home, a successful career, being informed on the culture and trends—it's got to be exhausting at times. A Frenchwoman earns all the vacation time she gets (and they get a *lot*).

"Yes, we're more balanced, but then the expectations are very high," explained my friend Nathalie, a photographer whose popular blog is devoted solely to Avignon. "The pressure is always on, in all areas of a woman's life. It can get very stressful."

However, as goes American culture, so goes the world. Mommy blogs are becoming popular here and women who speak English read ours. Elisabeth Badinter, one of the foremost feminist writers here, writes about the coming of our style of guilt-driven, perfectionist "eco-mothering" as she calls it, and the division between these moms and working moms. These women, in both countries, bring to motherhood the same skill set and drive to excel that served them in the professional world, with the resulting toll on mind, body, and psyche. Yes, there's a call for sanity in the United States; there's recognition (or resignation) that *you can have it all, just not at the same time.* But that doesn't stop us from missing whatever it is we're not doing at the moment, whether we're in the boardroom or nursery, or from feeling guilty.

There are longer-term consequences awaiting these moms, something many women my age are already experiencing: being able to choose both worlds—the professional and the domestic—means a lot of women will strive, struggle, and judge themselves in *two* worlds. Moms of the past used to take stock at midlife by looking at how well they raised their kids and managed a marriage and home; now we get to add to that the midlife crisis men have always had—did I choose the right field, make enough money? Did my job mean anything, did I measure up?

France may not have our mommy war yet, but the divisions are form-ing. During the week, we'd attended a *spectacle* at a more working-class elementary school in town. It was like a trip back in time, with the kind of barely organized madness these things had at my own elemen-tary school, back when parents and kids moved in separate orbits and perfection wasn't a goal for either group: kids running loose on their own, music blaring, slapdash costumes, half the kids forgetting their lines or steps, a rickety stage, parents laughing and socializing among themselves.

A week later we stand amid well-dressed, hushed parents at Antoine's more upscale suburban school, outside a barricade surrounding a huge blacktop that serves as the *spectacle* stage. Antoine's lining up with a big group of boys for his number. There's tape on the ground to spot the dancers.

It's a grand, elaborate reenactment of *The Lion King,* and the kids must have all been practicing as long and diligently as Antoine; almost all are focused and serious, sporting matching, beautifully hand-painted loincloths, spears, necklaces of feather and stone, and face paint.

Several teachers stand right among the kids to guide and remind, mouthing the lyrics, racing to put someone in the proper place, even sticking out their bottoms and wiggling them as a prompt. It's like watching dog obedience training—the dogs are rarely obedient but the owners, *damn,* you never saw such synchronized precision.

The parents are intensely focused on their kids. These are the parents who will sweat bullets and pay tutors to assure their teens pass their *bac* (short for *baccalaureate,* the big exam that determines if you go to univer-sity) and go on to run industry and nation; parents like myself and most parents in America today—very invested, involved, intense.

When the show is over, Mia and I head to the refreshment area to wait for Chrystelle. Antoine rushes up to us, says something I can't un-derstand, and hurries off to roughhouse with his friends.

I say to Mia nostalgically, "I remember how much fun these things were at your school."

"Not as much fun as it is here," Mia says, eyeing the tables.

There are gourmet cheeses, gorgeous desserts—and wine and beer. Antoine calls out for us to watch a crazy flip he's attempting to do, then hollers to watch a karate kick he executes on his playmate, then insists we watch another feat. How different a boy's energy is! So much more physical and independent, yet still looking over to see that Mom (or Mom's substitute, in this case) is watching.

I'm caught off guard by an ache that's become familiar in the last several years—what it would have been like to have a son. When Mia was five, Paul and I went through a difficult time, and I chose to abort a pregnancy, something I've always regretted terribly. Looking back, I see how little thought I gave it. I made a choice based on emotions and current circumstances, which included Paul's resistance, rather than a firm vision of how many kids I wanted.

I wanted a son, and I wanted Mia to have a sibling. I just assumed I would have one "someday." And I just *knew* in my soul that the child I would have had was a boy. For a long time after that, I had recurring dreams with a little boy with curly black hair and big brown eyes.

The way Paul and I handled it marked the beginning of a pattern our relationship took on; he would be upset by something and rather than talk about it, he would withhold, be passive-aggressive, the emotional bastion of the polite and saintly. Which left me feeling bewildered and abandoned, but I had nothing to pin it on—that's the beauty of passive-aggressiveness. And the frustration would make me angry, sharp, often at the wrong things and the wrong times. Which bewildered and upset him, and the cycle went on, waxing and waning as the years went by, unraveling threads in the tapestry of our marriage, leaving thin spots. It's a testament to our mutual love for Mia that she was the one thing we've never argued about; even during the terrible years, we were a solid team as parents.

I don't like that the ache I still feel for that lost child is tinged with anger at Paul. He had the right not to want another child, I've no cause to be angry at him. The only purpose it has served is to avoid being angry at myself, because, ultimately, it was my choice; almost everything in life is.

"This reminds me of when you were little," my mom says, looking around the yard of Antoine's school at kids running around, playing noisily, and small clumps of parents warmly greeting each other and conversing animatedly.

"You mean minus the ashtrays and beer?" I ask, dodging a group of squabbling boys. "My God, if I ever have kids I don't think I could handle boys. Just chasing after them is a full-time job! Maybe it's selfish, but I don't want my whole life to be my kids."

"All kids are a full-time job, Mia—it's called parenthood. Your whole life shouldn't just be your kids. You were there when Chrystelle and I were talking about that at dinner the other night—"

"I know," I tell her. "I heard you guys. I kept thinking how much it was like what that woman Martine said, too, about motherhood being easier in France."

Last week, I found myself in deep conversation with a woman at the table next to me in Bar les Célestins. She was in her early forties, dressed in a chic black outfit and chain-smoking while bantering with friends. Her straight, dark hair, deep-set olive eyes, and sharp, angular features reminded me of a slightly more masculine Anjelica Huston, a look the French call jolie-laide *(pretty-ugly) to describe women who are striking yet not conventionally pretty. She intrigued me. She had a confident, perhaps even cocky air to her, but there was also something sad and mysterious about her.*

We struck up a conversation, and I learned that she'd spent ten years in San Francisco after falling in love with an American, whom she married and had three children with. At first because there was no maternity leave at her job, and then because she loved it, she stayed at home with her kids. Her husband's income allowed it, particularly as he moved up the corporate ladder.

Several years into the marriage, he developed a taste for cocaine, their marriage fell apart, and she ended up moving back to France to be closer to her parents. She received some alimony but not enough to continue staying home with her children.

"I love my children, I gave myself to them completely," she'd said, taking a deep drag from her cigarette. "They're great kids, happy and healthy. As a mother, I feel good. I know I did well. As a woman . . . well, I teach high school math. It's not a bad job but I have a Ph.D. My friends from before I left France are where I should be, university professors, getting published, giving lectures, better salaries. It's awkward between us sometimes, you know? They pity me now. I pity myself. I'm a successful mother and a failed woman."

She stamped out her cigarette, exhaled deeply, and shrugged her shoulders. I could tell she'd delved as deeply as she wanted.

"It scared me," I relay to my mom now. "It seems like you totally lose yourself when you have kids."

My mom shakes her head.

"There are lots of ways to lose yourself—motherhood's just one of them. That's why it's so important to be conscious and intentional about your choices. And it's not like you have to go to every single Mommy and Me class, or bake cookies for class parties. You see what works and doesn't work and modify it for yourself. Oh, hey, there's Chrystelle."

Chrystelle's pulled her car up across the playground and is waving at us. She drops us off at Place Crillon, a plaza not far from the Palais des Papes, but not before Antoine takes my face in his hands, firmly kisses each cheek, does the same to my mom, and then hollers, "Au revoir les Américaines!"

"Let's go to the bluff, Mia, I don't feel like going home just yet," my mom says, and we turn onto the quiet, cobbled road leading to the bluff and the palais.

"You know what the most important thing about having kids is, Mia? If you listen to nothing else I say, get this—you have your kids on your terms."

I'm taken aback by the sudden intensity she says this with, her voice and expression almost terse.

"Don't put your career on hold when you have children. I didn't and it's one of my biggest regrets. I worked, I'm a Writers Guild member, but I didn't pursue screenwriting full-time and I never accumulated the body of work I should have. While your husband's career keeps climbing, yours stalls and it's almost impossible to catch up and compete. I stayed too focused on motherhood to see any life for myself outside of it once you were gone.

"Start getting clear on your vision of your life now, *and when you're ready,* you *choose how many kids you want. It's your body and your life. Marriages don't always make it and kids leave home, so you have how many you want, when you want. Your terms."*

"You always told me I was planned, so that would have been on your terms," I point out, wondering why I'm suddenly getting lectured.

"Oh, you were planned, you were just ahead of schedule. I wanted to finish my degree before having kids, but after the ectopic the doctor told me that the longer I waited, the harder it would be to get pregnant. Boy was he wrong—I got pregnant five *different times after that, four on birth control, mind you!"*

I think for a minute, because something's off.

"Um, not to point out the obvious, Mom, but me, plus the miscarriage, plus two ectopics equals four *pregnancies. And I'm pretty sure the answer was no when we were talking about abortion rights that one day and I asked if you'd ever had one."*

"Well, darling, I lied. Sorry. I wasn't ready to share that. It's something I still regret, I always wanted to have another child and we never did."

"Why did you decide not to keep it?" I ask gingerly.

"It was a rough time in a lot of ways, mostly between me and Paul."

The bitterness in her voice unnerves me. I don't know what to say. That sucks? I'm sorry? You can always adopt? I always thought I was good with thorny topics, but I have no idea how to even begin to relate to something like this.

"I will, Mom," I say, turning to look at her. *"I'll try to get really clear about what I want in life."*

"Good. Because it'll feel really shitty later if you don't."

We'd been headed toward the bluff but my mom suddenly turns and heads quickly for an alley we rarely use.

"Hey, where are you going?" I call after her, then realize by the suddenness, by the way she's holding her body, not to mention the word "shitty," that something's wrong. I hurry beside her and take her arm.

"What's wrong?"

She's crying.

"Mommy, it's okay."

She suddenly stops and looks at me, puzzled, hard in a way I've never seen.

"Okay? Of course it's not okay."

She finds a tiny stairway to a street below and sits on the top step.

"It was never okay. And it was never okay to pretend it was. Or to pretend it didn't hurt. It did. It does. A lot of things do."

She puts her head on her knees and cries. After a while, she takes a deep breath.

"Some things will simply never be possible for me again, ever. With life, work, kids. I know it in my head, I've talked about it but I've never let myself feel any of it. I'm sorry."

"Mommy, don't apologize. Just cry."

Most of our dreams never really vanish. Our deep, unrealized wants just languish until we're old enough or slowed down enough by some crisis for our skin to have thinned a bit. Then they appear like pentimento, the artist's regret. The cost of their burial just aches right through.

And you can't therapize it or deny it or New-Age it away on some retreat with platitudes like *it was all meant to be.* With rare exception, I think *we* make meant to be. I made certain choices, paid certain consequences, and then chose the mask. And now it's time to pay the piper. I can choose the cost of glossing over, of continuing to deny what hurt, which already has a long running tab. Or the cost of admitting it.

Which feels so horrible it's almost too much to bear—admitting I wanted to be a doctor, that I wanted a big, happy family, a son. That

I wanted a lot of things I was too polite or too afraid to ask for. Jobs I didn't take, things I didn't do because Paul didn't want to, or because I sometimes lacked confidence, though usually it was clarity I lacked rather than confidence.

Nothing earth-shattering, certainly nothing like the events of Mia's childhood. But those events were explored, expunged, learned from—I felt all the emotions that went along with them.

These are the kinds of regrets all women have, mistakes and missteps, paths not chosen, opportunities gone. Youth gone. Forever. And until I honestly acknowledge how this regret feels, acknowledge that I'm *not* okay with how some of my life went, it's like having a fake past, and a fake present, which is surely a prescription to a fake future.

And it precludes grace, my life's slate wiped clean by granting myself tender mercy. You can't forgive what you don't face.

After a while, I heave a sigh. I'm glad I'm not alone. Whenever I cry, which isn't often, I do it alone. I don't want to make anyone uncomfortable or force myself to stop crying before I'm ready. With Mia, right now, I feel free to be honest, vulnerable, to let it all out.

"Thank you for being here with me, for just letting me cry," I tell Mia, wiping my eyes on her sleeve for a change.

I told my mom earlier I wanted to know more about her and I'm getting more than I'd imagined, or perhaps bargained for. Never in my life have I seen her upset like this, there's a resigned and bitter quality to her anguish that's extremely difficult to watch. She has so much anger at herself that I'm not sure how I never noticed it before. Either she deliberately hid it very well or she's simply never allowed herself to feel it. Part of me wonders if impulse-buying the house was my mom's unconscious attempt to re-create the family life she wanted but never had.

Living with my mom this summer feels a little like being a fly on the wall of a director editing footage. She's shifting through scenes, finding patterns, seeing how things could have been alternately filmed. From the moment she called to say that she was going to France, something in her voice told me she was going through a big change, and that the summer would be a pivotal time for her.

Moments like these make me certain that I did the right thing in coming here; I'm learning more about her than I ever otherwise would have, and our relationship is completely changing, opening up, and becoming much richer.

chapter ten

Avignon

Those Who Matter Don't Mind

Imagine this life: every drive home is through rolling fields of grapevines and sunflowers, dotted with centuries-old farmhouses and garage-size rolls of dried hay. Your lavender-lined driveway ends at a terrace with an enormous tree shading a long rustic table filled most weekends with a bounty of food, family, and friends; your home is a huge old restored farmhouse with a big writing office that looks out on your husband's dream come true, an organic vineyard of award-winning artisanal wines. When not tending your two beautiful children and home, you're writing a hugely popular blog on France and the French language.

Oh, and you're stunning, beloved, and feel God's presence in your life. *And* your husband is a sweet, smart Gallic hunk. Voilà, my girlfriend Kristin's life. One that she'd dreamed of since she was an adolescent living in the shadow of a freeway near Phoenix. She'd just gotten her first diary and seen a Bain de Soleil commercial and knew her destiny: she was going to be a writer living in France. Which she is.

She was so determined to live her dream that she created a blog before there was any real Internet. While working as a bilingual secretary in Marseilles post-college, she crafted vignettes describing life in France that she sent by regular post once a week to Francophiles in the United States who might be interested in her weekly "Café letters." Once she started a blog, she drew fans worldwide, along with a publishing deal for a memoir.

She picks us up at the train station in Orange, looking breezy and radiant with her long, white gauzy skirt, intensely blue eyes, and tousled blond locks. I insist Mia sit up front, as it's her first time meeting Kristin. She and Kristin are full of questions for each other, about college, life in France, writing, dating. I love watching Mia get to know my friends. They elicit different things from each other than I do, and it's a chance to learn new things about each of them.

Kristin's normally reserved but she and Mia are chatting away like old friends. Mia has the ability to make anyone open up; she's genuinely curious and listens well, beneath the words.

On my last visit, I marveled at how such a soft-spoken, somewhat shy woman could do all the things Kristin does in a day (full-time blogging and photography, speaking, writing short stories, mothering two kids, helping Jean-Marc with a grueling harvest in the fall and a stream of vineyard clients and visitors all year long). What's allowed her to realize her dream where so many others fail, including me for many years, is how carefully and sanely she chooses *exactly* where to spend her time and energy. On the way from collecting us at the station to her home, she'd shot enough photos for a few blog posts at the cost of only two minutes' extra time—the old bicycle leaning against the *boulangerie* wall, an old tobacco ad painted on a crumbling building, a cat stretched out on a sidewalk. She threw together a wonderful lunch in ten minutes ("instant couscous tastes the same as the longer kind"). Her house is fresh, typically Provençal, and looks neat but lived-in. She wears simple, pretty clothes, a great haircut, little or no makeup, and no nail polish.

Basically, she'd become a French mother—disciplined about time where it counts most and not too worried about the rest. Though the rest isn't always something she and Jean-Marc agree on.

"For example," she tells us as we walk to the river where Mia and

Kristin's giant retriever, Braise, run ahead to have a swim. "I can speak French fluently by now, but my accent is terrible, even after twenty years."

It's true, she has a strong American accent. We've twisted our towels around our heads like turbans to keep the sun off our faces as we amble along a stony dirt path. On our right, Jean-Marc's grapes are just beginning to turn purple.

"It drives Jean-Marc crazy that I don't even try. But why spend my time focused on that? Everyone understands me just fine."

Kristin's life illustrates that it takes more than passion and a lot of work to make a dream work—it takes focus. What you think about matters, a lot. Your thoughts drive your actions. When I think about much of what I've focused my thoughts on in the last few years, I cringe. You stick a perfectionist who hates domestic stuff in a fixer-upper and what you get is someone constantly obsessing on things she isn't going to do. The thing about that, aside from premature aging, is that focus = *time*, something most of us don't really, truly consider. Those are minutes, hours, and days of your life gone forever.

There is a balance to be struck, however—a trade-off for such big accomplishments.

"Some people think I live this dream life. Don't get me wrong, it is what I always wanted, it's a beautiful life, and I'm deeply grateful. But every minute is taken up and my mind is always busy."

I told her it could also just be her nature, that maybe it's the other way around—her life is busy because her mind is; she'd live a very full, busy life in any career or country.

"That's probably true. But I do pay a price; some part of me is almost always worried about something or someone. I'm still upset about that guy last night."

She'd shared earlier about a local journalist who had shown up unannounced. She'd had a long day and all she wanted to do was finish an article with a hot cup of tea.

"But that voice in my head kept saying, *Am I being kind enough, or humble enough, I should be nice to him.* So of course I invited him in and was a good hostess for the evening, all while shaking under my skin."

Because she'd also had a vague instinct that he might not be sincere about the article he said he wanted to write. But another voice kept chiming in, this time rooted in her faith.

"I kept thinking of that Bible verse in Hebrews, *Be not inhospitable to strangers, lest they be angels in disguise.* I'm always afraid I'll misjudge someone. But you know what? He studied everything, but wrote nothing. He just came to snoop. I was so angry at myself—for not respecting myself, for not following my instinct—that I hardly slept all night."

I know *exactly* how she felt, what it feels like to mouth the words *Sure, I can do that* or *Of course you can join me,* while some part of me shrivels. What woman doesn't have that script memorized? Why don't we say, "Thank you, but I'd rather walk alone today," or "I'm sorry I'm not able to accommodate you right now," without having to justify or explain? Why are we so afraid to be hungry? After all, in the words of Bernard Baruch, those who matter don't mind, and those who mind don't matter. Otherwise the person who ends up not mattering is us. That journalist was just doing what he does; she had the choice to turn him away.

Why do so many of us choose to be good girls going for gold stars, instead of clasping tight the gold of our lives by living as we truly desire? We accommodate, we wait our turn, do what we *should.* Over a few decades of adulthood, you accumulate so many *should*s, I think some of us feel like our own walking, talking avatars, images of ourselves.

As if we had all the time in the world, as if our lives would never come to an end.

We tend to think it's just the sweet, over-accommodating women. Most of us can't imagine women with strong personalities, like Kristin or me, not speaking up for ourselves. But all of us learned very early on that honesty and boldness cost us relationships.

Girls are about connection, belonging, and approval; without it, we form a core belief that we're not worthy enough, not cool enough, not funny or pretty or smart or successful or whatever enough. Even the pushy girls. So we abandon part of ourselves rather than risk losing connection. We may become outspoken, accomplished women, but in many ways we've gone a lifetime racking up gold stars. By the time we consciously make the compromises of motherhood, we've long been making unconscious ones, for peers, boyfriends, husbands, family.

I think of the scene near the end of *The Bridges of Madison County*, where we see Meryl Streep throwing herself back into her ironing and her family after walking away from Clint Eastwood. How many women must have lain awake after seeing that film! Afraid that they'll one day know what life they *really* wanted only by having lived the life they didn't.

I think one of the greatest challenges of motherhood is this: how to be a good mother without being a "good girl." Not just for ourselves. For our daughters. So they don't learn from us how grown-up girls play pretend.

"The map says to take this right."

"You're reading it wrong, Mia. We're supposed to be headed east. If we turn right, the sun will be on our left, signifying we're headed north."

"Mom, I know how to read a map."

Here we go again. Estrogen. The open road. A tiny French car. We piled into Kristin's car after lunch to visit Sault, a charming village nearby, and are now completely lost.

We take a right onto a road leading to a town so small there can't be more than fifty structures, all of which we see in about thirty seconds, the amount of time it takes to circle the area and end up exactly where we started. Which I know because we already passed these same three older gentlemen, sitting on the same ledge, still smoking, talking, and watching the passing traffic—us.

They're so quintessentially French that I'm surprised Kristin didn't hop out and take a photo. The most vocal of the bunch seems to be the oldest, a still-handsome man in his seventies with snow-white hair, a white beret, and a striped sailor shirt. To his right is a barrel-chested man in a sleeveless undershirt, with a shiny gold medallion, who pauses every few seconds to pat away beads of sweat with a homemade handkerchief. To his left is a man that looks like a thinner, much older Geraldo Rivera, with eyeglasses the size of saucers and a forehead that's a sea of worry lines.

"We've just made a circle," I say.

"*I know,*" *Kristin replies,* "*but the map does indicate that this is the right road. Let's go around again and see—maybe the turn-off is just really small and we passed it.*"

Around we go, their heads turning in unison as we pass, and when a few minutes later we pass them yet again, Kristin stops the car and puts it in reverse. As she does this, they shuffle from their ledge to the curb. We pull up beside them, they look at us expectantly.

"*Bonjour,*" *Kristin says, and explains what we're looking for.*

There can't be more than one way out of such a teensy village but, being French, they passionately debate among themselves before reaching consensus, and he directs Kristin where to turn. She thanks him and drives away, but within a few minutes we're back again. Out of a sense of chivalry or pity, he hops into an old, beat-up car parked under a tree, sticks his arm out the window, and motions for us to follow him.

Finally on the right road, we relax and Kristin and I settle into an easy banter while my mom watches the countryside pass by. When my mom first told me about Kristin, she emphasized (because it's something she hopes I'll emulate) that from a young age, she had a clear dream that she never allowed circumstance or self-doubt thwart. That's fine and well, assuming you have a dream. I've never been particularly pulled toward anything. The only thing I can think of wanting to do when I was little was to work with animals, a dream that ended when I was seventeen and my mom pointed out that unless I wanted to study zoology (the sciences aren't my forte) and become a vet, I'd probably end up dealing with a lot of poop as a vet tech. Or sleeping in a dung hut as a safari guide. Either way, there was some version of poop involved.

Most days, not having a clear vision of my future doesn't really bother me; I figure I'll find my way. But sometimes I'm envious of people who've always known exactly what they wanted to do when they grew up. That was always the sticking point for me, not so much the "doing" as the "when I grow up" part of the equation.

I had somewhat of a lightbulb moment about this the other day when I was talking to Steven, the waiter at Bar les Célestins, and I realized that part of the reason I don't feel grown-up is because I don't know what I want to do.

Steven had told me that he was nineteen, which greatly surprised me be-

cause I thought he was at least my age, not six years younger. I don't consider myself or my friends immature but when I thought about us at nineteen, we were nowhere near as self-possessed or reserved as him. And, like our Malaysian cabbie Aza, Steven's not the exception to the rule. One thing that's obvious to anyone who stays very long in France is that Americans my age and younger are often less mature than our foreign counterparts.

The saying that "Americans live to work and the French work to live" didn't come from a vacuum; a career is central to a person's identity in America. In France, for example, you don't generally ask someone in conversation what they do for a living; it's considered poor form, and boring. Far more interesting to them are the topics of culture, food, religion, philosophy. In America, "What do you do?" is usually one of the first questions asked, even when making small talk, possibly because our lives are less balanced, but also because it's how we tend to define ourselves.

A culture that so closely ties who you are with what you do is fundamentally problematic for many twentysomethings, given that where we're at on the professional ladder is often the equivalent of a glorified gofer. And that's for those of us with jobs! The rest of us are temps or bartenders, or avoid the job market altogether by entering grad school or the Peace Corps. Knowingly or not, maybe we confuse not knowing what we want to do with not knowing who we are.

When I think about my crisis of confidence about writing, it wasn't entirely unreasonable. Fifty-six rejections is a heck of a brick wall to hit, artistically and financially. But there are many ways to deal with brick walls. You can make them mean anything.

We pretty much make up everything about the events and people that comprise our lives, and then we take all that and make decisions. Our choices depend on whether our basic view of life is of ease and possibility, or if we choose from a place of fear and lack, of believing we're not quite enough when push comes to shove.

After several years of growth and creativity, and having worked as a writer most of that time, I allowed a major event to plunge me right back into my doom and gloom, victim alter-ego, affectionately dubbed Morticia. Noticing that *by the way* I'm fifty-one no doubt intensified my paralysis. Whatever I endeavor to do, writing or otherwise, I have less time to do it, less time to make any more big mistakes.

I had all the garden-variety fears and doubts, rational or not, that midlife women are vulnerable to at three in the morning. Except it started to feel like three A.M. all day long. But again, it's never about the circumstances; it's not truly about my age or my career or my house. One can create a new life from a tent camp. Lots of people have accomplished amazing things after devastating injury, after war, rape, acts of God. First they survive, then, if they have a vision, they thrive.

Without a vision of what's on the other side of the brick walls we all hit, there's no reason to find a way around them, because you don't think there's anything on the other side. A vision has the wondrous, empowering quality of keeping you both clear and focused on the future *and* fully engaged and taking action in the moment, no matter what; it prevents a brick wall from becoming a destination, a permanent address for a victim, with a BMW in the driveway (Bitch, Moan, and Whine).

Without a vision for my life as an independent middle-aged woman, when I hit that brick wall I fed the little black beastie that springs from my shadows a feast of her favorite dish—fear.

She's the really bossy one; and she's not quite the glamorous gal she wishes she was. Calling her Morticia is generous. She's more like those little humanized monkeys in *The Wizard of Oz*. She puffs up her black, ratty fur to look big and scary and I believe every word she says: life is hard, life's a problem to be solved, you're not enough, not really, just look at what you've done buying that house! She can be vicious and soul-sucking, because she wants company in her cage.

Our little beasts have the power to run our life right into the ground. That's the power of our unconscious beliefs. They make you believe all kinds of lies about yourself, about life. And nothing scares our beasts like a powerful vision, one we're passionate about.

My favorite example of an authentic woman with vision has actually been dead over two hundred years: Marie-Louise-Élisabeth Vigée-Le Brun, the celebrated court painter to Marie Antoinette. Though she's best known for her enormous paintings of the queen and the royal family, she created an astonishing body of magnificent paintings that hang in museums all over the world. Fortunately, she left behind letters, a diary, and an autobiography, which she penned before she died at age eighty-six.

Born in Paris to an artist father, she fell in love with painting as a child, and made it her life come hell or high water. And hell came: her beloved father and teacher died when she was twelve; at her mother's urging, she entered into a marriage of convenience to an art dealer who spent or gambled whatever she earned as a painter, which was considerable; a bloody revolution that took her friends' lives and forced her to flee France; in exile for years, as a single mother; a devastating break with her only child, Julie, followed by Julie's tragic death at forty-two. Not to mention she was a female at a time when women had almost no rights and were denied access to formal education. She had to work twice as hard and be twice as good as a man to get half as much notice.

Yet she painted almost every day of her life, with a joy she found in nothing else except motherhood. Two centuries before there were workshops and gurus for self-empowerment, Le Brun marched through life as if she owned it—because she fully owned herself. She was a woman who knew who she was and what she wanted and did whatever it took to live a life of her own choosing.

What better place to look to Le Brun—and Kristin—as role models than where we are right now. And I know of no better, or more enjoyable, way to start than creating a vision map, something Mia and I have decided to do. We've spent the last week collecting magazines, brochures, and postcards, cutting out images and making a grand mess in the afternoons when it's too hot to be outside.

A vision map is more than a map of dreams, it's a process of clarifying what you want to focus on, a statement of intention. And, as I've learned, it's something not to be taken lightly.

The first time I made a vision map eight years ago was at the end of another workshop on—what else—vision, with—who else—Barbara facilitating (Barb's one of those E. F. Hutton types; when she speaks, you sign up for it, whatever it is). I threw myself into it with complete abandon, not so much because I had absolute faith in it, but because we had only two hours to do it and only a couple of boxes of magazines for fifteen of us.

There was a method to the madness. Such a short time bypasses the brain, where we tend to analyze our dreams into dust. And there's a reason for cutting and pasting images like third-graders.

We may not always immediately know why we respond to certain people, places, things, and situations, but we feel the pull nonetheless. Our brain will usually respond to images of those same things just as intensely. Which is what makes vision maps so powerful. They bring into consciousness what the thinking mind may not see as a possibility, either because we don't give ourselves permission to, or there isn't yet conscious awareness of a desire, or there is and we don't think we're deserving.

One of the biggest images I included on my old map was of a woman on the beach with a laptop and the words A CALL TO ACTION. I'd had no clue I'd ever write *Come Back,* but part of me was very clear that I intended to use my writing to create awareness, make an impact.

But there's the *be careful what you wish for* part, especially if you're like me, not so much a type A as type F—if you tend toward the freight train, you'd best be darn sure of the ultimate destination, because you buy your ticket with your intention, even if it stays in your unconscious, especially so. You can't write on the beach in L.A. most of the time, it's too cold. But you can in the beachiest, hottest state in the United States, which is where I found myself several years later, long after I'd forgotten about the map and against all common sense and my own personality.

That's where your *conscious* mind plays an important role, in clarifying, asking questions, gathering support and information, so you can keep the *qualities* of the experiences you want while fine-tuning to allow for everything else on the map, for your life to work. Which is what I should have done and didn't.

Just as important is what's *not* on your map. The one thing everyone else had on their map that I did *not* was, sigh, a house. I knew myself, I knew it was not where I wanted to put my time and energy. I'm not a nuclear gal, I'm that restless electron always seeking valence. I could live in a nice hotel room as long as it had a desk and a view.

This afternoon Mia and I are working in the studio, each lost in our own world. I've organized my images and words in categories: home, relationships, career, travel, mind/body/soul, legacy.

As Mia and I gather images, I show her a lovely photo of a curvy nude woman, seen from behind, sitting in a lush alpine meadow with a deep blue lake. I'm really drawn to the image, but I can't figure out where to place her.

"Hey, Mia," I ask, holding up the woman. "Where should I stick her?"

She studies it a minute.

"Well," she replies, "did you cut it out because you want to live somewhere like that? What do you like about it?"

"Well, it'd be a beautiful place for a home, but I was mainly drawn to her—she seems so serene and content, at home in the world."

"Oh," she answers, matter-of-factly. "She goes in your 'you' pile."

"What do you mean the 'you' pile, it's *all* me."

"No," she says, "those are things you want to do and have. Where's *you*, you know, the person creating all that?"

I walk to hers and sure enough, there is my daughter right in the middle, an image of a strong-looking young woman surrounded by words like "blissful," "powerful," "confident," "giving," "brave." Her core self, with everything else radiating out from her. Of course.

It's like God just keeps flunking me back to third grade over the last five years. Mia is right—I had lots of *evidence* of myself, what I'd create and enjoy, and leave behind, but I forgot my very essence, the *me* that will experience all of that.

Mia shakes her head and goes back to her area. Aside from my being a mother at twenty-five, Mia has had so much more life experience, both positive and negative, than I had at her age. I think Mia would agree my generation was more mature and capable in terms of life skills in our twenties. We expected to be self-sufficient; we didn't expect our first jobs to be fun or well-paying. And most of us would have rather slept at the YMCA than move back into our parents' homes.

But that's just about how we interacted with the world. In terms of self-awareness and psychological savvy, she knows more at twenty-five than I ever did. It never occurred to me to do the kind of soul-searching and self-examination she's doing now. And her life is going to be much better for it.

As I look at my piles, patterns emerge, recurring motifs and themes. Nature, mothers and daughters together, powerful women, authors I admire, libraries, a *Finance for Dummies* book, cities of the world, desks looking out on vistas, interiors with French doors opening to gardens, art, books, outdoor fitness, yoga, meals under trees with lots of people.

I realize how like writing a memoir this process is. When I looked back at all the major events of my life while writing our memoir, at the highs and lows, certain themes and patterns also emerged. Not what I thought or wished my life was, what it actually *was,* the results that told me what I had really been committed to all my life. I could see where I'd mistaken drama and conflict for life, which meant years of living reactively instead of generatively, a life I let be determined by circumstances and the choices of others. We like to *think* life happens to us, but pretty much everything in your life is there because you wanted it, even if unconsciously. Results, I have learned, don't lie.

I look at the pile of images for my relationship with Mia. Nature, books, travel, family, art, food, as well as words for our shared values: "love," "respect," "fun," "adventure," "art," "knowledge," "support," "accountability," "honesty," "communication."

I have a pile of moms and kids, oddly enough, given I've traveled half a world away to figure out who I am apart from being a mother. My favorite is of a woman around seventy with her hands cupping the face of a woman around forty. When I was cutting it out, I had to swallow hard, because it reminded me of my mom. But it's not just the younger woman

I identified with. I also identify with the maternal feelings of the older woman. Part of me knows I'm headed that way, closer to being seventy than thirty.

"What is *that*?"

I look up to see Mia holding a print of a fifteenth-century etching of a hairy little beast, probably what a northern European artist who'd never seen a monkey imagined one would look like if it also happened to be the devil.

"Hey, show a little respect," I answer. "That's Tish!"

"Morticia?"

"Yes. I'm going to put her in a pink tutu, so look for images of ballerinas."

"You're kidding! How cute!"

"Well, she's not going anywhere, so I'm making her presentable and sticking her with family."

Yeah, Tish can sabotage me if I let her, but mostly I think she just wants to be loved and reassured. I want her out in the open where I can see her coming. Lest I mistake her fears for reality. To fully reintegrate all the parts of myself, including little Tish, means all the feelings that go with them, even the painful, despairing, or shameful. Everybody has to come to the party for there to be a party at all.

She laughs. "You'll be like that pope with his little black demon following him around."

Spending the past few days immersed in a grown-up's version of arts and crafts has been great. Not just because it's fun skimming magazines and saying, "Yes please," to whatever tickles my fancy, but because it's nice to feel excited about the future again. Feeling unanchored is one thing, not knowing why I felt that way is another altogether. This trip's clarified, specifically, what wasn't working for me, and I feel like a horse behind the starting gate.

My mom gets up from where she's been working and walks over to study the images I've chosen. Many are lifestyle-related, friends laughing while hiking, countries I want to visit, a beautiful city apartment, photos of the kids in Rabin's SOS Children's Village Jorpati, in Kathmandu, to represent organizations I want to be involved with, an artist's studio, a library, a chic couple eating at a scenic restaurant, words like "adventure" and "excitement." Other images evoke feelings I want to regularly experience: a woman riding bareback on a galloping horse, a woman relaxing at a spa looking comfortable in her own skin, words like "relaxed," " joyful," "inner calm."

"What?" I ask, noticing my mom's skeptical expression. "Why do you have that look on your face?"

"Well," she says, squatting down beside me, "I love all of it, it feels very you, but, remember how you pointed out—quite wisely, I should add—how my map was missing a big section?"

"Yeah," I say slowly, sensing an impending lecture.

"Tell me if I'm missing it, but where's your career? You know, the part about how you'll finance all this stuff."

"Oh, that," I say matter-of-factly, reaching for a picture of a bedroom that looks particularly inviting. "I'm skipping it for now because I don't know what I want to do yet."

"Shouldn't you be thinking about it? Travel and fine dining aren't cheap."

"Mom," I sigh. "Why do you have to make everything so serious? This is supposed to be fun, I'm not thinking about career stuff."

"This isn't an arts-and-crafts project, Mia. It's an exercise in creating an intentional future for yourself. You don't want major professional regrets, and financial stress feels terrible, trust me. Not thinking about retirement funds when you're young almost guarantees you won't have one when you're old. But, mainly, doesn't a successful career excite you? Don't you envision that for yourself?"

Here comes the lecture.

"Of course I want a successful career, but I have no clue what I want to do. I'm not about to cut out publicist pictures since I don't want to do that long-term, and I don't want to paste a giant question mark, so I'm just skipping it."

"Mia, you're not 'skipping' anything, nonaction is an action. You're making a conscious choice to omit it. You don't know where you want to live, but you *cut out pictures of interior décor and pretty bedrooms, right? Do the same for your career. Forget the exact title, just think about the elements you want in a career. What excites you? What do you gravitate toward? Do you see yourself in a busy office or working from home? What qualities do you want in your colleagues? I saw some great images of professional women in beautiful offices. Why don't you—"*

She interrupts herself a second, bends down, and squints.

"Is that Tinkerbell??"

I look at the winking pixie in a cloud of fairy dust and feel somewhat sheepish.

"I happen to like Tinkerbell—she's a perfect symbol of feeling lighthearted and free."

"Honey," she says, looking at me, "you're an accomplished and wise young woman."

She walks back over to her area, sits back down.

"But in some ways you really need to grow up."

I look down at my map, which isn't really even a map yet but just a pile of images I now feel like tossing out the window.

"Well, thanks for ruining a perfectly nice afternoon!"

I walk out of the apartment, closing the door loudly behind me, and stomp my way downstairs to brood on a bench in the park across the street. Throughout the park, people are papering tree trunks with posters advertising upcoming plays.

Every July is Le Festival, *a monthlong theater festival that typically draws some hundred thousand people, and it's all anyone's talked about for the past few weeks. Bar les Célestins rolls in large shipments of wine and beer every day, and new faces are increasingly peppered among those we've come to recognize.*

By the time flyers for The Penis Monologues *have been strung above me like popcorn garlands, I've cooled off enough to see my mom's point. I initially avoided adulthood because I associated it with the loss of carefree, childhood fun. Within the past two years, however, I think it's less to do with fearing adult responsibility (it's not the most fun thing in the world, but I know how to live responsibly), and more to do with fearing I don't have what it takes to succeed. There weren't images of professional women because I often don't have faith in myself as one. I'm bored with publicity but it came easily to me and I know I can do it. If I switch fields, (a) I have to figure out what else to do and (b) I may be terrible at it.*

Until about two years ago, it never seriously occurred to me that I could fail. Not failure along the lines of borrowing a hundred bucks from your parents to make rent, but really, truly, failing. I spoke to my mom about this, expecting her to be sympathetic and regale me with anecdotes about times her idealistic bubble burst, but she was rather amused. Of course I knew I could fail, she said, we all did, we'd failed plenty as kids—we got flunked, we got detention, we didn't get picked for teams. It was a lifelong reality that motivated us to work hard.

Granted, I can't help that failure was hardly part of my generation's educational vernacular; most of us were taught early on that we could do and be anything. Praise, meant to foster high self-esteem, was the staple of many millennials' upbringings, both at school and at home. As Jean Twenge wrote in Generation Me, *we were applauded just for turning our homework in and frequently told how smart, talented, and special we were. Is it any wonder we anticipated relatively easy and immediate professional success?*

But when rewards aren't tied to results, I think it actually fosters insecurity. Kids aren't dumb; on some level you know you don't deserve the accolades and you start questioning your abilities, in part because you're never sure exactly what they are. I'm sure that's partly why, after a few rejection letters, I stopped submitting articles altogether. I often give up when things don't come easily to me, a pattern I want to change. Sometimes I feel like my self-esteem is similar to a beautifully constructed house of cards; the slightest of shakes and everything falls flat.

chapter eleven

Avignon

If It's Not One Thing, It's Your Mother

April 4, 1671, in a letter sent from Madame de Sévigné to her daughter:

> *I told you the other day about Madame de Nevers's new coiffure . . . this hair style is just what will suit you, you will look like an angel and it is quickly done . . . Now, imagine the hair parted peasant-fashion to within two inches of the back roll; the hair each side is cut in layers and made into round loose curls which hang about an inch below the ear; it looks very young and pretty—two bouquets of hair on each side. Don't cut your hair too short, because the curls require a lot of hair as several ladies have found out and are example to others. Ribbons are arranged in the usual fashion and a large curl on top which sometimes falls down the neck. I don't know if I have explained it very well. I shall have a doll dressed with this hair style and send it to you.*

November 1, 2007, in an e-mail sent from Claire Fontaine to her daughter:

While at the hairdresser, why not get some soft highlights put in? It's kind of mousy now and some brightness in your hair will light up your whole face. Your eyes and eyebrows will pop more . . . Also did you ever buy new foundation? That'll help with rosacea and breakouts because yours has got to be laden with bacteria (from your fingers to face and back to bottle, yech). I'm ordering the copper cream today and the mineral powder foundation will be my gift as well.

Some things never change.

I've just met my mom at Bar les Célestins with a freshly cut head of hair and she's aghast.

"It's not great, I know," I say, pulling up a chair. "They cut hair really bizarrely here—she used a man's electric razor."

"Not great?" she says, getting up to see the back of it. "Mia, she totally botched your hair. Why on earth didn't you tell her to stop when she pulled out a man's razor?"

"I figured that's just how they cut hair here."

"Of course it's not, the French are known for their great cuts, and even if it was, should that matter? You should have left."

"Whatever, it'll grow out."

"No kidding it'll grow out, but what are you going to do until then?" she asks, brow furrowed with genuine concern.

"Mom, why do you care so much? It's my head and the haircut was your idea!"

I was sixteen when I first realized my mom was more concerned about my appearance than I was. I had broken my nose, and the next day I was called out of the classroom and told to go to the director's office. Nervous (when you're in a boot-camp school, it's not quite the same as the high school principal calling you in), I walked in the room and heard my mom's voice on the other end of his phone yelling, "Her nose is in the middle of her fucking face." As if he didn't know.

Sometimes it's nice that your mom cares about details that no one else would,

like what you ordered to eat on a date or what errands you have to run today.
But that same eye for detail is also why I'll be talking to my mom and realize
she hasn't heard a word because she's studying my face to see if the foundation
I'm using is a good match for my skin tone.

Last week I snapped at her after she reminded me—for the third time—
that I should get my teeth whitened when I'm home because of how much coffee
we've been drinking here. It seems like there's always something I need to im-
prove, my nails, my weight, my hair, my clothes. I told her living with her was
like being attached at the hip to John Madden. Who's he? she asked. A football
commentator, I replied, who evaluates a player's each and every move. Em-
phasis on every.

"YEEOOOWW!!"

"Oh, stop being a baby!" Mia barks as she tries to grab a half-attached
wax strip from my upper lip.

I slap her hand. "Get away from me!"

With the weak dollar, Jolen Creme Bleach here is twenty-five dollars.
Hence, I let my daughter talk me into waxing. She tries to grab it again
but I duck and turn.

"No! I'll melt it off or something! You lied, it hurts like hell! You just
want revenge for the haircut!"

She suddenly starts yelling, which makes me turn back to see what
that's all about and—RRRRIIPPP! A sneak attack!

"Owwww!! You little bitch!"

Both our jaws fall and our eyes pop. We burst out laughing hysteri-
cally. I start crying at the same time because my upper lip is on fire. "That
was so not nice, Mia . . ." blubber blubber waaah waaah.

"My God, what a baby! Nobody bleaches, Mother. A blond mustache
is still a mustache. You'll get used to it."

"No, I won't!"

"Oh, please, it's a teeny ping and it's over. You should get a Brazilian,
then you can complain."

"Oh, of course! The moment I get home! I can't *wait* for Ludmilla to rip my pudenda and then slap it!"

My girlfriend Chris and I first learned about Brazilians when we went out with our daughters for sushi and sake one night. If the girls hadn't corroborated each other, we'd never have believed that women let a complete stranger first rip the hair off their *labia* and then *slap* it to ease the pain. *Then* they make them flip over on their side and stick a leg in the air so they can rip the hair from their hind ends, all the hair, even around *the*. Chris and I were laughing so hard we practically slid out of our chairs. The sake didn't help.

Whatever happened to a bikini-line wax or a shave and trim? I personally was never a fan of hairy armpits or the Jane-of-the-jungle look in the nether parts, but come *on*.

How is it that one of the things we most feared when we were young—being seen as unattractive—causes our daughters *more* trouble now, instead of less? We are the first female generation with media influence, our own money, political clout. Shouldn't we have made it better for them? Instead, the trauma, trouble, and time women expend in the name of feminine allure has grown exponentially.

Girls wear more makeup and sexier clothes and do more to their head and body hair in junior high than most of us ever did in our twenties. And as mothers we've allowed it. We've modeled it. We've sold them down the river—we've actually *bought* them down the river, because we often finance it, even as we lament it.

Where's the Whole Foods mentality for our girls? We support organizations and have whole branches of the government to keep our land and water clean. We censor what they dump in the lakes but not our kids' minds, and our girls are paying. And we do have the power. Corporations and the media are loath to offend mothers, who do most of the buying in the country.

Then again, why would we insist on something for our daughters that we accept for ourselves? Most of us have bought into the same mind-set. We've always seen ourselves as an ongoing self-improvement project, first for vanity, then to keep our jobs. Being seen as older isn't just a social hazard, it's professionally dangerous.

What difference will all the Take Your Daughter to Work days, getting more women elected, and achieving professional equality, make if we teach and model "not enough" in the most basic, gut-level way? How do we expand the definition of beauty for our daughters, and sons, instead of narrowing it?

Given my mom's shock at Brazilians, I'm glad I never told her about pole-dancing. Not that I did it for any length of time; it took me all of twenty seconds to clamber up a few feet, cling desperately, and—because a pole is a slick, cylindrical object and I am not a tree frog—drop like a rock.

I'd been curious about pole-dancing for a while and when I saw it listed on the classes offered at my gym, I thought, Why not? Home stripper poles had been featured on Oprah; *Teri Hatcher and Kate Hudson touted pole-dancing's firming benefits. Maybe it'd put an extra bounce in my step, make me turn a paler shade of green when passing one of Manhattan's many gorgeous models.*

So, after a day of negotiating with Elle *editors,* NPR *producers, and other people that reassured me my student loans hadn't gone to waste, I found myself flanked by a mélange of sweating and panting professionals, performers, students, and stay-at-home moms. As it turns out, the pole itself is only part of what's included in a pole-dancing class; the rest of it involves lots of hip-thrusting, hair-tossing, crawling on your hands and knees while making bedroom eyes at the mirror, and, as I was learning, floor-humping. When the perky instructor ordered us to lie on our backs, go spread-eagle, then flip to our stomachs and hump the floor, some went at it with reckless abandon, others mimicked the instructor in earnest, and the rest, like me, flip-flopped like fish gasping for air on a slippery deck.*

Two thoughts, meanwhile, were running through my head. One, my mother (who only ever let me play with Doctor *Barbie) would die if she ever saw me like this. And two, am I seriously humping one of the germiest surfaces in Manhattan? A surface, by the way, that I pay ninety-five dollars a month to have the privilege of humping.*

But I took the class for me! To unleash my inner beast, as the course description promised, because being sexy feels fun and powerful! Leaving the class, however, I felt anything but, and as I walked home I wondered how I actually came to think that crawling on my hands and knees would boost my confidence.

I may have fared better in the era of salons, when a woman with the quickest wit drove men wild, and less was considered more. Or rewind several hundred years earlier, to the days of courtly love, of troubadours and ardently delivered poems and window serenades.

Actually, courting rituals like that originated close to where my mom and I are staying in France, and were pioneered by a mother and daughter. Courtly love was already a growing tradition in Western Europe, but it was under Eleanor of Aquitaine, the powerful twelfth-century French queen, that the movement became famous. Eleanor set up her court at Poitiers and, because courts hadn't previously existed in that region of France, her younger courtiers were as unruly as college freshmen. Running a kingdom being time-consuming and all, Eleanor called in her daughter, Marie de Champagne, for help.

Peer pressure has always been an effective means of coercion and, recognizing this, the savvy Marie changed the culture to one where it was no longer cool for young men to be bragging and boorish, and young women to be swooning and promiscuous. Rather, the most enviable women were the ones with mannered, chivalrous, and respectful men pining after them.

Marie accomplished this by hiring a prominent cleric to write a rule book outlining new codes of behavior concerning love. The book was modeled on Ovid's Ars Amatoria (The Art of Loving), *but while Ovid told men how to dress, approach, converse with, and toy with women, Marie's book placed women squarely in control, advising them of the rules they should set forth for suitors and exactly how and when to judge them.*

This came none too soon; during Eleanor and Marie's lifetimes, Europe changed from a feudal society to a medieval one. While feudal Europe was undoubtedly patriarchal, women there still had legal rights; once the Church came to power in the late twelfth century, we lost the right to own property, and ourselves became *the legal property of fathers or husbands.*

Newly powerless, women across Europe used Marie's text to turn them-

selves into perfect coquettes, harnessing their seductive powers to move up the political and economic ladder. They became well-versed in the intricate and highly stylized dance of seduction, and masters in the art of pleasing, both in dress and manner. By the fourteenth century, France was the fashion and perfume capital of the Western world precisely because of the critical role appearance played in the art of seduction.

And appearance didn't necessarily mean beauty, nor did pleasing imply anything sexual; wit, charm, intellect, and style counted far more. Upper-class women were educated not just for their own benefit but because it gave them an edge in the art of conversation and courtship. The incredibly powerful mistress of King Louis XV, Madame de Pompadour, rose to power thanks to her exquisite charm and good taste, and Ann Boleyn, attractive but no great beauty, used the coquetterie *she learned growing up in the French court to snag the title Queen of England.*

Women in those days had to learn to make men their emotional pawns because, legally, we were theirs. Clearly, women aren't men's legal pawns anymore, but I wonder to what degree we're cultural pawns. Until the rise of advertising and male-driven corporate culture, salons—which were almost exclusively run by women—created and determined culture. Which writers, philosophers, or artists came to prominence was largely determined by who was invited the most frequently to the most influential salon. Maybe it's time to bring some of this back.

If you were standing in Place Saint Didier right now, you'd be treated to this little performance: a young couple banging on one of the closed glass phone booths, yelling *Frelon d'Asie! Frelon d'Asie!* at the madwoman sealed inside, who is bouncing off the glass, flailing one arm and hollering.

The city is alive with scenes like this, actors performing bits of their plays to entice you to attend. Many integrate themselves into city life so well it takes a moment to figure out that the drunk on the carousel hollering epithets is acting out a scene.

Most are definitely *not* part of everyday life: a group of prisoners bound together by a rope marches through the streets begging their cause on one block, screaming curses on the next. A dozen flight attendants in matching red suits scurry about as if on a secret mission, whispering in the ears of passersby. A somber, doomed noblewoman in eighteenth-century finery sits imprisoned in a wooden cage carried by a few scruffy *citoyens*. Following them is a poker-faced priest in a voluminous black robe billowing in the wind, handing out flyers for her cause (and the playwright's).

The woman in the phone booth, however, is not an actor, she is *me*. One minute I'm on the phone with a friend, next I'm screaming with pain and confusion, because out of nowhere it's like a humongous red-hot poker was shoved up into my armpit! I don't know if I'm bitten, have blown a blood vessel, or been shot.

"Frelon d'Asie!" the couple outside keeps yelling, pointing at some great big moving thing by my feet. *"Frelon d'Asie!"*

I smash my foot down on it. *Frelon* (hornet) my butt! Whatever it is, it's so big that by the time I'm done stomping on it, it looks like a flattened Hershey bar. And what the heck does Asia have to do with anything?!

"Arrêtez (stop), *madame, arrêtez!"* they urge me, which I finally do. They shove the door open and I fly out of there like a bat outta hell. I take off for the studio, flapping my arm up and down and sobbing unashamedly. I'm such a big hit with the crowds, I swear I hear clapping.

"Sssst!"

That sucking in of breath through closed teeth that the French do when shocked is what the cute little pharmacist does upon seeing the cantaloupe that is now my armpit. I actually had to walk here with my arm held up.

Last night when I stumbled into the studio after the hornet attack, Mia and I couldn't find any stinger or bite marks. There was, however, a small hole. No pharmacies were open, we couldn't find a doctor, and we couldn't reach Chrystelle. So we disinfected it, I took four ibuprofen at once with a huge glass of wine to knock myself out, and I went to sleep with an ice pack strapped on. By morning, voilà, *un melon*.

Oh lá lá, cluck, cluck, cluck, the pharmacist says, the hornets from Asia! Poor thing, cluck, cluck, cluck, you are very lucky, it can kill you, this one! *Comme ça*—like this, she holds up her fingers to demonstrate almost three inches big. No kidding.

The pharmacist is the first line of defense for the French. Many go years without ever seeing a doctor. Pharmacists here can diagnose, prescribe most medicines, give shots. Though they're well-trained in holistic remedies and recommend them, the French love Western drugs. I had a raging sinus infection last time I was in Paris with a fever of 104 degrees and a very real desire to shoot myself in the head. I was prescribed, and took, no fewer than five powerful drugs, two of which are still not approved in the United States. I was stoned out of my mind but better in one day.

Without a doctor's visit, this petite young woman has given me antibiotics, something probably stronger than morphine, and the promise of a shot if it isn't better by tomorrow. All for the cost of a cappuccino and a croissant.

Once we tell her how much more drugs cost in our country, I leave there with a year's supply of hormone replacement therapy. The hormones actually require a visit to a doctor but, *Bouf!* she says with a wave of the hand, you 'ave a right as a woman, you don't need a doctor to tell you what you need! And voilà, a year of hot-flash relief for one-eighth the cost.

It's another thing about the French I just adore. They love to make lots of rules and then they love to break them if they're seen as unnecessary or an affront to their rights as a *citoyen*. Strangers will argue passionately with one another in defense of their rights at the drop of a hat. Last time I was at Charles de Gaulle Airport in Paris, a *très* petite woman in a pink Chanel suit got into it about her rights with a brawny young customs agent (in the States you wouldn't say boo to any official who can throw you in jail). Four of his massive, handsome coworkers came, all waving *les* fingers, poufing, and yelling at her in unison with him. But, let me tell you, she held her own. In five minutes, they all reached agreement, which is what they desire after all, and she was waved through with a smile, which she returned as she clicked her sling-backs through the turnstile. Typical.

They'll also argue *your* rights. Chrystelle argues for ours regularly. She recently admonished a librarian who wouldn't let us use their Internet. They are writers, madame, *artistes*! Last week we were walking on a nearby trail when a restaurant appeared smack in the middle of the path, with a sign forbidding passage. *"Bouf!"* a diner exiting the place told us as she waved us in. "Who do they think they are? It is your right!"

Sitting at Bar les Célestins at night feels like having drinks at the office. Except instead of sitting in the dim recesses of the bar waving our laptops around to pick up *le wee-fee* (wi-fi), we're at a wobbly table in the plaza, where festival-goers and performers swirl around us in every direction. Roman whisks over with our drinks, snaking (as only those long, skinny legs can) between tables and humans.

Across the street, a shirtless man who looks like Popeye leans out his third-floor window, tattooed arms crossed on his sill; his plump, elderly neighbor peers down over her geraniums. Three hundred years ago you could have gazed up and seen this exact same scene. Except, of course, for the posters plastered on the building wall between them, portraying two actors, one of whom looks remarkably like Rupert Sewell, with his finger up the nose of the other.

The trunk of the giant plane tree in the plaza is wrapped with flyers and posters for concerts, recitals, classic plays. In the theatrical equivalent of the Salon des Refusés, the exhibit the Impressionists held after being refused into official salon, Festival Off is held outside the walls, and includes every other kind of play—lower budget, experimental, fringe; from the looks of the posters, most seem to involve a lot of yelling.

Just beyond us, a young woman sings "La Vie en Rose" to little applause and even littler tips. She's not bad, but Avignon's academies turn out dozens of world-class vocalists every year. Avignon during the festival is an even tougher crowd. It doesn't help that she dressed with little thought. It's one thing to the French to *look* like you've dressed with little thought, quite another to actually *dress* with little thought.

Two men sit at the next table laughing and drinking; a freckled, wiry fellow with a red crew-cut, and a suave East Indian guy around my age who suddenly turns to us and asks, in perfect English, why two pretty young women are sitting alone on a Saturday night when they could sit with them. Who could refuse such a charming invitation?

Kamal, an *Avignonais* of twenty years, was born in India, speaks several languages, and seems to have lived many lives. Ryan is a gay Irish engineer around forty, who once lived here with a lover. He returns every few months to visit his friends.

After an hour, we've covered the usual cultural differences, with Kamal prefacing most of what he says with "You Americans . . ." and Ryan half-listening, half-lost in his own internal orbit. Once Kamal scoots his chair over to engage Mia in conversation, Ryan scrapes his chair over to me.

"Aie knew yair hair mother an all, but ken aie tale ye soomthing?"

He leans so far over there's nothing between us but his breath, rich with his tenth beer. I have no idea what he wants to tale me but his expression is suddenly deeply earnest. He puts his fingers in a V and taps under his eyes.

"Et's raight heer, ai'm tellin' ye," he taps and nods in Mia's direction, "aie ken see it heer," tap, tap, nod, "in the shadoos oonder hair eyes."

"Oh, that. She has allergies, they're allergic shiners. It's the pollen here."

He shakes his head at my apparent ignorance. He sighs and leans in again.

"Aie knew yair hair mum, aie knew, but sumwun has to say et. The gairl needs sumthin," he sighs, holding up the V sign again. Only this time he leans closer and taps them under *my* eyes.

"Et's raight thair in the shadoos. Ai'm sorry te have te tail a mum, but thair ye have it."

"Have what—I have shadows, too? We both have allergies," I manage, completely bewildered.

He sucks in his breath and then blurts, "*Sayks!* The gairl needs *sayks!* Ken ye not see et, woman?"

Lord, have mercy on me. *Somebody* have mercy on me. I have a fire-breathing gay Irishman in my lap telling me, loudly, that my daughter needs sex.

He sits back in great relief. Yooo knoooo, he says, a nice loover, just for the soommer, her being in France, after all.

"I need WHAT?!" I sputter.

I wondered why that man from last night was trying to poke my mom's eyes out, but that certainly wasn't on the list of possibilities. Yes, it's been a while, but (a) is it that obvious and (b) what the heck's she supposed to do about it? Order Roman for me instead of my next glass of wine?

"I know," she exclaims, "I couldn't believe what I was hearing."

"But what do your eyes have to do with anything??"

"Doon't ye mean tha shadoos?" she says, tapping them. "Oh, who knows! Men usually think that everything has to do with sex. The first therapist I ever saw asked me halfway through the session—completely out of the blue—how often I was having sex. He said it was an important part of patient history. Right."

"That's what Tracey's did, too!"

Tracey is a family friend, a very successful writer in a very happy marriage.

"She said that every male therapist she ever saw asked about her sex life no matter what she was there to talk about."

We both shake our heads, laughing as we weave through boulevards crowded with street performers, doing our best not to inadvertently walk through the middle of someone's play.

"So. Have you ever thought—" my mom pauses—"you might meet someone here?"

"Meet someone . . . ?"

"Come on, Mia, you're twenty-five, you've got to feel like going on a date or something."

"Oooh, you mean do I need sayks!" I laugh.

"Don't talk so loud," she says, scowling. "I don't know. I mean, if you were living here by yourself you might take up a . . . a, oh I don't know, a sooomer loover."

I know she was going for nonchalance but hearing my mom say the words "summer" and "lover" in the same sentence is painful, no matter how close we may be. Maybe Kamal's right, maybe Americans are more uptight. Maybe if we were French this conversation would be as natural and breezy as deciding on what to buy for dinner. What about a lover, honey, you need one of those? Oh, thanks for the reminder, I'm fresh out.

Of course Ryan had a point, and when I studied abroad in France during college I did have a summer boyfriend—something facilitated by the fact that my mother was across the Atlantic.

Kamal can call me American, a Puritan, or Cotton Mather for all I care, but asking my mother to vacate for the night so I can take up a lover is one line in the mother-daughter relationship I'll never cross!

I myself am no stranger to being asked to vacate the premises. College kids call this being "sexhiled," which I know because my sophomore year it happened to me so often that I was a near-permanent fixture in the student lounge.

Wanting me to vacate was Nina, my roommate, and when we first met I'm not sure who thought she had it worse. Me for having to room with the female Casanova, or her for having to live with a celibate who dressed like Ted Kaczynski (a year and a half in a Montana boot-camp school means you own a lot of plaid, flannels, and fleece).

Nina never left the room without darkly lining her emerald eyes, glossing her lips to a luscious shine, shaking out her long brunette waves, and arranging her most notable feature—all-natural, perfectly shaped double Ds—into a traffic-stopping display. People couldn't help but gawk and she reveled in it, something that amazed me because of how uncomfortable I was with catcalls or any form of sexual attention.

Moreover, Nina had quite a sexual appetite. Who knows how many partners she had over the year we lived together, but the most memorable included an El Salvadoran with family ties to a former guerrilla president, the navy cadet who later went AWOL, the five-foot-five Italian self-made millionaire, and, my favorite, her doctor (who turned out to be married). Clearly, their initial consult went well. I quickly learned when I heard Andrea Bocelli or opera music blaring (both disguised other kinds of wailing well) from our room, to come back later.

I heard a lot of Bocelli that year.

Nina was comfortable with and open about sex and sexuality in a way many women aren't. And she didn't sleep with so many men because she had daddy issues, or for acceptance and approval. She truly enjoyed it and felt—not just pretended to feel—fantastic the morning after. While most girls did the Walk of Shame quickly and quietly back to their dorm after spending the night in a guy's room, Nina catwalked it like a runway model. At the time, this fascinated, intimidated, and appalled me.

Not that it took much to scare me off; as a one-of-the-guys kind of girl, I never wore makeup, owned nary a hair product, and when I wasn't wearing L.L. Bean, I lived in a pair of shapeless, sexless Thai fisherman pants (they're amazingly comfortable). Which is why, fortunately, Nina blockaded the door when I went to meet a cute boy from my history class for dinner and a movie.

She took one look at me, ordered me to sit down, and rummaged through my closet until she came out with a long skirt and a tank top. While I changed, she pulled out her makeup kit, and only then did she let me out of the room.

And that's how I met Graham, my first long-term boyfriend. It was the first time either of us had been in love or dated someone for more than a few months, which was perfect, because it meant we both entered into it without any expectations. We wrote our own rule book based on what felt right to us, adjusting as was necessary, particularly for me, given I'd been sexually abused.

There was an innocence to us that reminded me of a high school relationship (or at least how I imagine them to be), where everything is new and you're shyly negotiating and renegotiating everything. It was like a virginity do-over, only with a best friend with whom there was mutual trust, affection, and respect. We were together for two and a half years, by the end of which (it ended very amicably, and we're still good friends to this day) I learned how to be in a healthy romantic relationship.

Dating Graham helped me immeasurably when it came to intimacy. Heineken, however, was instrumental when it came to the polar opposite. For women who are deathly afraid of catcalls or overt sexual attention (I froze at either), I highly recommend donning a green polyester minidress, white patent go-go boots and matching cap and parading through a bar passing out beer to mildly intoxicated men. Heineken had just launched their first light beer and, as a promotional model for the campaign, we were seventies-era stewardesses right off the plane from Amsterdam—we actually had to fake accents—to bring you this new beer! Hey, I was newly graduated with steep student loans, and promo modeling paid $25 an hour and consisted of handing out free beer.

It gave me an entirely new skill set, and, ultimately, it was a good experience for me. I used to respond to catcalls with an expletive-filled sentence or totally ignore them. Working for Heineken, we couldn't do either, and what I learned was that the classier and more polite I was in reply, the more embarrassed and subdued guys became. For the most part, catcalling has little to do with you and everything to do with impressing the other guys, and when you recognize it as the pathetic ego-boosting ploy it is, you're far more relaxed. In a strange way you almost feel maternal toward them. And because you're not flustered, angry, or embarrassed, they don't get the reactions they're hoping for and quickly lose interest.

It was total immersion training, but now I can walk by any construction site without breaking a sweat.

"I absolutely love this dress!" Mia exclaims.

We're in a shop on the crowded Rue de La République and she's tried on a long sea-green sundress with pieces of fabric across the bust that create flower petals. It's a beautiful dress but it doesn't really flatter her.

She turns for me to see it all around and says, "What do you think? Isn't it beautiful?"

"Well . . . it's not the most flattering weave."

"Really? I love the fabric, what's wrong with it?"

"Well, it kind of clings in the behind."

"Oh," she says, disappointed, then brightens. "That's just the back, who cares? How about the rest of it?"

"Well, to be honest, it kind of clings all over. It's just not the greatest fit, honey."

"But the color looks so good on me, and these flower petals are so cute!"

She's so excited about the dress, but she did ask my opinion and it isn't very flattering even in this dim light. I know Mia, once she has it on outside, she won't be happy that her tummy is completely outlined.

An American woman dressing next to us has been watching. She joins in Mia's enthusiasm, saying, "I think it looks fabulous on you, and it's perfect for your coloring."

"Really?" Mia lights up. "Thank you!"

"It's so clever how they did the petals. I think you should get it," the woman says, giving her a big smile before leaving.

Mia is ecstatic. I don't say anything else as we gather our things and head for the register. I'm too stunned—at what a complete idiot I am.

A total stranger was a better mother to my daughter than I was. She made Mia feel like a million bucks. All she saw was how happy Mia was wearing that dress. All I saw was the flaws, what wasn't "perfect."

What if perfect is wearing something that makes you feel fabulous and beautiful? Anyone who's more focused on how a dress clings to Mia's hips than seeing her glowing, happy self isn't worth her time anyway. Today, that anyone would be her own mother.

My perfectionism reared its ugly head again, and I've never felt it so viscerally. Seeing my own child's face light up when another woman saw *her,* not a dress, a stupid dress, was like a kick in my gut. A very well-deserved one.

And not just today, over a dress. It's been a lot of days in her life, over a lot of things. How awful that must feel to Mia! To always be seen with such a critical eye. Yes, sometimes our girls need the unvarnished truth. Sometimes Mia *insists* on it. But now wasn't one of them. I lost sight of what was truly important.

I follow Mia out into the heat and noise of the crowded, *merde-*y *rue.* We duck quickly into one of the tiny passages leading home.

"Oooh, what a relief!" she says of the dim coolness.

"Mia, I'm really sorry about the dress."

"Sorry? About what?"

Which makes me feel worse—is she so used to it that it doesn't register?

"You look radiant in it, really, the color, the design, but most of all you love it, it makes you feel good. All I was focused on was one stupid little thing that didn't matter at all."

"I asked your opinion and you gave it, that's okay."

"No it isn't. I saw the dress, I didn't see you. I think I do that about a lot of things."

She's quiet for a second. "Not as much as you used to."

"I'm so, so sorry. I feel really horrible. There's always something that could be better, everything has to be perfect. What you wear, what classes you choose, how you do or say something."

"I know your intentions are good, Mom. You want the best for me."

We reach the other end of the passage and turn toward our plaza, which seems like another world, tourist-free and quiet. I stop her.

"Don't make excuses for me, Mia. You must feel like nothing's ever good enough, or worse, like *you're* never good enough. It must feel like shit."

"Oooo, now I know you're sorry," she says, amused but clearly pleased I'm acknowledging it. "Well, yeah, sometimes it does feel really lousy, but I usually just ignore it. It bothered me before, because I took it personally, but it's really not about me. You're almost never satisfied with *yourself*, you're always thinking about how things could be different or better. At the end of the day that's a lot harder on you than it is on me."

"It is, and yes, I'm much more aware of it now. But this isn't about me. I've always known, in my head, that I'm hard on you sometimes. But seeing how you responded to that woman in the dressing room . . ." I feel my throat get tight. "You had the same happiness in your face that you did as a little kid. Ohhhh, man—I can't even think how to express what it felt like. I feel like I could apologize to you every day for the next year and it wouldn't be enough."

"Awwww, Mom." She puts her bag down and hugs me.

"I'm so sorry, Mia," I whisper, hugging her tight.

I arrive at our bluff at my favorite time, just as the pale gold stones of the city begin to gray, as if to better turn your attention to the sky. Before sitting on the low cavalry step, I glance over the wall, a hundred feet below. Mia said she'd meet me later in the plaza by the puppet show and she's there already, sitting cross-legged on the ground behind some children.

As usual, the bluff isn't crowded, just a scattering of a dozen or so people. Farther down the wall, a young man with a felt fedora plays guitar softly. Also as usual, everyone's silent or whispering, out of respect for where they are—sandwiched between Christ, Mary, and a predictably beautiful sunset. This evening the sun has melted into a bowl of red-orange between two low mountains on the horizon. The sky deepens into indigo above it.

Suddenly the heavens do something I've never seen before. Sunbeams are normally rays of light radiating out from darker clouds. Today the reverse occurs—dark blue-violet rays shoot out of that molten nectarine glow. A sky full of inky sunbeams.

After a few moments I hear some high whispery twittering I recognize instantly. Only young girls make that lovely noise. I turn slightly to see three little girls in flared dresses, each its own shade of pink. They're gripping the wrought-iron railing around Mary's feet, staring up at her as they whisper urgently, as if discussing some expected miracle they'd been talking about all week on the playground, *Is it true, about the Virgin and miracles and resurrections and pestilence and angels and sins, will she share secrets, see how special I am, hear my wish?*

The girls then rush to the wall in front of me, with their prayers still fresh in their mouths, twirling to sit cross-legged with their dresses spread around them. They gaze up in excitement, lips pressed tight against their smiles (they're really pushing for somber piety here). They close their eyes and press their hands together in unison to mumble silent prayers. And then, in unison again, they bend at the waist over their crossed legs, until their foreheads touch the ground in front of them. Three little devotees arranged like petals of a rose, waiting.

Their mothers are far off to the side, oblivious to this little drama, one holding an infant who burps up. Without a break in conversation, one woman wipes baby puke from the mother's dress, the other wipes the baby's face.

I hear a murmur from the little girls' bowed heads and they suddenly lift their heads to stare at the statue with a look of both absolute faith that whatever they were expecting to happen was really going to happen—and the beginnings of the kind of doubt that every mother would recognize: you see your daughter has begun to know something about the world, something that she knows you always knew and never told her.

Of course, you didn't. There are so many things we never tell our young daughters. Most of them things we'll never end up telling them, we don't need to, we know the world will tell them. The world is always telling them, and each moment that they're first able to hear is a moment we mourn in a small way; because it's one moment closer to them being us. And for us, one moment farther from who we once were. For we will no longer have our girls in which to see our *own* young, innocent selves. We know that when she leaves the girl she is behind, she takes the girl we once were with her. A part of both of you is lost to the world.

This is both the joy and the heartbreak of raising a daughter. Your heart melts at the sight of their absolute innocence, but your mind knows they have to live in the world, and that the most precious thing about them is also the most dangerous.

The longer we're here, the more obvious it is that two women in search of themselves and each other could not be in a better place to do it. For Avignon is a woman if ever a city was. More than that, a *French*woman, as much a coquette as any that beguiled a king. For, like a true coquette, she reveals herself only slowly—you must work to get to know her. But she rewards your efforts; her streets reveal hidden gems.

I've been happy to trail behind The Navigator all summer, letting my gaze dance from one visual treat to another: above a luggage shop sits an ancient stone carving of a cow's head mounted on cleavers, axe, and bellows; farther down a sheep's head and a giant stone fish, each creature surrounded by the various tools of their demise, all evidence of the sixteenth-century guilds once housed here; in a dim breezeway beneath them is a sad little plaque commemorating the Jews in this area who also met their demise, during World War II. Three eras in one eyeful.

At knee level, a painted Mickey Mouse peers above an architectural detail. Below our feet, small stenciled messages on the stone pavers: *FAITES COMME CHEZ TOI* (Make yourself at home), *ET SI DEMAIN RIEN?* (What if tomorrow nothing?). Scrawled on the wall in beautiful cursive writing: *LA CULTURE C'EST LA MORT DE LA SUBVERSION* (Culture is the death of subversion—apropos in one of the world's capitals of culture); another bit of graffiti adapts a faded Art Deco–era ad forbidding the parking of airplanes. And we must have passed these red words on a wall dozens of times before I noticed them:

BE HAPPY*
*Free game, no purchase necessary

Even the massive buildings themselves hide layers of history easily missed when passing. There's a charming little park at the end of our block behind an amusing costume ball of a complex that covers several blocks. We were here weeks before I noticed it was one structure, the semi-ruins of a huge fourteenth-century Benedictine monastery, with a different era's façade on each block. The front sits on the grand Rue de La République, which Mr. Bonaparte III's designer obscured with a smooth-stoned nineteenth-century affair. I dunno, maybe just to show it who was boss, which was just, you know, so Napoleonic.

At certain angles it looks like the face of a young girl pasted onto Aunt Hilda's ancient pockmarked mug. As if you wouldn't notice those gigantic crumbling buttresses poking out all over her medieval hind-end in the park, like Madame Pompadour's wooden panniers when she lifted her skirts for the king. And just pay *nooo* attention to that tall pointy hat sticking up with all those gothicky pinnacles and ribs.

In 1700, an architect slapped a snooty neoclassical façade on the far end of the monastery's side. There was no attempt at integration—seen from the side, it just sits there like a rococo Venetian mask.

Avignon constantly surprises with such things-behind-things, little mysteries, and always the suggestion of more. For me it is the light that most enchants. As the afternoon sun lowers, it's hard to look at anything other than *the air* here. The intense Provence sunlight bounces off this sea of stone from a thousand angles, rendering it into a kaleidoscope of dove, mushroom, beige, chalk, and honey that gives the very air itself substance, a creamy velvet density that makes your lids want to lower. It feels like you're walking through a laundry line of an Edwardian lady's filmy lingerie.

Only when you find yourself in the open plazas or on our bluff does the sunlight look like her usual golden self again, deepening as she leaves for the day, giving us sunsets on our bluff that are as luscious and rosy as a ripe fig, one more feminine visual that adds a sweetness to our life here. And, of course, the graceful madonnas always above our heads.

Avignon's feeling of feminine mystery and invitation is even reflected in the women's style here. They take layering to another level, often wearing a few days at a time: an apron-type dress over a longer dress over loose linen pants, or a slip dress over another dress over jeans, a sexy bra strap peeking out. Top all that with a long, wispy cardigan and a flowing scarf and voilà, *le style Avignon*. The near-constant wind seems to conspire in the whole effect, blowing aside one gossamer layer to reveal another.

It would appear unstudied, but everything about a Frenchwoman's appearance is studied; girls here are taught style with their ABCs. What they call *déshabillé*, the sexy, artfully disheveled look Frenchmen love, can take hours to achieve. Not unlike the city herself, an enchanting *déshabillé* that's taken centuries to achieve.

chapter twelve

Budapest

Dark Shadows

I would always know when it was coming on. I'd come home from school and the shades would all be drawn and the Platters would be singing," my friend Melissa shared. "She'd play that album over and over. I knew not to disturb her."

That's how my girlfriend Melissa knew her mother had sunk into one of the depressions that so frightened her as a child. She was afraid to say anything, afraid she may be the reason for it. Until Melissa shared this with me, it never occurred to me that Mia suspected my depression, or if she did, how it affected her. She never even told me how much it used to frighten her until I wrote about it while we worked together on *Come Back*. Our daughters learn young to tiptoe around our darkness.

Mia and I are in Budapest, where we've come for a couple of weeks both so I can show Mia where my mother lived and was in hiding, and to escape the increasing crowds of the festival. As you travel east in Europe, the forests literally grow darker and denser and the rational, linear lines of Western architecture swell and darken into mercurial bloodred onion domes. Even the colors of the buildings are moody here, with their saddened pinks, jaded greens, and yellows that purr rather than sing. There's a melancholy to Central Europe that I settle into like a warm bath.

I wish that I'd been more honest with Mia about my depression when she was young, been able to tell her that Mommy was going through a sad time that had nothing to do with her, that it would pass. Not just to ease her fears or to model emotional honesty for her, though those are significant reasons, but so that she might learn to feel okay with, and learn from, her own shadows, to whatever degree they may show up. To teach her to acknowledge and integrate negative emotions, not fear or deny them.

One of my biggest lessons as a mother has been that it's not what we do or say that has lasting impact on our children. It's our very essence. We *are* their instruction manual on how to be a human being. And who we are stems from our core beliefs about ourselves, programmed into us from our own childhood. Our kids, especially our daughters, internalize our beliefs about ourselves and about life from the moment they arrive, the limiting beliefs most of all, because they're unconscious.

My very way of being taught her that to be a person is to be fragile; the programming was that denial and suppression are what we do with negative emotions. No wonder she ran away when her shadows loomed large at fifteen—in a very real sense she'd watched me do it long before that.

Apart from that, Mia seems to have broken the mold. She occasionally gets anxious, a trait she shares with my mother, but aside from those few years as a teen, there's no darkness to her. She's always been a bright spirit, with a vibrant, loving quality that everyone responds to and that makes her a joy to be around.

As for my own shadows, though much has been written about depression and children of the Holocaust, I'm not sure mine has its roots there, or not entirely. While I suspect a genetic component, on both sides of my family, I believe part of it is rooted in geography and ancestry. Hungary, for example, has long had one of the highest suicide rates in the world. Sabrina, a young Hungarian-American acquaintance who was raised in both countries, reflected on this with me recently, sharing how the temperament is echoed even in their sayings. "Don't worry," you tell someone who's just had some really bad luck, "tomorrow it'll be worse."

France enlivens me, but this part of the world stills me, it fits the darker parts I have learned to value. I liked *Dark Shadows* as much as *Gilligan's Island* and that's never going to change. I no longer fear the sadness I sometimes fall prey to, or feel it needs to be fixed. I like being able to fish around at the bottom of my dark pond for a while, scan for items of interest.

And one thing is certain: for better or worse, depression is authentic, true and honest to the bone. I have to wonder sometimes if it's my body's way of shoving my ego and illusions out of the way to let me empty the reservoir of emotion that's dammed up.

The Eastern European landscape is dark and dramatic and intense and beautiful, and it reminds me of my mother. Not of my mother now, but of a side of her that I still see from time to time. For the most part, my mom is bright and lively and on some days she's so upbeat and optimistic I want to smack her. But she also has a very dark side and I can see from her relaxed energy and tone that she feels very much in her element here.

When I was eight and nine, my mother went through a terrible depression. It was only when we were working together years later that she honestly talked to me about it. She described waking up with a pillow wet with tears from crying in her sleep, crying all day long while I was away at school, and feeling peaceful only when deciding how to best kill herself. I have to wonder if she'd have succeeded if Paul hadn't worked at home so she wasn't alone. She told me how she forced a happy face on for me when I came home because she didn't want me to see her in pain—she thought it would frighten me.

I finally told her that I always knew, and that her silence about it was worse; I assumed whatever was going on was too terrible to even speak of. The intensity of her sadness terrified me, living in our home like a silent sibling, consuming as much of her time and energy as I did. I remember coming home from school those years and hearing Michael Nyman's sound track to the film The Piano. *It's beautiful music, but it's very dark, and even after it was turned off, the chords and melodies lingered in our home like smoke. I didn't understand the term "clinical depression" then, but I knew my mother* saw the world through a dark veil, and I didn't know what I could do to push it aside.

She eventually got help and normal life resumed, but childhood has a way of magnifying events in your mind's eye and I've always been very sensitive to any sign of sadness in her. I remember reading what my mother had written: "I knew a hole has opened up in the terrain. And that if I wasn't careful, I could fall in." She didn't realize that I knew that hole was there, too. And that I was afraid that if she fell in I'd be pulled down with her.

It wasn't until my sophomore year of college that I finally saw The Piano. Stumbling across it in my campus library felt like finding an invitation into my mother's world, to that missing piece of the puzzle.

I took the film back to my dorm room, turned off my phone, and watched it. Afterward I sat motionless and silent for a long time. In my mind's eye was an aerial view of our old apartment, a pale woman curled in the fetal position on a yellow bedspread, a listless expression on a tearstained face. I felt the heavy tiredness, the indifferent acceptance of death, the dread of having to hide what she was feeling from the ones she loved. It was the first time I fully saw my mother.

When we are children, seeing our mothers upset is as frightening as it is confusing. When we become adults, while we may understand what's going on, it's no less disturbing. I think back to a few weeks ago, when my mom sat down in the middle of an alley and started crying about lost children and other big regrets of hers. I've very rarely seen her that raw and unraveled, and when the person who's always been your rock drifts out to sea, life suddenly feels unstable and uncertain.

Like a lot of daughters, I imagine, I have a complex relationship to my mom's emotional state, particularly to her level of happiness. On the plane here I read A Woman's Story, by French writer Annie Ernaux, about her relationship with her mother, and I was struck when she wrote: "I was both certain of her love for me and aware of one blatant injustice: she spent all day selling milk and potatoes so that I could sit in a lecture hall and learn about Plato."

That sentence helped me see that it's hard for me to separate how much my mother loves me from how much she's sacrificed for me. Now, when I picture my mom lying listless and depressed on her bed, I can't help but think about the bed itself.

At that point we were living in a one-bedroom apartment. My mom wanted me to have the bedroom, and she and Paul turned the living room into their bedroom. The sacrifices my parents made for me, how much of themselves, both emotionally and financially, they invested in me. It makes me feel like they deserve a return on their investment, that they know all those sacrifices weren't in vain.

I think kids often feel that their parents' happiness hinges on their own, and that they judge themselves based on how you're doing. Our failings are their failings, our successes their triumphs. Knowing that someone determines whether they were a success or failure as a human being based on how you turned out can be really stressful.

My mom and I have talked to hundreds of women about their moms in the last few years and one thing we all seem to have in common, no matter what age we are, is a genuine and unselfish desire to see our moms happy. I have to wonder, though, if some of our wanting them to be happy is needing *to see them happy, for selfish reasons—the happier and more fulfilled our mothers are in their own lives, the less likely they are to be impacted by—or scrutinize—ours.*

"Menjen már onnan, illetlen külföldi! Ha még egyet megfogdos, lecsapom a mocskos kezét! Honnan jön, Amerikából? Miért nyomogatja meg egyenként mindegyiket! Állatok ezek!"

(Get away from there, you rude foreigner! If she touches one more, I'll slap her filthy hands! Where did she come from, America? Why is she pushing each one individually! Animals, they are!)

It's always produce.

First in Provence, where I was publicly scolded for picking out my own tomatoes (the *merchant* picks your produce for you), and now a six-foot-tall peasant woman in Ma Clampett getup wants to smack me upside the head for touching her enormous, gorgeous, homegrown tomatoes. I was just feeling, *very gently,* for ripeness when she blew a gasket*bekek*.

She and her amazing tomatoes aren't the only giants in Nagycsarnok, the soaring, Eiffel-style, glass-and-metal-covered market in Budapest. Everything here is bigger. The people, the produce, the volume. There are squash bigger than my thighs, cherries the size of apricots, apricots the size of apples, and poppy-seed strudel as big and heavy as shot puts. All of it so delicious, *we're* going to be bigger by the time we leave.

Architecturally, Budapest is an elegant city largely patterned after Paris, but where France is neoclassically delicate, Hungary is voluptuous; a sort of baroqueified Eiffel, by way of the Ottoman, the Byzantine, and an embarrassment of fabulous Art Nouveau. The occasional blocky Soviet hulk actually serves to throw the beauty of everything else into sharper relief.

A highlight of our trip thus far is the Hungarian National Museum. Because the artifacts and artwork are displayed not by type (paintings, sculpture, costume) but chronologically, Mia and I have just moved era by era from the dawn of the Magyar culture to the current day.

My favorite space is on the grounds of the museum, in a serene, shady patch of the gardens. Actually, it's my favorite place in the entire city, because it's where my mother used to while away her free hours as a young teen, before the Nazis invaded Hungary in 1944.

While Mia wanders about shooting photos, I'm sitting on the same wood-and–wrought-iron bench my mom sat on as she knitted the striped sweater she wears in a beautiful photo of her at sixteen. She's smiling and happy, with her thick, wavy blond hair styled into the big swoop of bangs popularized by Betty Grable. It makes me smile to think of my mom as a typical teen, a girl who loved movies, singing along with the Andrews Sisters and mooning over Gary Cooper (who, of course, spoke fluent Hungarian; movies have always been dubbed here).

The feeling of sitting *exactly* where she sat before the bombs fell, where she laughed with friends and clacked needles, is so big in me that I hardly know what to do with it. Sadness, delight, fascination, but mostly longing, a deep, knotted ache. For my mother.

The sad or clouded look I was anticipating on my mom's face is notably absent when I approach her. If anything, she's in a pleasant mood, reaching for my hand as I sit on the bench beside her.

"*Being here isn't strange for you?*" *I ask.* "*Or hard?*"

"*It's comforting,*" *she answers softly.* "*In a way, it's the closest I've been to my mom in three years. I wish I'd brought some yarn with me; it'd be nice to sit and knit here, or teach you to.*"

"*I know how to knit. Or maybe it's crochet . . . what's the one where you only use one needle?*"

"*Crocheting—but since when do you crochet?*"

"*I don't, but I know how—a girl from the psych ward taught me [I had a two week stint there during my wayward years]. They didn't allow knitting, but I don't exactly have warm and fuzzy associations with either one!*"

We both start laughing and my mom shakes her head. "*Yeah, I don't suppose they'd give you two pointy objects there.*"

"*No. Good grief, that place was abysmal. To this day if I hear that Paula Cole song about cowboys I want to run screaming—it played on the radio all the time then. And remember how beige everything was?*"

"*I more remember that you were a total snot to me and Paul, and couldn't fathom why it wasn't okay for you to live on the streets with Cloud,*" *she says, rolling her eyes.*

"*Yeah, that wasn't my finest hour.*"

"*Are you looking forward to visiting Morava?*" *my mom asks after a moment's pause.*

After our conversation at the Sénanque Abbey, my mom and I talked about my going back to see Morava, which is a few hours from Budapest, as a way of gaining further closure.

"*I am. I'm a little nervous, maybe even sad, but it's more that excited-nervous feeling, you know?*"

She nods and I follow her as we get up and walk toward the street. Thirty minutes later, we're standing in front of a simple, elegant nineteenth-century apartment building several stories high with white stone detailing and ornate wrought-iron railings. It's pale yellow, and a square courtyard inside the building allows you to see the stairs and walkways on each floor. It's the building my grandmother hid in during World War II.

It was an eventful building; while in hiding there, she overheard deals

being made between Adolf Eichmann, the S.S. commander who extermi-
nated Hungary's Jewish population en masse, and Raoul Wallenberg, the
Swedish diplomat who tried to save them. It was largely the wealthy Jews
who were saved—most couldn't afford to have someone like Wallenberg buy
their freedom from Eichmann—and it's chilling to think that human lives
were bought and sold not twenty feet from where I'm standing. Especially
because the numbers of those saved were minuscule compared to those de-
ported.

When Germany invaded Hungary in 1944, they knew they were losing
the war. Exterminating Hungary's Jews was a race against the clock for Eich-
mann, who sent them to Auschwitz with dizzying speed. More Hungarian
Jews were killed in Auschwitz, the closest death camp to Hungary, than Jews
from any other country—somewhere between four hundred and six hundred
thousand.

Bubbie survived because, first, she was living and working in Budapest
when the Nazis rounded up everyone in her village and, second, she had some
serious chutzpah. Without any false papers to replace the gold star she removed,
Bubbie relied on her blue eyes, blond hair, and perfect German to bluff being
a gentile.

"Bub always said the Hungarian Nazis were worse than the German Nazis,"
my mom finally says, staring intently into the courtyard. "I think her exact words
were, 'German Nazis were quite civilized when they weren't killing you.'"

I smile at my grandma's dry humor.

"At some point in the war she did slave labor and there was a soldier, a
teenager, who used to slip her bread. Near the end of the war, German soldiers
weren't all willing; by then they were drafting even fifteen-year-olds. I know
some of the time she worked at a distribution place where they sorted through
the things taken away from Jews that were deported."

"That must have been awful."

"Not as awful as Auschwitz."

A small shop of some kind has been built right into the courtyard of the
building, and as my mother and I talk quietly, a tall man in his forties with
salt-and-pepper hair and big, dark eyes leaves the shop to walk toward us.

"*I can help you?*" *he asks in broken English, clearly wondering why two foreigners have been staring into the courtyard for so long.*

"*Good afternoon, sir. My mother used to live here, in the forties, during the war.*"

He brightens. "*This was an important building,*" *he tells us.* "*Kastner (a well-known Hungarian Jew later indicted in Israel for also dealing with Eichmann) lived here. Also during war, a writer live here in hiding. Nagy Lajos. He write book about it.*"

"*Really?*" *my mom asks, excited.* "*He was in hiding here? My mother hid in this building, too. Do you know if this man survived? Or if he's still in Budapest?*"

She's over the moon at the thought of meeting someone Bubbie was in hiding with and she looks crestfallen when the man calmly shakes his head no.

"*After war, Communists come, they execute him. I don't know why.*"

"*Do you know if any of the other people who lived in the building then still live here?*" *she presses on.*

He shrugs his shoulders and shakes his head no again, but with a kindly look in his eyes. You can tell he senses my mom's looking for something important to her. We thank him for his help and walk away, my mom chattering about how she can't wait to find out if Bubbie remembers the writer, and how exciting to meet a man who knew some of the building's history, and wouldn't it have been amazing if the writer had lived and we could have met him!

My mom's always been so hungry for information. Junior high marked the beginning of what she dubbed her Hitler years, when she began reading whatever she could find at the city library about the Holocaust, which wasn't taught in school curriculums much then. When I was growing up, I remember looking at the cartoons in Maus, *not really understanding them until I was old enough to read and comprehend the other books on her shelf,* Hitler's Third Reich, Children of the Holocaust, The Rise and Fall of the Third Reich.

"*It must have been so surreal for Bubbie when she first came to America,*" *I think out loud.* "*It's not like she could relate to other housewives on her block.*"

"*Sure she could. Our neighborhood in Cleveland had lots of survivors, and there were people like her friend Renate, who was German but not a Nazi.*"

Now, when we moved to Anaheim, that was another story. Aside from one or two other families I think we were the only Jews in a twenty-mile radius. My mom was so thrilled when she found a pediatrician who wasn't only Jewish and spoke Yiddish, but another survivor. I loved when Dr. Abrams came over. He was this short, roly-poly man, and they would drink coffee and eat my mom's poppy-seed pastry and laugh for hours. He once said that you can't not be funny speaking Yiddish—humor's just built into the language."

"Was there a lot of anti-Semitism then?"

"Not really, no. One girl used to call me an Italian booger for some reason but I only had two experiences of anti-Semitism, both in fourth grade. First was this kid named David, who probably went on to become a serial killer. Boy, was he one miserable kid. He was always more dressed up than everyone else, buttoned-up shirts, cardigans, and rock-hard leather buckle shoes instead of sneakers like the rest of us. I stayed late one day after school to help a teacher, and all the other kids had left, so I was walking home alone. He came up behind me, calling me a dirty kike, and kicked the back of my legs black-and-blue for an entire block."

"What? Why didn't you just run?"

"I was so scared I froze, and he was much bigger than I was. I'd never experienced anything like that before. I think I figured if I ran he'd catch me and really beat me up. My legs were bruised for weeks. I never told my mom, though. I thought it would really upset her, you know? But then a few months after that, Stuart, who lived on my block and was normally only a mild jerk, rode by on his bike, called me a fucking Jew, and threw a rock at me. It hit me square between the eyes." She pauses to point to the small scar between her eyes.

"That's how you got that?" I ask, wondering why I'd never asked about it before.

"Yeah. Anyway, I saw a trend developing that I didn't like so this time I ran home crying, blood running down my face, and told my mom. Well, she took one look at me and without saying a word, she put on her shoes, grabbed my hand, and marched over to his house.

"Now, you have to remember, my mother was extremely shy then. But when Stuart's father opened the door—and we had never seen his dad; they

were from Germany and always kept completely to themselves—my mother gave him a talking-to in flawless German. My eyes just about fell out of my head. Bubbie spoke six languages but I'd never heard her speak German. I'm sure he was just as surprised. I had no idea what she was saying, but the father just kept nodding politely and speaking very softly. And whatever she said worked, because right after the door shut, you could hear the hollering and little Stuart squealing."

It's funny hearing her describe Bubbie as shy and quiet. I guess raising five kids and a lifetime of experience knocks any timidity out of you, because one of my earliest memories of Bubbie is crossing the street with her, and hearing her tell a honking driver to "Go toot up your ass—this is a crosswalk!"

"His dad must have beat the living daylights out of him," my mom continues, "because the next day his face was all puffy and he could hardly sit in class. He was super-polite to me the rest of the year. I actually felt bad for him. But I remember being so proud of my mom. I felt so good that she did that."

She smiles as she says that last sentence and I like hearing the warmth in her voice talking about how good Bubbie made her feel that day. It balances the sadness and frustration she usually feels when thinking or talking about her mom. It's a great image to walk away from this building with, my mom's little schoolgirl self, Coke-bottle glasses and braided hair, skipping behind her mom, feeling happy and safe and proud.

No matter how old we get or what the relationship is like, we never stop wanting our mothers. I think that's why women often say that the moment they felt fully grown-up was after they'd lost her. For most of us, no one makes you feel safe in the world like your mom, at any age. Mortally injured soldiers cry out for their mothers on the battlefield. Even women who you would think would hate their mothers, such as those who write to tell us that when they were growing up their mothers turned a blind eye while their fathers were molesting them. Twenty years later, they go to family dinners and keep silent, knowing that's what everyone wants.

I wonder if they fear that if they shun their mother, move on, it means their mother doesn't matter to them anymore, and we need our mothers to matter. I've observed that women whose mothers were cruelly abusive, or who looked the other way, will often go through hell in their own minds, willed ignorance and denial of epic proportion, to allow themselves to be with her—living a kind of reverse Persephone myth, the daughter coming up from hell in search of a mother who has taken away her own daughter's spring and summers. *(If you're a mother who looked the other way, I beg you to put this book down now and pick up the phone. Acknowledge what you did, apologize, and ask how you can make amends. And then listen. Don't try to justify or make excuses. There are none. Just listen. And then do whatever she asks of you. Whatever pain or shame you feel is nothing next to what you caused. You will give life again to your daughter, and to your relationship.)*

For many women, however, it's not an abusive background, a shattered, or even strained, relationship that haunts them or causes sadness, there's just a vague disharmony, a distance. It seems to me particularly true for boomers, I believe because most of us bought into the culture of the times.

We were the first generation who not only wanted different lives than our mothers in almost every possible way, but were able to do it. The majority of us were largely contemptuous of their Donna Reed lives, with the culture's encouragement, certainly with Madison Avenue's and Hollywood's. Most folks don't know that The Gap started out in the sixties as The *Generation* Gap. It was when we were teens that it became cool to reject our moms.

Then, as adults, with the therapeutic community's blessing, we discovered we had inner children. The thing about inner children is that they see the world through a child's eyes, but with a grown-up's ability to inflict harm. Children don't have a well-developed understanding of cause and effect. Not to mention they're immature, usually selfish, and know Mom forgives everything. Which made us perfect victims, and Mom a perfect target.

First we made our moms and their way of life irrelevant, not worthy of influencing us, then our inner tykes made them *über*-relevant by saying they had too much influence. We blamed them for everything wrong with us, for our "issues." We took our cues to denigrate our mothers for not having coddled us enough from the very same therapeutic community that told them in the 1940s, 50s, and 60s not to coddle us, not to be too loving. During the twentieth century, even the government bashed moms; Judith Warner points out in her excellent book *A Perfect Madness* that during World War II the military blamed the fact that one in five young men flunked the draft on "smothering" mothers.

Freud set the tone in America early last century: *Femininity, the necessary turning away from the mother, is accompanied by hostility; the attachment to the mother ends in hate.* Do we really believe that anymore? If it were true, why is it only in the United States that healthy psychological development depends on separation from the mother, emotionally *and* physically? Why is it only in our country that letting your daughter *go* is synonymous with letting her *be* who she is? Women in first-, second-, and third-world countries become successful, professional, emotionally healthy adults while living at home till marriage.

How could an entire generation of American mothers all be wrong, and an entire generation of kids all be right? They washed our diapers before they had disposables, made clothes from scratch, washed floors, and devoted their lives to us. Then society changed all the rules; it took away alimony but wouldn't allow them to get credit in their own names once their husbands began to dump them, while we were off watching Pink Floyd, changing the world, and too busy to care. By the time any of us had an inkling of what many of our moms' lives were like, if we ever did, decades had passed.

They didn't nurture enough or criticized too much? Oh, now that we're older and wiser, most of us will say, "They did the best they could." How big of us.

What if the best they could was pretty damn good? Our moms must have done something right, because by and large they raised and shaped what is arguably one of the most successful, creative, influential generations of all time. We went off into the world with a sense of self-esteem, life skills, independence, and confidence that evades a lot of our own kids. And they did it without the guilt of today's moms; they didn't second-guess their every maternal move, do our homework for us, or worry much about our self-esteem.

I've lamented that the culture is the biggest parent of all for our children. But parents are just as much a product of our culture and era, for better or worse. I've read about twentysomething malaise, but only in observing and listening to Mia on this trip am I beginning to grasp what it's like for them, and see the impact of the changes in motherhood that we've adopted since the sixties.

I spent years complaining about my mom, yet when I look back at some of the smartest things I did as a parent, I see that I learned them from my old-world mother. Like putting Mia to nap wherever I was, so she'd train herself to sleep through anything, instead of putting her down in a quiet room so she'd train us all to drop dead while she napped. Like not to worry if Mia didn't eat all day (relax, no little kid ever starved themselves to death), and to use a playpen so I could take a shower or cook unimpeded (lots of moms would label that abusive today, but Mia loved her little "housela," and I loved being able to go number two uninterrupted). My mom taught me not to feel guilty for holding her as much as I wanted ("You're supposed to baby them when they're babies!") or for letting her cry when it wasn't important ("She'll never learn to comfort herself, she'll cry over everything").

My mom taught me to be a relaxed mother, which, until the *caca* hit the fan when Mia was a teen, I was. I certainly had, and have, my flaws as a mom, and I did join the Kumon math bandwagon (against my mom's counsel) with a daughter that couldn't care less about math, but I never questioned that I'd know what to do with a baby or that I'd be a good enough mom. I read only two books on mothering, beat-up copies of *Dr. Spock's Baby and Child Care* and Selma Fraiberg's *The Magic Years*. From my mom I learned that mothering can be as natural to a woman as breathing.

It certainly was for her, which is remarkable, given her history. She lost her own mother at twelve, went to live and work in a strange city, all alone, at thirteen, survived a war and the murder of her family before

she was eighteen, lived for three years in a displaced persons camp in occupied Germany from the age of nineteen, endured an unhappy marriage
to my dad (definitely no picnic), and raised five kids in a foreign culture.

She never once complained about any of it to us, not once. It used
to bother me that she rarely talked about her wartime experience. How
selfish and foolish of me! I was too busy thinking of my own curiosity
and "right" to know to think about how it might pain her, or how wise
she was to know that it would probably have been *more* damaging to her
children to talk about it. What six-year-old needs the horror of the Holocaust in her brain? And adults' and children's worlds were more separate
then; parents then didn't want or need to be their child's friend.

I also see now that in the sixties, in Orange County, California,
sewing dresses and baton uniforms and making tuna casseroles for a big,
healthy family, laughing with the neighborhood moms at their kaffeeklatsches, knitting on the sofa and watching her crush, Elliot Ness, my
mother was *happy*. She always said that all she ever wanted to do was be
a mother and housewife. And she succeeded, she made a happy home;
other than the two bullying incidents, my elementary school memories
are of sunshine, Kool-Aid, Simplicity patterns, playing freeze tag till
dark, my mom's beautiful soprano filling the house all day, and homemade fried chicken at the beach.

Then the seventies hit and we became teens. Raising American
daughters who suddenly acted like they no longer wanted or needed her,
in a culture of sex, drugs, and rock 'n' roll, with almost nothing from her
own childhood as a guide—my God, she must have felt as if she woke
up on Mars. A few of her kids gave her major heartache. My older sister
and brother were pretty even-keeled and respectful. I was a studious girl
who never got into any trouble, but I went through a long phase of being
pretty bitchy to my mom; one of my younger sisters was sweet to my
mom but, if they had programs like Mia's back then, she was a candidate;
Vivian was a good daughter but at sixteen, after ignoring a sore throat for
two weeks, she got scarlet fever, followed by encephalitis, and went into
a coma for weeks.

The doctor told my mom in a hospital hallway, bluntly, with no one there to support her, that if Vivian did live, which they didn't expect, she'd be a vegetable. He used that word. When I flew home from college and got to the hospital that night, I walked right by my own mother. She'd aged so much overnight that I didn't recognize her. Her face never looked the same. Miraculously, on Thanksgiving Vivian came out of the coma, stared at my mom, then chastised her for having a third eye. She couldn't add two and two for a year, but we're a tough bunch—she eventually went on to get a master's degree. I went back to college the following semester and since then have never lived in the same city as my mother.

None of us do. Only now do I think about how lonely her life must have been for *twenty-five years*. Only in the last year have I gone over the whole of my mother's life in my mind, over and over again. It has taken me a lifetime to finally, fully *see* my mother. Not as I wanted her to be, but as she was. And she was pretty amazing.

I want desperately to say all these things to my mother, to apologize for unintentionally, and occasionally intentionally, hurting her when I was younger, for not really acknowledging or appreciating her when she was older. I want to tell her how sorry I am for not slowing down to walk at her turtle's pace the last time I was with her. I'd crawl at a snail's pace to walk beside her now.

Walking through the empty hallways of Morava, my old boot-camp school, feels like wandering through the watery remains of a sunken ship; the rooms and furnishings are just as they were but it's eerily silent and still, all signs of life long having floated away. I suppose the life left Morava ten years ago, when sixty American teens packed their bags to return to the States.

After I opened up to my mom in Sénanque about still feeling badly about my teenage years, she suggested that while we're in Budapest I take a side trip to visit Morava. I arrived in Brno, the city on whose outskirts Morava sits, earlier this morning and was met by Peter, an old staff member who hadn't changed one iota; the same bold blue eyes, cropped blond hair, and boyishly handsome face. We toured the city that morning, which I'd never actually seen despite having lived there for six months (you had to reach a certain level to go off-grounds, and considering I was scraping leaded paint from the walls to snort it for the buzz, I didn't exactly qualify). Brno is an ancient bustling city, and it was nice meandering with Peter through its charming historic center, updating each other about the whereabouts, careers, and family lives of the students and staff we've kept in touch with.

It's late afternoon now and as Peter drives toward Morava I'm surprised by the beautiful homes and gardens interspersed with small farm plots and big black sheep. I have zero recollection of any of this. The last time I drove by I was furious, beginning to withdraw from drugs, and trying to memorize the street signs so I could run away. It's strange driving past and seeing it as any tourist would: beautiful.

Morava Academy, boot-camp school for troubled teens, is now Hotel Jelenice, a pension whose sole current occupant is Francesca, the raven-haired Gypsy cook who's been there forever. She bundles me in a great big hug, kissing me on both cheeks, while Peter translates that ten or so former students have visited Morava over the years, and how much she loves seeing us.

She takes us inside, talking to Peter and smiling at me while she leads us through the dining room, to the room we used as a classroom, to the space where we exercised. As she does, it's like the rooms re-create themselves, textbooks pop back up on shelves, seats rearrange themselves into schoolgirl rows. The air feels heavy, almost like it still carries the suppressed shouts and laughs of teenage girls not permitted to speak.

It's well past dark by now, and Peter and Francesca both have to get home to their families, but they agree to meet me in the lobby tomorrow morning. I'm the only person in the entire hotel, something that would normally unnerve me, but this used to be my home and I'm actually glad for the solitude. It's easier to imagine how it once was.

I start at the bar near the entrance, sitting on the same stool where I had my intake done, glowering at my mom while a staff member took me away to go over items I was and wasn't allowed to keep from my suitcase. Two liquor plaques stand where hand-decorated motivational quotes used to be, but other than that it looks exactly the same. Earlier, Francesca beckoned for me to walk behind the bar and opened the cupboard where our medications were stored (the bar used to serve as the nurse's station). Still on the shelves' sides are pieces of tape with students' names written on them; she never had the heart to take them down.

I open the cupboard now and take a photo; I know the other girls I've stayed in touch with will get a kick out of seeing their names still taped up. I walk down the hallway toward the bedrooms, remembering standing in perfect lines and doing head counts before leaving the area, remembering the smiles, nudges, scowls—there was a language spoken even in the silence.

In my room, it's the details that bring it all back, the brick-colored tiles in the shower and bathroom floor, the mottled brown-and-cream fuzzy fabric, the lace curtains. I get down on my hands and knees to remember picking up lint without a vacuum, which we were only allowed to use on Sundays. Getting ready in the bathroom and slipping under the covers still feels like a familiar routine even after all these years.

I remember what my mom said back in Bulgaria, about people tending to be motivated by going toward pleasure or away from pain. It's true, I'm very much a go-to person—I'm inspired to act when I think about the future, about what things I want to do or have, what places I want to see. I have never liked looking back and I've always had trouble with endings. Even as a kid, I'd rarely finish books or movies that seemed sentimental to me, like A River Runs Through It *or* Where the Red Fern Grows, *for the same reason it's easier to slip out the door than say a tearful good-bye.*

But sitting here on my old bed I'm realizing how much is lost by not doing that. Looking forward carries with it a sense of urgency and movement that almost creates an adrenaline rush, but remembrance has a certain warmth; I never realized how cozy nostalgia can be. Yes, there's a tinge of sadness, but it's not the kind of sadness associated with pain or suffering. It's a wonderful kind of sadness that I have no desire to avoid or escape.

Lying here in my old room, the same place where I first learned to be silent and find myself, I feel as though I'm watching a movie called Morava *through to the end. Quiet exits may be easier, but some moments in life are best experienced in full.*

There's a chill in the air when I wake and I nestle into the covers, looking at the pale gray shadows cast on the wall by morning light filtering through lace curtains. I trace my finger along the patterns, enjoying the minute-long vignettes of my old life here that are coming to mind.

I hear the faint clanking of pots and pans, and after a quick shower, I walk into the dining room and I laugh out loud. Whether it's for my benefit or because it has and will always be the usual fare, the breakfast laid out by a smiling Francesca hasn't changed. Thin slices of salami, triangular wedges of La Vache Qui Rit cheese, and six-inch-long, cylindrical bread rolls dubbed by incarcerated teenagers das penis brot.

How history repeats itself in families. In Mia's case it skipped a generation. In many ways she's more like my mom than I am. Both have the same blue-gray eyes and an impulsive nature that had them running away and landing themselves at fifteen in Brno and Budapest, cities four hours apart. Both are extremely smart and love to read, but neither cared much for school the way I did.

Mia's always understood my mom in a way my sisters and I haven't. My mom used to stay in Mia's room whenever she visited, and the two of them could talk and play cards for hours. My mother talking to *anyone* for hours is a rarity, but she's happy and relaxed around Mia.

During one visit when Mia was seven, as we were about to head out for a Saturday outing, my mom announced that we couldn't leave till Mia made her bed. Mia took my mom's hand and patted it gently, saying sweetly, "It's okay if I don't make the bed today, Bubbie. Really, it is. It can stay like that all day and everything is going to be juuuuust fine." Completely disarmed and charmed the Bubster. Nothing's changed between them.

Mia has that talent with everyone. She's always been wise beyond her years about people; she sees right through to who you are and speaks to that person, intuiting almost immediately the right thing to say or do. I am sometimes concerned that she puts others before herself more than is good for her. Mia rarely asks for anything for herself, never has, materially or otherwise; she can be content in almost any situation. It can be a healthy attitude and approach to life.

It can also be a way to settle for less, from others and from yourself. I've often expressed this to her, and she listens, but I know it doesn't have much impact; she's always been one to insist on finding out things on her own, often the hard way. I'll have to simply trust that she'll create whatever life experiences she needs to get whatever lessons she needs to grow.

I'm excited that she's gone back to Morava; it was such an important part of her life. And I'm glad she went alone; the experience was entirely hers then and should be now. And what an experience. We've heard from countless others who've graduated from schools like hers to thank us for writing about something that's impossible to explain or understand unless you've lived it.

What emotional fortitude it must have taken, even in her then-drugged-up state, to be locked up across the planet, with strangers, in near silence, forced to look at herself in a way very few adults ever do. It wasn't until I spent three weeks with the kids at the school she was transferred to in Montana that I had even an inkling of what it must have been like; doing everything but school and therapy in silence (on the lower levels), walking in lines to go anywhere, the complete and utter lack of freedom, month after month (it took quite a while to earn privileges).

I remember walking in line with a group on a gorgeous winter day with the snow falling lightly, surrounded by pines and mountains. It was the kind of day that makes kids want to throw snowballs and cavort in the snow. And they couldn't, at least not spontaneously. And I knew it was like this every day, all day. It felt like an actual weight on me, a lead suit. Yes, they did fun things, they earned trips home, but how she got through twenty months there, I'll never know. Neither Mia nor I regret my sending her, but I've always been aware of the price she paid, of the downsides.

I hope she's enjoying Brno with Peter; it's not as big or spiffed up as Prague but equally beautiful. I don't know how I survived the time I spent there after leaving her at the school. I'd stayed a week thinking I'd be able to visit her, only to learn they wouldn't allow it; too many kids manipulate and guilt their parents into taking them home, where they'd get into even worse trouble. I wandered around bereft and lost, in a sleep- and food-deprived haze, both on foot and, miraculously, in a rental car, which always seemed to elicit terrible yelling in other drivers. On my last day I learned that what I thought were stop signs were NO STOPPING HERE signs on what I thought was a two-lane road but was really a freeway. And those friendly police officers standing on the shoulder waving at me every time I passed weren't being friendly—that's how they tell you to pull over to be ticketed. I was a complete mess for a long time, in every way. I ultimately came out a better mother and human being, but initially the terrible sorrow, anger, fear, and self-recrimination just about did me in.

I'm strolling along the Danube, which is not particularly beautiful today, just a wide, brown, muddy river. I'm at roughly the same spot where my mother used to see Jews and intellectuals shot and dumped in the river during the war. "You had to just keep walking along. You couldn't show any fear—the Nazis could smell fear."

Most of what she's shared about Budapest over the years has been positive, however. How sophisticated, cosmopolitan, and lively it was, how beautiful the architecture and museums were.

I step onto the Liberty Bridge to walk to Margaret Island, another place she loved. The Liberty is, in my opinion, the most beautiful of Budapest's famous seven bridges (all of which were blown up by the retreating Germans in World War II, since restored)—a grand and graceful Art Nouveau chain bridge, painted a pale jade, with huge bronze falcons atop ornate pinnacles.

Just as it must for my mother, this part of the world holds both beauty and suffering for me. For her, the happiness of her youth in a city she loved and the horror of war. For me, there is the shadow of that history, and coming here to leave behind my only child when I couldn't save her myself. Thinking of this as I leave the bridge to wander up the stairs to the hilltop on Margaret Island, I'm struck by something so obvious I can't believe I didn't see it before.

When I first read of Vigee Le Brun's history I was captivated, by the woman herself and by her talent. I read her memoir, all the biographies on her, visited any museum I could that exhibited her work. It only now strikes me that she resonated with me for another reason. As drastically different as our lives are, they're almost exactly alike in one significant way—as mothers. Both of us devoted our lives to our only children, who were both daughters who chose to self-destruct before our eyes, both in extreme ways; and we both left our girls in this part of the world when we could do no more, with our hearts completely shattered.

After fleeing the revolution, Le Brun and Julie lived all over Europe, and Le Brun wasted no expense to develop her daughter's talents. Both because she wanted Julie to know the pleasure of her own accomplishments—something Le Brun deeply understood—and because she herself was proof that a poor match could lead to financial and social ruin. But Le Brun was truly one in a million in her talent and ability to generate great wealth of her own in an era when women of her class depended upon men or inheritance to survive.

Though Julie did show literary inclination, which Le Brun encouraged, she lacked her mother's talent and ambition. Given that so did 99 percent of the female population in the eighteenth century, Le Brun was probably unfair, and certainly unrealistic, in her disappointment. I have to think that Julie must have felt that keenly, because she began to rebel against her mother. At twenty, she took up with a partying, reputation-ruining crowd that included Gaétan Nigris; secretary to a Russian nobleman, Nigris was a handsome aesthete with no money, no title, and little ambition.

Le Brun was understandably distressed; herself aside, in that era a reputation and prospects were all a woman had. She also saw what her love-struck daughter was blind to: he was arrogant, petty, and selfish.

But, because reverse psychology is so hard for a mother, she did what so many mothers do, and God knows I certainly did—protest and forbid. And the more she denounced, the more Julie defied, soon becoming engaged to Nigris.

One has to wonder if this was Julie's power play, her way of stepping out of Le Brun's shadow, of gaining freedom from her. Le Brun begged and wept, but Julie held her ground. Le Brun attended (and paid for) the wedding, then waited for the train wreck.

I have to admit, I know the anguish and anger she felt. It's the kind of fury only a mother helpless against her own child's self-destruction can understand, even if she is partially to blame for it, perhaps especially so. Le Brun's spirit was so badly broken she fell into a profound depression:

> The whole charm of my life seemed to be irretrievably destroyed. I even felt no joy in loving my daughter, though God knows how much I still did love her, in spite of all her wrongdoing. Only mothers will fully understand me.

During a visit to her daughter soon after the marriage, Le Brun could see that Julie was already becoming disaffected with Nigris. She also saw Julie wouldn't leave him, so she bit her tongue and soon left Russia. A few years later, Nigris dumped Julie after a move to Paris, leaving her in great debt. Le Brun continually rescued Julie financially, but despite repeated invitations, and the fact that they saw each other almost daily, Julie refused to live with her mother, preferring an increasingly wanton life with a very low crowd (to use the parlance of the day). How well I know how Le Brun felt; I wanted to pull my hair out and scream to the heavens when Mia ran away to live in a truck with druggies; it was beyond comprehension to me then. I can still feel the frustration behind Le Brun's words:

> Whether it is through my fault or not, her power over my mind was great, and I had none over hers; it is therefore

understandable that she so often made me shed bitter
tears.

Sadly, Julie died of pneumonia at forty-two, with her mother at her side.

Le Brun's life parallels those of so many modern mothers, it's uncanny: working, successful, single mom, overparenting—and overshadowing—her daughter. But while it would be easy to see Julie's behavior as simply rebelling against a powerful mother, and it may well have been true, that is seeing her through modern eyes. It can't have been the only reason. For a young woman to be a party animal now is hardly unusual; it's practically a rite of passage at college. Back then, however, there were only two sides of the tracks—and once you were on the wrong side, you could never go back. You didn't go on *Oprah* with your tale of triumph; you didn't get a second chance at a good life. Your teeth rotted, you had no heat, you got third-world diseases, you almost never bathed, you went hungry, you were scorned, seen as a disgrace. Life at court wasn't just about eating bonbons; it gave a woman literal, physical safety and health. What Julie did was extreme in a way we can't even imagine.

I have to wonder if her lifelong impulsiveness and wild behavior were also biologically driven; it certainly is typical behavior for a young person with depression or bipolar disorder. Or perhaps she suffered some kind of trauma or abuse as a child; it was no less common then than now, one in three girls, and, again, her behavior is so typical it's almost textbook. How sad that we have no record from Julie, no journal or diary to understand her unhappy, too-short life.

I cannot even imagine the pain of mothers whose daughters don't recover the way Mia did, mothers whose children continue to self-destruct into adulthood. This is where I struggle with the advice given mothers of addicts, as does my friend Maureen, who's written extensively and eloquently about her struggle with her adult son's debilitating, decades-long drug addiction. Mothers are told not to give their

adult children money or assistance when they're in the gutter, to let
them hit rock bottom. As if hitting rock bottom always does the trick.
Often we're the only thing standing between life and the rock bottom a
mother fears most: death. It's true the addict needs to make the choice
to change. I think it's our job as mothers to keep them alive till they do,
no matter how old they get. We're not their drug counselor, or proba-
tion officer, or shrink. Le Brun did what I and most other moms I know
would do: use our instincts, our hearts, our resources, everything we've
got, to save our children.

Our daughters can break our hearts a hundred different ways. One
of the most memorable e-mails I received from a reader was one that
contained a haunting, uncredited quote: "A daughter cuts her teeth on
her mother's bones." That may be true, but, as Chrystelle would say,
the thing of eet ees this—a mother doesn't much care. We would give
up none of it, no pain our daughters cause us, to have our bones whole
again.

*The train carrying me back to Budapest hums and squeaks as it chugs along
through the Czech Republic, Slovakia, and eventually Hungary. I watch the
land fly by, soil from the same region of the world that my grandmother and
her family are from.*

*There's a strange symbiosis between life and death, crisis and opportu-
nity, death and rebirth. In nature, death and destruction nourish new life;
one animal eats the dead flesh of another, and what's not consumed by fauna is
consumed by flora as carcasses sink into the earth. Decaying and moss-covered
trunks of fallen trees are where new seedlings grow quickest.*

*My family's ashes are scattered throughout this part of the world, the same
area that, metaphorically and perhaps literally, gave me new life. Sometimes I
still can't believe how callously I treated what so many people tried, and failed,
to cling to. I'm not sure I'd say I was ever suicidal but I was reckless enough not
to care that I was playing Russian roulette.*

Until about thirteen, I was happy and vibrant, and it's remarkable how quickly that vivacity was leeched away and replaced with a violent self-destruction. Child abuse isn't child abuse; it's people abuse, because children grow up. No matter how many years pass, or how much or little you consciously remember, history like that is akin to a forgotten landmine that sends shrapnel tearing from within once triggered.

I've never told my mother or grandmother this, but Bubbie actually helped me through it. My grandmother endured a hell that only genocide survivors can truly understand, and, strange as it may sound, I took comfort in her experiences. It would be wrong and disrespectful to compare our situations, because the scope was vastly different; I was a single person, she was part of a mass extermination that was far more brutal, bloody, and devastating.

A similarity, however, is that we both experienced a very dark side of humanity unusually young. My biological father taught me that people you trusted could turn on you, that the world could be dangerous and illogical and cruel. And because I didn't realize how many other kids had been abused, I often felt different and emotionally isolated from my friends. Knowing what happened to my grandmother made me feel less alone, and I must have seen her as a guide of sorts, because she used to show up in my dreams.

Growing up, I had terrible nightmares of being chased and hunted, sometimes by my dad, sometimes by Nazis, other times by someone I couldn't see or name but knew wanted to hurt me. Perhaps because in real life Bubbie successfully navigated dangerous and frightening territory, she often appeared in my dreams, pulling me behind an alley or revealing a secret hiding place just in the nick of time. Sometimes she'd wait with me until the danger passed, other times she'd appear long enough to stash me away someplace safe, and then vanish.

There was always a subtle defiance in her eyes, and she was watchful and calm, never nervous or scared. In real life my grandmother is often worried and anxious, yet growing up I only ever saw her as a fighter as wise and brave as Minerva.

"Hát nézzenek ide, csak ötig tud számolni! Ha egyenként adnánk a szil-vát akkor Amerikával is tudnánk üzletelni. Mennyi eszük van ezeknek a buziknak . . ." (Well, lookie here, she can only count to five! If we sold the plums one by one we could make business with America! How "smart" these cretins are . . .)

If it's not tomatoes, it's plums. How was I to know you can't buy *five* plums because he'd rather sell you half a kilo. Or it's train tickets. When I gently pointed out to the guy who sold us Mia's ticket that he was over-charging us *double*, he stood up to his full six-foot-six height and *shrieked* at us to leave, GO! GO!! GET OUT!!! because he was the *best ticket-seller in Budapest!!* I thought Mia would faint dead away.

Although of course there are kind, helpful clerks in Budapest, there are so many who aren't that I've gotten used to anything involving pur-chases as being hit or miss. I just think of it like opera—getting yelled at with no idea why. I've also gotten used to being followed in stores, because they think I'm a Gypsy. I mean, they don't even try to hide it— no, they *want* me to know they're watching me, no doubt because they think it'll prevent me from stealing. Sometimes I mess with them and try to look shifty.

But I'll be damned if I'll get yelled at while I'm stark naked. So before we get in line in the famous Gellert Baths, we study the long menu *very* carefully. The less you say the better. It ain't easy. We're contending with a menu that wishes us *a pleasant relaxation to this fun-damentally refreshing service of Swedish.* I see the word *therapeutic* and assume it'll be deep-tissue and Mia chooses *refreshing massage,* hoping for a light touch.

We line up behind a bunch of tourists. It's not looking good. Each one in the group of tall, handsome Australian fellows in front of us leaves the cashier looking more stricken than the last. When I reach the counter, I point, say two words, hold out exact change, and get blasted anyway, for no reason I can see. This time I just mutter along with her, *yeah yeah yeah right sure yeah sure.* I don't even care if she un-derstands me.

Once in the women's spa, it's another world. Soft robes and white fluffy towels, hushed voices, sweet smiles, madame this madame that, follow me to massage place madame, smile smile, sweet sweet. They escort us to a big room of white subway-tiled walls from the Gilded Age and blessed silence, then they help us lay our naked selves down in separate, partitioned-off massage areas. *Ahhhhhhh* . . .

Then Prince's "1999" BLASTS out of speakers above us. *Très* relaxing! A huge woman walks into Mia's area and a teeny one walks into mine. *Therapeutic* must mean "hothouse orchid" here, because she proceeds to do nothing more than press me lightly hither and thither like she's testing me for doneness.

Then comes the sound of a water hose blasting from Mia's area, followed by loud clapping sounds, more fire-hose sounds, then wet, whacking sounds, flopping sounds, more blasts, and cupping sounds. No sounds from Mia at all, which is alarming.

This goes on for half an hour. I'm ready to jump out of my skin and Mia must have grown fins by now. Incredibly (well, maybe not), the Red Hot Chili Peppers' "Torture Me" comes on as I'm led out. Mia's standing there, bright red, wide-eyed, swaddled in a wet white sheet, and shaking her head to say, *Don't even ask.*

Thank God the bathing pools make up for it all. Two pools under a dome of ornate Nouveau tiling and dim, twinkly light create an almost magical feel. The water is scorching in one, just pretty damn hot in the other, but after you sink in slowly, it's heavenly.

There's a beautiful blue-tiled fountain against one wall, with water cascading down from the ceiling above it feeding the pool. A nude, Rubenesque young woman with long, blond hair and big, pendulous breasts hikes herself up on the edge of the fountain. She leans her head back to let the water fall onto her head and run down her body. She's magnificent, utterly at home in her body, letting the hot water take her cares away.

Women of all ages talk and laugh softly. All are nude, most are Hungarians. Some are obviously mothers and daughters, displaying the same figures thirty years apart. There is an ease and closeness between generations here that's really wonderful. Mothers have never been seen as "uncool" in this part of the world. Even when I dropped Mia off in the Czech Republic ten years ago, pink-haired, pierced teens held their mother's hand and Sunday is held sacred as family day in Eastern and Western Europe. Your role as the matriarch and emotional rock of the family endures until you die and forms what is hopefully the core of a close relationship with your adult daughter; however, being "best friends" with her is neither common nor desired. There's a sanctity to the mother-daughter relationship that precludes it.

It's seen as equally inappropriate in France, according to my French friend, the photographer Nathalie.

"If you were trying to be your daughter's best friend, you would be seen as quite off track. Your job is to be her mother. I don't want to know about my daughter's dating life—she has her peers for that. Nor would I talk to her about mine. And I certainly don't want to know about my own mum's private life."

She thinks that's part of why American kids aren't as respectful to their parents—a line is crossed. I turn to talk about this to Mia. Her head is back, resting on the lip of the pool, her eyes closed, her limbs relaxed and floating.

"Hey, Mia, I've been thinking."

"Thinking is good," she mumbles without opening her eyes.

"I wonder if the reason so many American moms and daughters strive to be best friends is because it's a way to bridge the gap in the relationship that our culture creates when you're eighteen and leave home. I don't think it's all that natural. Mothers and daughters want to feel close even when they grow up—not that moms should dictate their lives—"

"They shouldn't?"

"Well, I know you want me to dictate yours."

"Of course."

"I think in the absence of the kind of relevance you once had when your kids were young, you hope friendship takes its place, fills in the gap. A way of making sure you're wanted after you're no longer needed."

"So we don't put you out to pasture like an old horse?"

"Exactly. Where you'd punish me for dictating your life."

We giggle and let our limbs float lazily in the water. Till this trip, I assumed our strongest ties would always be the iron bonds we forged through shared trauma and triumph. But the silk threads we are weaving into our relationship now, through sensual things like food, this spa, sunsets, art, are bringing us just as close as any tragedy could. It makes sense, really; our first bonds with our daughters are inextricably linked to the physical, the sensory.

They go from our wombs to our arms, our breast, we bathe them, tickle and nuzzle and whisper to them. They throw their little arms up to be held the moment they see us, they puke on us, bite us, wipe their noses on us.

Sharing these kinds of pleasurable sensory experiences, the "girl-friend" thing, is a big part of the charm of having a daughter. And yet, it never occurred to me how much this was missing from our relationship. I used to find it kind of frivolous. How could the very first feeling that tells us "life is a good place"—pleasure—be frivolous?

To respond with pleasure, as an infant does when it nurses, is one of our first experiences in the world. A baby shrieks so horribly when it's hungry because it doesn't yet know it'll ever eat again, it doesn't know it won't die if it doesn't eat right away. Our first knowledge of the world is that pleasure *is* life.

Physical pleasure is so linked to the feeling of unconditional love, our first and most basic experience of being human, that not to respect it is a kind of self-denial that is almost a violence to oneself. I never realized it before, but to allow ourselves pleasure is literally the way we continue to mother ourselves—to love ourselves unconditionally.

Yet it's the first thing so many of us give away, whether through lack of time, stress, or putting our family first. We give up the "guilty" pleasures; we decide self-care is an indulgence. I have heard from those close to me, for years, that I don't take time for myself; it's true, I rarely relax. As I am to myself, so I have been with Mia. We've traveled together, but we rarely indulged ourselves together or had fun just for fun's sake. The fact that your relationship with yourself reflects in all of your relationships is never more true than in your relationship with your daughter. We play out so much of our own unconscious in our relationship with them.

I'm so glad Mia never took on this trait. She doesn't deny herself the things she enjoys, whether naps or ice cream or turning her phone off to read a novel. When she and her cousin Rose were eight and six, we asked them what they wanted to do when they grew up. Rose said in her somber little voice, *I want to be the boss*. Mia laughed and said she wanted to have a good time.

Nothing's changed. Rose now assists neurosurgeons and sees patients as a physician's assistant, and while Mia works hard as an author, she sees writing as a way to do her favorite things: read, eat, and travel. She'd actually settled on her philosophy of life at five. I fed her such healthy food that one day Paul finally insisted, "She's five years old and doesn't know what hot fudge is. That's pathetic!" So we took her out for a hot fudge sundae.

We were watching her eat this huge sundae, and she had hot fudge all over her mouth. She was beyond euphoric—I mean, her eyes were just about rolling back in her head as she savored every mouthful like it was her last. Given that she'd just figured out what I'd been keeping from her all this time, she probably thought it was.

She was just so over the top with joy that we couldn't help asking her things like, "What part do you like best?"

"That it's so GOOD!!" she practically hollered like we were nuts for asking.

Do you like the chocolate or the strawberry better?

"Yes!"

Better than the cherries?

"No! Yes! What?"

It's like she was drunk on the stuff. Do you like the hot fudge all by itself?

She gave a great, fed-up sigh and said loudly and sternly through a mouthful, "Lithen (spraying chocolate), you two. It's jutht a—Wait a thecond . . ."

She shoved in another mouthful—"Jutht a matter of, of"—swallowing and gesturing broadly like *get this you idiots and then shut up*—

"It's just a matter of GOOD!!"

I'd say her take on life was and is as wise as any: "It's just a matter of *good*."

chapter thirteen

Avignon

Always Coming of Age

The thing of eet ees thees," Chrystelle says, turning to put her feet on the rungs of my chair and leaning close enough to look me in the eye. "You must be able to say *I 'ave done everysing I can, I can do nussing more.* And right now you cannot say that," she adds, raising *le* finger and an eyebrow.

The three of us are having lunch in a darkened Asian restaurant and Mia's mentioned an upcoming trip she's taking to visit her Bubbie. Chrystelle asked why I wasn't going, too.

"My mother won't even talk to me on the phone," I replied. "She's hardly going to want to see me in person."

"You don't know thees for sure. 'Ere's what you must do," she says with the finality and firmness of a French best friend with the answer to your troubles. The French want and expect unsolicited advice or assistance from a close friend; a friend who waits for permission to set you right or provide a solution is no friend—what, I have to *ask*?

"Yes, you 'ave called 'er, but you 'ave not gone to see 'er, so she can see your face again." She adds kindly, "Eet ees not so easy to close a door as eet ees to 'ang up a phone."

"I don't think she'd have any trouble at all."

"Maybe eet's true, but eef she were to die tomorrow, you will always weesh you 'ave try. You 'ave to know you do all you could or you weel 'ave no peace. So"—she raises the commanding finger again—"you weel arrange the treep with Mia and when you are there you or Mia say to your mother that you are close by een the 'otel. And then she can choose. And then you weel know in your 'eart that you do everysing possible."

She makes me promise to consider it. I know she's right; I'd never forgive myself if my mother died before we ever spoke again. I know far too many daughters who live regretting they didn't do more.

One lovely woman I know struggled her entire life with a mother whose bitter anger and darkness shrouded the light she longed for in her company. She shared with me:

> I never understood how she had so little love to share with her children. It was only after her death that I truly understood the darkness she felt in my company.
>
> I was responsible for my mother's effects after her death and among them were her writings. I came across one paragraph in a journal I almost think she wanted me to see. In it she talked about not liking me because every time she saw me I reminded her of the man she married and no longer loved. That was a moment of absolute clarity for me. I also saw that she was bitter about the loss of her youth and the choices she made in her younger years.
>
> I understood for the first time that a mother can feel competitive with a daughter and resent her youth and career. I realized that she resented the fact that we were free from the choices that defined her life, and that we could choose to be happy. I was relieved to find out that my suspicions about my mother waging a battle both darker and bigger than me was really nothing I could do anything about, except forgive her for it.
>
> I wish I could talk to my mother again and let her know that in spite of it all, I loved her. That in spite of her inability to love

her own children, we loved her dearly. She was the smartest, funniest, most beautiful woman in the world to me and all I ever wanted was for her to be happy.

The day I heard she died, I hadn't seen her for a long time. When I drove down her driveway I hoped I would wake from this terrible dream, but I saw the police cars and I knew it was true: she died before we had a chance to speak again.

I asked the police to let me see my mother, alone, and there she was, crouched in her bathroom with one hand up, almost in retaliation. I sat in front of my dead mother and asked her to hear me.

I told her I loved her and that I wished she had loved me back. I told her I was sorry we hadn't spoken in so long and that I stayed away because the story she had created was wrong. I asked her to let me know that she finally understood what the real truth was. It was the first time I could actually talk in her company and perhaps one of the only times she ever heard me.

I watched my mother get wheeled away on a cart by two strangers and, amazingly, it started to rain. A hummingbird flew to me from the window of her bedroom, in the rain, and swept back and forth in front of me. It then flew up to a window she loved with stained glass in the form of edelweiss. It flew back and forth in front of the window and came right back to me again, so close I could hear its wings flapping. The hummingbird went back and forth and back and forth right in front of my eyes, and then flew off to whatever heaven might be. She still sends me signs, in the form of hummingbirds. I only wish she and I had the chance in life.

It was heartbreaking to hear her story; her pain was so deep. And it made me realize how lucky I was. That my mother is still alive; and that she never resented our youth or our accomplishments—she wanted our success, however we defined it. My friend made me see yet one more thing I never appreciated about my mother, something I have never thanked her for.

I promise Chrystelle, and Mia, that I will reach out to my mom again, though I don't promise how. On the one hand, even after two years, I'm afraid a live rejection will devastate me. On the other, I'm not made of sugar, after all.

"Mother." It's the Voice again. "That is a definite *no*, trust me."

We're in the jam-packed outdoor market in Gordes, the premier hill-top village in the Lubéron. I'm holding a long, heavy strand of one-inch oval alabaster beads from a table of necklaces made in Africa.

"What do you mean? It's so elegant, and white goes with everything."

"Mother, it looks exactly like a tapeworm!" she whispers.

I drop it immediately. "Thank you, great, now I can't look at it." I smile at the tall, turbaned woman, hoping she didn't hear or understand. *"Merci, au revoir,"* I say politely before moving off.

Mia follows on my heels. "I saved you from yourself, trust me."

"You've saved me from everything I've picked up. How am I going to get any souvenirs?"

I've been to this market many times over the last decade; nothing has changed. The same chicken truck, buckets of olives and mounds of brilliant spices, the same tourist-priced Provençal linens and local-priced produce. Nadine still owns the tiny *tabac* with the giant American flag over the register (*"J'adore les Américains!"*), and Olivier's little olive oil shop is still there, where we stock up on the *gel douche* (shower gel) that smells exactly like the fields here. We buy our favorite Gordes treat, a croissant stuffed with almond paste, honey, and dark chocolate.

Mia stops at a huge stall in the middle, where stacks of pale, waxy soaps in every shade of pastel are piled up, emitting a choky smell.

"Why don't you bring some soap home? It comes in a dozen scents."

"No, this soap goes mushy and the scent doesn't last. I want to look for the family I always buy from."

We wiggle through the crowd to a little opening in a wall leading to a lot behind the square where a young father and his shy little daughter always sold fragrant, crescent-shaped bars of soap. She'd pack them up with a handful of dried rose petals and tiny silk flowers, tied with a ribbon. But they're nowhere to be found today.

"How sad! They were so special," I say. From the moment we reached Gordes, something in me knew this would likely be the last time I come here. I wanted to buy them one last time.

It feels strange to realize that you're getting old enough to sense that something you're doing or saying or someone you're seeing may be for the last time. We pick up water at a little grocery where the woman who owns it remembers me, which also feels bittersweet. I look at the buzzing crowd behind us in the square we have to go through to get to the car. It's not how I want to remember Gordes. Beyond the lot is a narrow rocky road cut into the hillside.

"Why don't we go the long way, Mia? Have I ever shown you this road? Hardly anyone uses it."

Soon the entire Lubéron valley is stretching out for miles far below us as we walk, with its checkerboard of farms and hilltop villages.

"This was the back road I'd take into the village from Fontainille," I tell her. Fontainille was the *mas* (farmhouse) that our friends Cristina and Jordana would have every August. It was where I was staying just after Mia went to Morava and I would sing lullabies out the window, wishing them all the way across the ocean to her.

We stop to peek into the town's little cemetery in the hillside, with its old tombs and war monuments.

"There's a really neat place where we can eat these before they melt," I tell Mia.

"Too bad the girls don't have the house anymore. It would be nice to go back."

"I don't know, it wouldn't feel the same," I reply. "Maybe you're too young for this, but you know how memories can go from the active file to the 'that part of your life is over' file? Where you can't feel the weight and sound and feeling of the moments in your body anymore, and the events finally die and become like an old black-and-white photo?"

"I do. Certain places in L.A. felt like that the last time I was there. The park where I played soccer. It made me smile to drive by it, but I didn't feel a connection to the park, I felt connected to the memory of it."

"Here we are." I stop at a little gap in the cypress and pines and turn in. "Come on."

We push through bushes and overgrowth to where jutting out from the trees is a wide, flat stone completely hidden from the road. It seems to float over the valley. We sit cross-legged, *very* far from the edge, and take out the croissants, which are gooey by now. The honey oozes out at first bite.

"Mmmm," Mia sighs. "Just as good as I remember."

"We're going to be a mess—I forgot napkins."

"What, you, forget something?! You have to walk home!"

"Fair enough," I laugh, licking the honey running between my fingers.

"My goodness, now you're licking your fingers. Before you know it, you'll be talking too loud and burping with your mouth open."

"Don't hold your breath, missy. By the way, do you know where we are?"

"No, should I?"

"This is where Cristina scattered some of her dad's ashes."

"What?" She stops eating. "And we're sitting here eating pastries?!"

"Why not? Bob would have loved that we're enjoying ourselves here. This was one of his favorite places in the world. I never saw him happier than when he was in Gordes."

She thinks a moment, then resumes eating. "Well, I suppose that's a nice way to think about it. Kind of like Pashupatinath, death is just part of everyday life. Probably a healthier attitude." She pauses. "Hey, Mom, not to be morbid or anything, but, well, aging eventually leads to death—"

"And I *am* aging, right, yes, go on . . ."

"Well, I've never told you this, but one thing I want you to do before you die is make me a CD of the songs you sang to me when I was a kid."

"Awww, that's so sweet! Of course I will!"

"Not just the lullabies, but Joan Baez, Joni Mitchell, stuff you sang around the house."

"Any other requests? I mean, what with my practically decomposing by the minute and all."

"Well," she says, hesitantly, "actually, yes. We've never talked about what you want me to do when you die, if you want to be buried or cremated or whatever."

Whatever?

"If you want to be cremated," she continues, "please don't ask me to keep your ashes. I love you to pieces but I refuse to put you in a decorative urn on my mantel."

I laugh. "Me, queen of wanting as few things to dust as possible? Never!"

"I don't want you in a box in my closet, either," she adds warily.

"Don't worry. I'm sure I'll come up with something very creative and fun by the time I kick the bucket. I don't want to spend eternity next to your flip-flops, I assure you."

This kid.

Avignon's newest arrival is Sarah, a family friend of ours whom my mom and I have missed sorely since leaving L.A. The first time I met Sarah I was seven years old and panicked about having been assigned to her second-grade class. I'd just seen Roald Dahl's The Witches *and was positive that this tall lady with long hair, fair skin, black boots, and a black outfit was a witch. Witch or no witch, however, she won me—and the whole class—over in no time, thanks to teaching math in a Dolly Parton accent, turning forest clearings into outdoor classrooms, and singing history lessons on her guitar.*

My mom was the second-grade art docent that year (budget cuts laid off art, music, and P.E. teachers, so parents stepped in lest we become overweight and uncultured), and she befriended Sarah, who quickly became part of the family. Today, Sarah's a mélange of sister, second mother, and mentor.

My mom and I have enjoyed acting like old-hand tour guides to a city we knew nothing of three months ago, taking Sarah to the bluff at sunset, shopping at the Villeneuve farmers' market, introducing her to Chrystelle and the Bar les Célestins gang.

Sarah and I took a walk down Rue des Teinturiers the other day, and she said how appreciative she's always been that my mom shared me with her. "She never tried to get in the way, or was jealous of how close we became. I'm not sure if you realize how unusual that is—she was even thrilled that you sent me a Mother's Day card one year!"

I'd never thought much about it, but my mom did always let me form bonds with her friends and encouraged me to find female mentors. I think she felt that people have different life experiences, different dreams, different talents and interests, and the more exposure a child has to these, the richer their childhood may be, the broader their horizons.

Having Sarah in my life nurtured and developed parts of me that my mom didn't understand or relate to. As a talented painter and artist, Sarah identified with my love of sculpting and using pastels. She loved horses and riding just as much as I did, and has the same spontaneous-borderline-reckless streak that would have had her swimming with elephants, too. During the years that my mom was depressed, it helped to have Sarah take me on adventures, tramping through the woods in Topanga Canyon, swimming in the ocean at Paradise Cove, swinging from rope swings over waterfalls at Will Rogers State Park. She's also très pas comme il faut, and couldn't have cared less if she'd seen me sleeping in a hotel lobby clad in sweatpants and flip-flops.

Today, the three of us are at Kristin's house, talking and cooking in her kitchen, which overlooks a valley floor filled with the even rows of bright green grapevines.

"Let's go outside for a bit, get some fresh air," Kristin suggests, wiping her hands on a dish towel. "It'll be hot, but I'll get us hats. We can walk to the river."

The elements hit us the moment the door opens: the pulsing hum of cicadas, the dry wind and beating sun. By the time we reach the river, the ice-cold stream is a sweet relief and we splash around for a while before heading back to eat the meal we prepared earlier. While waiting for Jean-Marc to finish his work in the distillery, Kristin lays out a large sheet for us in the shade of a giant tree in her yard.

Sarah's soon catnapping, and while my mom and Kristin talk quietly, I pull out my camera and scroll through today's photos. On the walk, Sarah had pointed out how crisp and sharp the afternoon sun had made our silhouettes, and we clowned around with different poses and formations. It's impossible to tell who's who from the silhouettes; the photos just show curving female forms with arms extended upward, outward, one looking like an upright snow angel, another striking a yoga Warrior pose. There's an ageless quality to them, a snapshot taken at just the right moment of four women at play, a capturing of laughter and wonderful female energy.

Growing up, all I wanted was to be a boy, and I still envy certain things about them. They can pee standing up; they don't have to deal with periods, labor pains, having men talk to your chest, or failing to attain the promotion or salary you deserve because of your sex. They don't have the same fears of rape, of not feeling safe when traveling alone.

But they'll never know how uniquely powerful female kinship can be, it's less permissible for them to express emotion or cry. They'll never experience how amazing it is to know that your body can nourish and sustain human life. One time, when I mentioned to Chrystelle that childbirth sounded perfectly awful, she just smiled and said, "Yes, eet's painful, but you weel not care. With Antoine, when the nurse first put 'eem to my breast, I know that I am never alone again een all my life."

I'm thinking of one thing after another that I absolutely love about being female and feeling better and better about myself after each one. I know what it's like to reach a place within where I truly love and appreciate the unique qualities that make me me, but I've never felt a general gratitude and appreciation for my gender. It's not about pitting one sex against the other, or deciding who has it better or worse—it's just fuller and greater appreciation of femininity and womanhood.

Womanhood. There, I said it.

I say it to myself a few more times.

I am a woman. I am a woman.

It feels right this time; I'm pretty sure I could say it to someone else without rolling my eyes or wincing in embarrassment. Maybe in part because I've just spent an entire summer with women from all different age groups, something that isn't always encouraged, or easy to do.

Magazine spreads frequently advise us how to dress or take care of our skin based on what decade of your life you're in (this usually spans from your twenties to your sixties, although I once saw a spread including the seventies; I guess they think we're just beyond help at eighty). Nor do we tend to have close friends running the gamut in age; my friends in their twenties are almost exclusively close friends with other twentysomethings.

I look at my mom and Kristin laughing, at Sarah stretched out in the afternoon sun, at a group of women in our twenties, forties, fifties, and sixties, women who are constantly evolving as we figure out who we are and what we want. Things that I've been grappling with, yet assumed were unique to my age and having just started out in life (conveniently, I also assumed they'd magically disappear as I matured).

I think when I go home, I'll see female colleagues less in terms of our age differences and more in terms of the shared experiences of our gender. I think I'm comfortable calling myself a woman because I understand that adulthood isn't a destination, it's a process, and, as women, we are always coming of age.

"It's ironic that a religion that so deified Mary for her ability to do what God denied man the ability to do," Mia says as she trudges along behind me in Avignon, "went on to so totally disempower women."

I love the way Mia's mind works, how ideas are more important than things for her. We're on one of our daily meanderings and, for a change, she's deigned to let me lead in weaving through the spaghetti of passages and streets.

"It's *because* men don't have the ability that they did," I answer. "I think it terrified them and left them feeling utterly inferior. Someone pulling a live human out of their very person? It's the ultimate thing to be jealous of and want to control."

I lead her to an unassuming archway in one of the endless stone walls behind the palace. I can tell she's never seen it before, not that she'd admit it, Miss I-know-every-corner-of-the-city. We slip through it into a long, cool rectangle of sandy gray pebbles enclosed in ancient walls that are lined with huge sycamores. A hidden courtyard, another little gem I already know I shall miss come September. There's a row of fifteenth-century windows with taupe-colored shutters overlooking the far wall; beyond the wall on our left rises one of the massive rear walls of the palace, blocking the lowering sun.

We're directly behind one of the biggest tourist draws in Europe, and somehow, miraculously, it's absolutely silent here. It's empty but for some pigeons and a couple sharing a book on a bench beneath a tree, holding it close between them to read. Mia's as surprised as I was when I stumbled in accidentally last week.

"Here's the best part," I whisper, pulling her along to a spot between the trees on the right. She gasps when she sees it: a brilliant gold life-size statue of a man with his head thrown back laughing. Not a saint or a revolutionary hero. A regular modern-day Joe (I'm sorry, but he looks more Connecticut than French) in a short-sleeve shirt and khakis, barefoot, holding a book. Like your handsome English Lit teacher at a barbecue. It's a perfect metaphor for a city that's both a seat of learning and power as well as gritty and working-class, old money alongside North African immigrants, with a big gay community thrown in.

A ray of sunlight blazes on Joe's wavy gold hair. It would be a traffic-stopper in Manhattan or London. In this forgotten courtyard in Avignon, it's astonishing, genius really.

I cock my eyebrow and look at Mia. There are some advantages to stumbling around lost for a while. It allows for discovery.

Call me a cheap date, but this simple little studio has pleased me more than any five-star hotel. Other than the floor, there's almost nothing to clean or dust, which is freeing. There's nothing in it that reminds me of anything, anyone, or anyplace I know, which is a kind of mental and emotional freedom.

Most of us aren't aware of how much of ourselves is bound up in our visual landscape—the chairs, dishes, clothes, the "stuff" that makes up a woman's life—until we leave it. And while it may be true that you don't always know what you've got till it's gone, it's also true that you don't know if what you've got really matters till you realize you don't miss it. Other than people, I don't much miss my life back home.

As I rise to have breakfast while Mia sleeps another hour, I suddenly realize what my crazy urge to take everything out of the studio was about. I want to wake up Mia and say *Hey, Mia, it's the room in* Sister Act! I know she'll remember.

There's a scene in that movie where Whoopi Goldberg's character is first shown her room in an abbey. It's all white and utterly bare but for one chair, one desk, one cup, one bowl, one spoon, one bed, one pillow, one outfit. I can still actually *feel* the elation I had when I saw it. The utter simplicity of the room, and the life that went with it, felt like a soul stripped bare, and my soul gave me a kick in response, saying *Pay attention, notice!* How it feels to see stillness and honesty in a place that would elicit the same in the character. Thankfully, we were at home, because out I blurted, "Yes! One cup, one bowl! I love it, *one* dress, one chair! I want that life!" We all wondered if there was something in the takeout.

With nothing more than a simple instinct—and trust—I created a snowy cocoon of stillness I must wake in and return to every single day. I wasn't sure *why* I wanted the walls bare, but for once just the wanting was enough.

It may be minor to someone used to always knowing exactly what they want and why and how and when. But to a woman who spent a good part of her life accommodating, protecting, living years where I was authentic in my mothering but in no other part of my life, it was no small thing at all.

I slip quietly out of bed and head to the sun-washed kitchen. I set out a brioche and Chrystelle's grandmother's thick homemade apricot preserves and sit down to a view I'd only find in coffee-table books at home: a sea of medieval terra-cotta rooftops beneath a piercingly blue sky. If I look left, it's nothing but a chattering wall of green, thanks to a flock of big, boisterous magpies. With their natty tuxedo coats, they dot the tree like fat, sassy penguins tossed from a wedding party for drinking too much. They holler and hop around, making branches dip under their weight, entertaining me while I eat.

In the yard below them, the tops of two once-white lawn chairs poke out of the tall overgrowth that has swallowed them. A set of French doors behind them is a still life of broken panes, cords of twisted ivy and broken boards. They belong to an eighteenth-century town house, long abandoned; the stone is blackened, the windows boarded up with long-rotted planks. But you can see those ubiquitous blue shutters behind them, a color unchanged in centuries.

It's a beautiful place, even in its decay. Voluminous silk skirts and petticoats no doubt rustled up a storm in there a few centuries ago. After an often-bloody civil war here between papists and those loyal to the French Revolution, Avignon was finally integrated into France, just in time for both the Red Terror *and* the White Terror.

I think of Le Brun, whose wealth and association with the queen made her a marked woman during the French Revolution. She barely had time to grab her daughter, switch their satin gowns for the servant's clothes, smear their faces dirty, and make a dash for the border in a cheesy carriage, sitting knee-to-knee with a reeking drunkard.

Were the wealthy women behind those blue shutters safe, when even smelling of expensive perfume could cost you your head? How far to save one's life, what kind of cleverness, or ruthlessness? Once that was over, did the women hold salons of the old guard, or welcome the new, embrace the romantic over the rational? Were mothers and daughters split on these issues, like the rational royalist Le Brun and her romantic and emotional daughter, Julie?

Once she returned from exile, what went through Le Brun's head as her carriage rolled over the very spot where her friends' heads had fallen into a blood-soaked basket before being picked up by the hair and held high for the cheering crowd? Perhaps she'd see Madame du Barry's lace scarf round a shop girl's neck. An artist selects her subject's clothes; she would know it among thousands, Belgian lace whose every detail she rendered. Ten years later, she'd recognize the scent of a one-of-a-kind perfume stolen from the queen's boudoir. That's a beautiful plot point, I muse to myself, recognizing Marie Antoinette's personal perfume on someone a decade later, but, wait, not on a shopgirl, on another noble-woman, an old friend of the queen—that has much more intriguing story possibilities.

My mind wanders to perfumer Annick Goutal's answer when she was asked what was her greatest luxury. To be warm, she said. I just loved that answer. Warmth. Not something you have or do, something you feel in your bones. She died of breast cancer not long after that, at only forty-two. I wonder if knowing her time here was limited brought a realization that one needs so little, really, but it's that little that is true luxury.

For me, this is that kind of luxury, this silent, sitting-still-ness, and the inner portal it opens, like a train window full of prairie sunrise, a view to world after world, in my mind's eye. How wonderful to let my imagination play again, without simultaneously thinking of everything I *should* be doing or forgot to do or don't want to do. Scenes and characters, images and dialogue, are quietly back, effortlessly and unsummoned, like flowers blooming in a dead garden.

I'm almost tingling with the sense of curiosity and delight that only writing brings me. How did I ever think I could continue writing with-out stillness, silence? Well, I didn't. I simply stopped writing. Was it a way to keep myself busy to avoid any midlife self-reckoning? Or is it nothing that complicated, just simply the lifelong habit of an undisci-plined, too-busy mind?

Either way, even now I can sniff the beginnings of "Okay, that was a nice few moments, thank you trees and birds and God, time to get up and get going, there's so much to do and think and ask and say, and why didn't I do this or get that or give more, give less, blog more, blog less, call my brother, find that earring, and Paul is crazy, the studs under the east bedroom window *are* sinking." A mind like a shark—swim or die.

Change happens in the small moments, when a sliver of light finds its way through the cracks. Until I did inner work the first time around, I had no *idea* how much discipline it takes to stay conscious and present, to put in the kind of every-moment-of-the-day work it takes to change your way of being. I taped affirmation cards everywhere, made Wheel of Life Charts on which I wrote down every single thing I did in fifteen-minute increments for three entire weeks (that'll shatter any illusions you have about how you spend your time, take my word for it). I asked myself a thousand times a day before acting—and, miraculously, speaking—What am I creating with this choice right now?

So what new choices am I willing to make, right now, to support this essential part of me? Same thing I used to do, set an intention, right now. Four hours a day in silence, minimum, with my notebook or laptop.

It feels good to be going back to tools that have worked for me in the past. Simple things but hard to actually *do*, like keeping commitments to myself, choosing from intention rather than feelings, excuses, or circumstances. But if I could do it before, for several years, I can do it again. I *weel* do eet again.

I'm not religious but hymnal music moves me like little else. It's stirring, the deep hum of collective voices, the way they seem to vibrate within stone walls and floors, up through your feet and into your bones. When I left our apartment for an evening alone on the bluff, I didn't expect to hear singing coming from inside Notre-Dame-des-Dômes, any more than I expected that toward the end of the church's vespers service my face would be tearstained.

A hand comes and rests lightly on my shoulder, and I look up to see a nun gazing softly at me. Embarrassed, I smile and apologize but she just looks kindly at me without saying anything. She radiates such calm and compassion that I don't feel compelled to brush away my tears or leave. They probably see a lot of this here, people in varying states of emotional rawness. After a minute, she tells me gently that the church is closing but that I am welcome back at any time.

I smile at her in silent thanks before walking outside and finding an open spot to sit on the bluff. In a world where we put up so many barriers, where we carve out different times and places for even the most fundamental of human emotions and experiences, spaces like churches give the gift of sanctuary, a place where unburdening yourself doesn't burden someone else.

It reminds me of a trip to Paris I took several years ago, when I'd stopped into one of the city's many churches. I was wandering through the side alcoves when I noticed a man I'd passed on the way in, a nondescript, middle-aged businessman. He was kneeling in a red velvet pew beneath a large oil painting of a saint, his hands pressed against his forehead in prayer as he quietly sobbed.

His back was to me, so I stayed a second, wondering why he was crying, and feeling badly for initially dismissing him as a boring older man. At seventeen, seeing a grown man sob was startling and uncomfortable.

I don't think I'd feel that same trepidation today. I wouldn't focus on my discomfort, or feel the need to do something, like I did then. Pain or sadness aren't repellents, they're a normal part of life, and shying away from them denies you a chance to deeply connect with, or assist, someone else. Even with everyone blogging and tweeting, I think families and individuals still privately suffer more taboo experiences like addiction, abuse, or mental illness— which only further contributes to all three.

I'm sure that's why of all the places I've visited Nepal stayed with me the most. I was fascinated and unsettled by how openly and unceremoniously death, grief, abuse, and poverty were displayed. I think often of the kathe children, how they roamed the city streets, competing with starving dogs for scraps of food in garbage heaps. Meeting the kids at Rabin's orphanage was all the more powerful because we'd had three days of seeing firsthand the fate they'd been spared from.

I remember falling asleep that night thinking about a short story I read in college by Ursula Le Guin called, "The Ones Who Walk Away from Omelas." Omelas is a beautiful Utopian city with a happy and prosperous population, save the fact that a nameless and naked child lives beneath the city, abandoned and locked in a basement. Even one kind word or gesture toward him would end Omelas; that is the balance required, the misery of one for the happiness of all.

The story stayed with me for days, not for the reason my philosophy teacher assigned it—an allegory weighing the benefits of utilitarianism (the greatest good for the greatest number of people)—but because Le Guin so vividly described the boy. I actually had dreams about him, crouched in a dark corner, a belly stretched tight from malnutrition, and skin scabbed over from living in his own filth.

The story affected me because I knew it wasn't fictitious, and it came back to me in Nepal because that boy was literally staring me in the eye. In America, far fewer kids live in such abject poverty, but millions of boys and girls—here and around the world—live equally bleak emotional lives. Often in plain sight, too; when families and communities willfully ignore abuse, they re-create Omelas by keeping peace for all at the expense of one. Although "peace" being kept is debatable; one need only look at crime and drug statistics to see that abused youth don't go quietly into the night.

I wrote my first book to help give voice to survivors of abuse, and, for two years following its release, I loved hearing other people's stories, sharing my own with lawmakers and policy-influencers, learning from child therapists, scientists, social workers, and child advocates. Child abuse can be a heavy field to be immersed in, and I was right in sensing I needed a break when I moved to New York. But I deliberately continued veering away from it, because I felt that someone my age shouldn't enjoy child-abuse conferences as much as happy hour with friends. I thought I'd regret not having "enough fun" in my twenties, although I'd often left speaking engagements on cloud nine. Interesting that my mom got herself stuck because she thought someone her age "should" own their own home; we both let numbers create false rules and benchmarks for us rather than making choices dependent on where we were at personally, not chronologically.

Viktor Frankl's book Man's Search for Meaning *is enduringly popular for a reason I clearly failed to grasp: creating meaning, rather than pursuing pleasure, leads to a happy life. Fun and happiness are by no means mutually exclusive, nor do they always equal each other. I do want to return to that field, although I have no idea when, in what capacity, or how it'll ultimately look for me: a full-time career, volunteer work, helping change laws, creating public awareness of its prevalence and long-term effects and cost.*

I never in a million years thought I'd see being abused positively (particularly before I'd healed from it) but there's no changing the fact that it happened, and I've come to accept and even appreciate how it's affected my outlook on life. It added a complexity that makes the world both more beautiful and uglier than I think I would otherwise see it, like increasing the contrast in a photograph so the darks get darker and the brights even brighter.

Trusting Aware Happy Loving Authentic Powerful Compassionate Serene
These words overlay the pale, nude woman in the lush mountain meadow that represents me; she's squarely in the middle of my vision map. Five months after that morning on the beach I feel these qualities in myself, or at least the possibility of them, in a way that had long eluded me.

To the right is a picture of a bottle of champagne and people celebrating, a symbol of letting go of my "waiting for the other shoe to drop" mentality, which has prevented me from celebrating much in my life. Having experienced weeks of pleasure with Mia, and alone, just *because,* has been new for me, and I've loved every minute of it. There are always other shoes in the air—that's life; and they *will* drop; no one escapes that. I've come to think that it's just ducky to celebrate for no other reason than that right now, at this moment, no other shoe has dropped.

Near a photo of me are images of authors, books, and women I admire, including Le Brun and Jane Austen. The words "love in action" are superimposed upon a woman at a laptop. I know I'll return to fiction, with great joy, and with no less commitment to my purpose to create awareness. I want my words to matter as much as entertain.

Thanks to Mia, I have a *Just a Matter of Good!* section ("Mother, where are your hobbies, things you enjoy?"): knitting, hiking, fencing, movies, things I love to do but haven't made time for.

My home area consists of a table full of food and loved ones under a huge tree surrounded by gardens, a huge room full of windows with only a big, champagne-colored velvet sofa and chair, a broad glass coffee table and reading lamps, a desk looking out on a dewy, green view. And a gorgeous hotel room overlooking a big city, for feeling at home wherever I'm at.

I'm just never going to be a very surrendery person. I'm a live wire, for better or worse, so I'm making my health and wellness section about "want to," not "should." There's a small image of a woman meditating on a mountain peak, and lots of big images of runners (I've never run a block in my life, but I want to), hikers, and outdoor athletes.

A big pair of hands, palms open, with the word *Give* anchors the bottom in what I call my G section (*God, Gratitude, Give, Grace*). I want to broaden my concept of authenticity. Being true to who I really am is obviously essential, but without acknowledging the web of relationships I live in, it can also become an excuse for self-absorption, for seeing others solely through the filter of my needs and wants. Which can lead to the kind of disconnect I have with my mother.

I've spent a lot of time here thinking about how we raise our daughters, within the context of culture and history, particularly how my generations shifted the focus from "*we*" to "*me*." I'm not so sure it was a good thing. Ask a person who's been trashed, hurt, or humiliated on someone else's blog how they feel about the writer's need to "speak their truth." Being authentic needn't mean hewing only to our true wants and needs; relationships, and just living in the world, require that we compromise and make sacrifices. And sometimes we *do* want the approval of others; it's sometimes called admiration and respect. And we often earn it by doing something we don't want to do but we *consciously* choose to do for a higher good. It's when we aren't conscious about our choices and intentions regarding those compromises and sacrifices that we end up crying in alleys, filled with regret. If I'd have set a conscious intention to create closeness with my mother (and forced myself to think a bit before speaking or writing), I would still be speaking with her.

That balance between authenticity and relationship is what having a child teaches you. I never authentically liked wiping up barf, singing "The Wheels on the Bus" a thousand times, or chasing an addicted teen all over tarnation, but I knew what I was in for when I signed up. I made those choices consciously, and oh what a joyful sacrifice. Had I but been equally conscious and committed about some of the other choices in my life, I'm sure I would have found equal satisfaction and meaning.

I've included images of mothers, daughters, family, my girlfriends, Paul. There's a section for my relationship with Mia. It's a collage of sunsets, gardens, travel, women having fun together, art, books, a beautiful home for her to visit, a bedroom in her favorite colors; our shared values for our relationship are superimposed: *Trust Adventure Art Love Respect Vulnerability Honesty Communication Celebration.* And a picture of a big ear, for listening; so I can be a better mother and friend to her.

We've become so much closer this summer than I could have imagined. One of the most valuable things about a close relationship between mother and daughter is the degree of safety you feel with each other. It allows for a kind of vulnerability that can take the relationship to a level unique among all your relationships. It also allows for the kind of accountability so many of us find difficult, but without which resentment and emotional dishonesty build and trust diminishes.

This trip has also made me realize that the depth and breadth of our bond still starts with me. Until I saw how much of my unconscious behavior showed up in Mia—particularly around vulnerability—I'd never realized how powerful an influence I am on her, even as an adult. I saw over and again how the degree to which I was willing to open my heart was the degree to which the relationship expanded and grew more meaningful. Kind of like the Peter Principle for mothers and daughters, only instead of advancing to the level of your incompetency, the relationship advances only to the level of your own emotional inaccessibility. We are role models for our daughters *all* of our lives.

I've also realized that there isn't ever going to be a "post-motherhood" me. Being a mother will always be central to who I am—and central to my relationship with Mia. As close as we may feel as friends, I *will* always have a more critical eye, even if I don't voice it. While respecting her as an independent woman is essential, I *will* no doubt also sometimes say things to her only a mother can say and get away with. And because I am her mother, I *do* expect a degree of respect and deference from her that I don't from anyone else. And she'll get things from me she won't get from another human being, ever, because a mother's love *is* unique—among all of our relationships it's our most primal, unconditional, and eternal.

I also understand more clearly that being a daughter is central to who I am. Among myriad things I've learned from Mia this summer, one of the most important is how to be a good daughter. Mia's taught me that the same kind of unconditional love I give her, I also get from her. I could not possibly have the beautiful relationship I do with Mia if she wasn't as accepting and nonjudgmental as she is. I have not been the same way with my mother, I judge her, I have expectations, I want her to be the way *I* want, rather than love and accept her just the way she is. I owe my mother the same degree of respect and deference I expect from Mia for no other reason than because she is *my* mother.

So today I've marched myself to the only public phone nearby that's working this week. Yes, that one, *Frelon d'Asie!* After making sure there are no hornets the size of sparrows, I punch in the Telecarte's requisite sixty-seven numbers and wait, very anxiously.

"Hello?" she says in the mildly surprised way she always does when answering the phone.

"Mom?" I say nervously.

"Who is this?"

"It's *die Grösse*," I say, using the Yiddish name she called me when I was little and she didn't want me to understand what she was saying (I was *die Grösse*, the big one; my younger sisters were *die Mittleste* and *die Kleine*, the middle one and the little one).

"Oh," she says blandly.

A painful pause.

"I wanted to tell you I love you," I add quickly before she hangs up on me.

"Well, I don't want to talk to you," she says before hanging up.

Yes! This is promising! Because she just *did* talk to me, for the first time in ages. Till now she just hung up without speaking.

It's a start.

I usually learn things the hard way (being court-ordered into a boot-camp school comes to mind) and, if I'm honest, it's something I've taken pride in. Learning from other people seemed unadventurous, cowardly even. If I want your advice, I'll ask for it! It's my life, and mine to make a mess of! I've made all sorts of immature proclamations over the years, mostly when I know I'm making a mistake but want to avoid facing the facts (or the repercussions).

Granted, when lessons come with a price they do tend to stick, but one thing this trip has taught me about myself is that there are prices I'm not willing to pay. I never want to feel how my mom undoubtedly felt that day when she broke down and cried in the alley about all the years she feels she wasted. And, as she pointed out, I'm creating my "should haves" right now.

It's hard to imagine truly lost opportunities at my age, because it seems we have tons of time to regain them. But dreams do die and ships do sail, and sometimes calling them back only sinks you. Part of me had been waiting for adulthood to click into place, for me to get "it" (whatever that elusive "it" is) before turning my attention to the bigger questions. But the only thing clicking is the days going by. Adulthood isn't something that just gels, as I had always told myself. Things don't just fall into place, they just fall, and most people then learn to live with an arbitrary arrangement.

Last week, when my mom and I were finishing the vision maps we started a month ago, it felt very different. I thought seriously about my professional and financial future, because I want to be conscious of, and intentional about, what I'm doing or not doing. I don't have concrete answers yet. I have no idea how I'm going to combine, or make a living from, everything I've cut out this time around—research libraries, airplanes headed overseas, kathe *kids, writ-*

ing desks, podiums and microphones, personal role models like Jane Goodall or Christiane Amanpour—but they're on my radar now. And if images are as powerful as people say they are, maybe looking at this every day will somehow help me knit them into a career and a life.

It's rare to have someone totally, messily, open themselves up to you—especially when that person is the one person that you've looked up to every day of your life. I haven't told my mom how powerful that day was for me, nor do I want to. Talk is cheap. I'd rather show her the impact she's had by going home and taking steps toward creating a life I love.

"I don't know how we missed this area!" I marvel.

We're on our last meandering walk together in Avignon. We've just stumbled upon a serene, enchanting little corner inside the walls we've never been to, a few residential streets of stately old town houses and lush foliage.

"Oh, Mom." Mia rolls her eyes. "There isn't a street here we haven't been on a dozen times."

"Don't give me that look. First, listen—" I tell her.

"To what?"

"Nothing, that's the point. It's dead quiet. Avignon isn't quiet any time of day or night. We've *never* been here."

As soon as we clear the overhanging leaves of a thick hedge, a huge ghost of a weathered, neoclassical church dominates the street, made of stone that's so pale it's almost white, like clouds with no honey.

"Oh, wow, even *I've* never seen that," exclaims The Navigator.

The gate is open and the courtyard empty. We enter and turn down a long, vaulted portico with a row of two-story arches and big doorways eight feet above the ground that have been walled in over the centuries. It's like walking back through time.

"Mother, look! *Extases*, it's here—this is the church!"

There's a tall poster with the charcoal images of women we saw on the brochure we picked up our first week here at the tourist bureau. Ernest Pignon-Ernest's exhibit of female saints and mystics lost in ecstatic reverie. We look at each other with the kind of excitement usually reserved for a shoe sale or free chocolate and scurry inside before it closes.

At the end of the long, dark nave, in a large, shallow pool of water where the altar would have been, seven female saints and mystics, breathtakingly executed in charcoal, seem to literally rise from the water, on ten-foot-tall white panels that undulate and interlace. Lit from below, the women are much larger than life, sensuously draped in white cloth, breasts bared, eyes closed in ecstasy. I recognize Teresa of Ávila, Hildegard von Bingen, Mary Magdalene, and Catherine of Siena, Madame Guyon (an imprisoned mystic who has fascinated Kristin of late). Monumental goddesses, magnificent in their self-possession.

Mia and I are so surprised and awed by their grandeur and beauty, by the unexpected and commanding way they're presented, that we spend a magical hour with them, and the artist's preliminary sketches along the walls, without speaking a word. It's such an exceptional synthesis of style, format, and subject that in my mind it trumps anything in last month's festival. How like Avignon to surprise and delight us like this a day before I fly home—to save the best for last.

After we leave, we realize that the lone woman at the door had let us stay well past closing time, something we've found typical here. Avignon has been so sweet to us; we've made all manner of linguistic and social gaffes and they've treated us with great goodwill and generosity. They've nursed, educated, and advised us, they've lowered prices for us, brought us jams, candies, the fruits of their own gardens. They've refrained from laughing every time I held up four fingers and said *cinq* (five). (Mia neglected to tell me this till yesterday. "I'm sorry, it was just too much fun.")

Mia's become very friendly with Steven; he's joining her at Sarah's for a dinner after I leave. Yesterday we ran into him in the park, where the two of them were off and running in French. All I could understand of their excited conversation was "Atatürk," the "defensive walls of Marseilles," and "there are times when cow brains are sympathetic." Time for old Mom to go home.

As we exit the church courtyard to the street, the capricious wind sends eddies of tiny leaves around the chin and outstretched arms of a small stone madonna mounted on a town house and a bar of sun angles an irregular path down the length of the street.

A woman passes in and out of the light, carrying a baguette and a tote of groceries, the neck of a wine bottle poking from the top. She's so utterly *Avignonaise,* tanned, fine-boned, with a pretty mess of brown hair in a loose chignon. From another street comes a man about thirty in a black T-shirt with a skeleton on it over skintight jeans, motorcycle boots, with a face right out of a medieval painting, with big, dark eyes, flat cheeks, a long face, and sharply angled jaw and nose. Behind him walks a young couple, she a neo-'ippy, he looking like a festival leftover in a Mad Hatter hat and magician outfit. In a moment the street is empty but for the wind and sun and ancient stones.

When we first arrived, the city seemed to confuse and intimidate. She's still a marvelous mystery, but now we feel ourselves enfolded rather than intimidated, we feel woven into the tapestry of Avignon.

Till now, I'd suspected that choosing it wasn't just because it's in Provence, near Chrystelle, and affordable. Like clearing the studio walls, I think there was a deeper instinct at work that I wasn't conscious of. I turn and look up at our bluff, high above my left shoulder. How fitting, how perfect that the place I came to cleave more closely to my daughter is watched over by a gleaming, gilded woman, her serene face the first thing to shine in the morning and the last thing alit at twilight. A mother.

Mia and I wind our way to our bluff for our last sunset together and find the entire palace area under heavy guard in preparation for an EU summit meeting. As the sun begins to sink, Mia grabs my hand and we run for the closest wall portal to watch the sun set from the bank of the Rhône.

Mia stands a few feet in front of me, gazing into the fiery Provençal sky with the summer-bleached tips of her hair sparkling in the light. Silhouetted by the sun, she's as majestic and awe-inspiring to me as the women Pignon-Ernest painted, as sweet and tender as the three little girls on the bluff, as courageous and compassionate as any woman I've ever known. I don't know what I was in a prior life, but whatever it was, I must have done something right.

I know that for every mother, there is always the possibility of three in your relationship with your daughter. You, your daughter the way she is, and your daughter the way you want her to be. I learned the hard way ten years ago that that kind of control is an illusion and a barrier. You can't even control the inner life of your daughter when she's a toddler; you can only control her environment, and not always even that.

Once she's an adult, the only environment you can offer her is *you*. I am, and always will be, the place called Mother for Mia, the river we navigate together for a time, never long enough, riding the waves and plumbing the depths, a river that will carry her for all of her days.

Only in France would you see someone swearing as they unsuccessfully try to light a cigarette while bouncing up and down on a galloping horse (sans helmet, to boot). Said someone is Margot, a heavyset woman whose large chest isn't helping matters, and considering the wind is frizzing and blowing her hair every which way, it's amazing she hasn't set herself ablaze with her lighter.

Margot lives in the building where Sarah had stayed, and when she heard I loved riding, she offered to take me to a riding ranch nearby. She's a riot, extremely funny, very animated, and with a penchant for flooring her car while swearing and honking at any driver blocking her path.

Either because Margot knows the owners, or because the French thumb their noses at rules and regulations, the ranch is surprisingly laissez-faire. There's no liability waiver to sign, nary a helmet in sight, and our guide didn't bother asking what level rider anyone was before kicking his horse into a full gallop, sending the rest of us thundering in tow.

There's an element of surrender to galloping that I love. When your horse takes off and you tuck yourself down into its mane, it's a completely sensory experience: rhythmically pounding hooves, rushing wind, surroundings flying by so fast they're just abstractions of shape and color. It's a rare combination of soothing and exhilarating—and when you're doing it through vineyards and châteaus, it's pure heaven.

By the time I'm back in Avignon and waving good-bye to Margot, I'm still on cloud nine, and decide on dessert for dinner. I stop by the apartment for the last of my Gourmandize candies, buy a triple-scoop gelato for the main course, and climb upstairs to the bluff to sit for a while.

My mom left last week and I've enjoyed having some days to myself before stepping back into my life. This summer was about bonding with my mom, but considering I've learned just as much from her as I have about her, it seems fitting to spend my final days more quietly and reflectively.

I walk back to the apartment slowly, enjoying how the air cools and silhouettes blur in the moments between dusk and dark. My gaze skips along the landmarks now so familiar to me, the sweeping plaza of the palais, *the clothing boutiques in the* zone piétonne, *the bell tower of St. Pierre. I walk past the* boucherie *at St. Didier until I see the glowing neon outline of Bar les Célestins come into sight, followed by our very first landmark, Le Petit House of Condoms, and, finally, turn into our little alley with its massive stone wall. I walk upstairs, let myself into the room, and then it hits me.*

Ever since we first moved into the studio, I've had a strong sense of déjà vu. It would spring up randomly, when I was turning on the shower, sweeping the floor, making the bed. Sometimes it was more of a sad, nostalgic feeling, other times it would make me smile and feel comforted. I didn't say anything to my mom because I had absolutely no explanation for it.

Now I understand. The naked white walls, the lack of furniture, the large window filled with green. It's just like my old room at Morava. Even the dark orange curtains echo the brown carpet. A medieval city is infinitely nicer than a Soviet-era hotel, not to mention the food's better, but here I've had a regular routine, been completely removed from my life, lacked television and radio, had little time online.

The circumstances are extraordinarily different, of course, but the outcomes are quite similar. I've come away from each feeling calmer and more confident. I have a deeper understanding of how I operate, what is missing from my life, and what I want for myself. I'm leaving with a more compassionate attitude toward people in general.

When you open yourself up to the world, she opens herself up back and you step into a space that's wider and brighter than you imagined it to be. People are hospitable in countless ways, and our common humanity often overshadows even radical differences in circumstance or culture. I've found you can often rely on the kindness of strangers, and I'm pretty sure that I could be plunked down almost anywhere, and find a way to create a life I like there.

I feel at home in the world, undoubtedly because I feel at home with myself. At two critical points in my life I've been lucky to have been able to hit the pause button and withdraw for a period of reflection and examination, both opportunities that were created by the person who best knew I needed them: my mother.

All relationships happen in stages, with varying depths, multiple layers. You invariably reach a point where you hit the ceiling of a certain level of intimacy and then have the option of staying there—which risks the relationship becoming predictable or stale—or you can take it to the next level. We did that this summer.

There are, and will always be, roles and boundaries, but room's been carved out for a mature friendship. The footing feels more equal, the connection more solid, and our understanding of each other much deeper. And it's nice knowing that, as I go through stages of life like motherhood or menopause, we'll continue connecting on new and different levels. My mother will pass one day, but our relationship will continue well past that, evolving and deepening until I myself go. And then, if I'm lucky enough to have one, it will live on through my own daughter.

fin

Epilogue

*T*wo weeks before leaving for China, I was having dinner with Soraya at Thai Eatery in Brooklyn. When the bill came, we reached for our fortune cookies and I cracked mine open to find this: You are about to embark on a most delightful journey. *Followed, of course, by what lotto numbers to play.*

It's not often that our expectations are met, and even rarer that they're surpassed, and while the lotto numbers didn't pan out, the fortune did tenfold. It's been a delightful journey in every aspect imaginable, one that continues.

Because structuring and writing a tandem memoir is best done when both writers are in the same physical space, following the trip I moved from Brooklyn to West Palm Beach to work on this book with my mom. Within a few months the walls of our office were a kaleidoscope of chapter outlines, Post-it notes for various scenes or emotional beats, and pictures (we re-created Avignon photographically to help keep it alive as we wrote).

As the book took shape, I grew along with it; some might even say I grew up. After cracking open Financial Planning for Dummies, *I opened a ROTH IRA, and have worked part-time as a publicist to actually contribute to it. I've taken advantage of coastal living by becoming a certified scuba diver, and I go to museums, lectures, and concerts regularly. My television watching has been whittled down to about four hours a week, and I've ditched reality TV entirely. I've also become a proud vegetarian (you try eating meat after listening to the entire audiotape of* Eating Animals *on a road trip with my dad) and am s-l-o-w-l-y learning to cook.*

I'm clear about my commitment to work with lawmakers and the educational community in an effort to prevent or stop child abuse, and I write and speak about my own experience as a way of helping other survivors heal and move on. This year I began research for my next project, a narrative nonfiction book that combines four of my greatest interests: travel, human behavior, history, and culture. I'll be writing this one sans Maman, *and starting next month I'll be sleeping on Soraya's sofa as I transition back into life as an author in New York City.*

The same week I got home I did three things. The first was to call my mother. It took a lot of calls but she did start speaking to me. I eventually went to visit her; it was as if no time at all had passed. Words cannot express how grateful and happy I am to have her in my life again.

The second thing was to join a boot-camp class. I couldn't run a block or do a single man's push-up. Nowadays I'm running five miles, doing fifty push-ups and a couple hundred sit-ups, all before sunrise. It's changed my life.

The third was to start learning how to assist others in changing theirs. Just before I left Avignon—ironically, as I was packing up my vision map—I got an e-mail from Barbara: did I want to train under her to become a performance/transformational coach? As she likes to say, there are no accidents. Still jet-lagged, I got on a plane to San Jose and a year later became certified. I then went on to become a certified relationship coach.

Sadly, a year after I returned, both the house and my marriage continued their slow decline. As much as we respected and loved each other, Paul and I weren't sure which was causing the other to further decay. We've separated and have never gotten along better. The week I left, he bought the paint color he'd wanted for five years (and I didn't). Dating in my fifties, for the first time in twenty-five years, will be an interesting adventure.

Having Mia live near me these last two years has been fabulous. I feel like I got back the two years we lost when she was fifteen. I've watched her grow as a woman in so many ways and I've grown and learned from being with her. Mostly, we've had fun together. That girl could make a stone laugh. Our editor won't want to hear this, but half the reason we took so long to write this book is that we laughed so much whenever we worked. We can't walk two blocks without stopping to laugh, and you can't ask for more than that, because like life, the mother-daughter relationship is, *après tout*, just a matter of *good*.

I'm currently living in Paris, researching a historic novel. I have no idea where I'll live when I return, and I'm not really bothered by that. Trust seems to be working pretty well for me these days.

Acknowledgments

Chrystelle Guisset, *chère amie* and chief muse, you are a constant source of delight for us. We cherish your wisdom, love, and support, your humor and your joie de vivre (not to mention your talent for logistics and efficiency). This book would not have been possible without you.

We're fortunate in having an agent who is also a friend (and a mother of four daughters, all under age five!). Stacey Glick, of Dystel & Goderich, thank you so much for being our cheerleader and champion over the years.

We're just as lucky in our brilliant editor, Cassie Jones, who's got the patience of, well, a mother. You make us look good, you make us laugh, and you call us "your lovelies." Doesn't get any better than that for an author. *Nous t'adorons!*

We're grateful to Jessica McGrady as well, for her smarts, efficiency, and care, especially when we're down to the wire (which is often). And to our amazing copyeditor Olga Galvin Gardner, whose sharp eyes and mind made this a much better book. Our gratitude and a round of applause to everyone on our team at HarperCollins—your support and hard work have meant the world to us from day one.

A very special acknowledgment goes to William and Pamela Chalmers. What Bill (aka the Ringmaster) has created in The Global Scavenger Hunt is sheer genius. How Pamela pulls it all together, and holds it all together on the road, is just as amazing. To learn more about this amazing annual travel adventure and competition, and the great good they do with the funds they raise for the Great*Escape* Foundation, go to globalscavengerhunt.com.

We would like to acknowledge and thank again everyone who donated to charities in our names. Your generous donations went to the organizations Childhelp and Protect.org, and, through the Great*Escape* Foundation, funded coed elementary schools in Sierra Leone, Sri Lanka, Ecuador, India, and Kenya, and gave to the Clinton Foundation, World Monuments Fund, and the September 11 Freedom Fund, among others. To learn more about the remarkable work done globally and in the United States by SOS Children's Villages, visit www.sos-childrensvillages.org and www.sos-usa.org.

To all the women who have so generously shared their personal stories with us, in person, through e-mails, and questionnaires, thank you—you have enriched this book, and our lives, more than we can express. Every one of you has touched us and made the journey that began with *Come Back* one of continuous discovery, inspiration, and growth.

A huge thank-you to the many folks who have supported, advised, humored, fed, and sometimes housed us during the writing of this memoir. In the United States: Nancy Marsden, crusading for our children on the Huffington Post; Chris Simpson; Leah Komaiko (who births a lot of amazing things over at leahkomaiko.com); Kelly Sterling, who nourishes us in every way (put on your apron and go to snailsview.com); the remarkably doublegood Karin Anderson; Robyn Tauber, mother extraordinaire who spreads sunshine everywhere she goes.

In France: Kristin and Jean-Marc Espinasse, who continue to enchant with their words and wine at French-word-a-day.com and rouge-bleu.com. The humor and kindness of Isabelle Oudin and Anthony Viro gave us more unforgettable memories than we could fit in here. Nathalie Daguet, for your keen insight and for giving us all Avignon on your gorgeous blog, avignon-in-photos.blogspot.com. Christine Witebsky, la belle Isabelle, and Xavier Robaux, for your kindness, friendship, and last-minute rescue. Thank you, dear Amy Plum, for the warmth and welcome of your home. And Bruno Lavollé, for your extraordinary generosity, warmth, and humor; you and your delightful family have made Paris feel like home.

A special thank-you to Maureen Murdock, Ph.D., therapist, photographer, and author of *The Heroine's Journey* and *Unreliable Truth,* among many others; Tracey Jackson, screenwriter, filmmaker, and author of *Between a Rock and a Hot Place*; Sabrina Faludi, for giving so generously of your time, care and expertise, usually at a moment's notice

We are grateful to Mindy M., Jill R., Amy H., Sue L., Tracey S., and Nikki R., for their wisdom and courage in sharing their stories with us.

For sharing their experiences and insight on the mother-daughter relationship in other cultures we thank Noni Darwish, Violet Mess, and Sabrina Faludi and her friends.

Un grand merci to those who've given us a home-away-from-home office, in France: the Fabulous Five at Bar les Célestins—Stephan, Christine, Edith, Jeremy, and Roman; and in West Palm Beach: the gang at the Clematis Starbucks, the Marulli family at the historic Harvey Building, Chef Scott Helm for care and feeding, and a very special thank-you to Molly Charland and her staff at the Four Arts King Library, a haven of tranquility and beauty.

We've had the privilege of speaking with book clubs across the country over the last five years. In the last two, some of you let *us* interview *you,* so a special thank-you to Queen Nancy and the Venice Book Club Chicks; Pamela and the Jersey Girls; Not Too Busy to Read in Plymouth; Sherri and Wendy of the Yale book club in Miami. The Chicago area has so many book clubs full of smart, funny women; please forgive us for not mentioning you all by name. If we've forgotten anyone, and we're afraid we have, it's only because we let Claire handle logistics and filing. Bad idea.

A huge thank-you to the warm and wonderful Dee Bloom, a cheerleader and friend who gave this book a critical read at a critical time, giving us, and you, a much better book.

To our Hungarian family—Alice, Zolie, Hajnalka, Eva, Gabby, and

Zoliku—connecting with you has been an amazing gift. You've shown us that love, laughter, and generosity require no translation.

Claire would also like to thank:

My first and greatest debt of gratitude goes to you, Mom, for all the things I never thanked you for, the wisdom I didn't see, the sacrifices I didn't notice, the quiet acts of loving kindness and devotion, the patience and joy you took in mothering us, all the ways you said you loved me that I was too foolish and wrongheaded to recognize. I see more and more each day how much I owe to you, as a mother and as a woman.

The great putter-upperer and, nowadays, fixer-upperer, Paul. Your patience, smarts, talent, and love have helped mother this book through a very long journey!

My four unique and wonderful sisters, with special thanks to Viv for your eagle eyes and insight in reading this manuscript. Sandy, my beloved big brother and Stacey, welcome to the family.

Barbara Fagan of SourcePoint Training, for your brilliance about *being*, and for your mentorship, love, and support over twelve years. You're a role model, an inspiration, and a treasured friend.

Lou Dozier of SourcePoint Training and Lynn Pollard and David Gilcrease of ResourceRealizations. I cannot imagine more effective and powerful training in the field of relationships than what you've lovingly created.

Cami McClaren, I'm grateful to have you in my life as a friend and colleague. Your willingness to challenge me has been invaluable.

Carole Watson, for your support, wise counsel, and for tracking me down all the way in France.

A big *köszönöm* to Violet Mess and her six A.M. boot-camp gang, for pushing me further than I ever thought I could go. You guys rock.

Denise Perez—we've laughed, cried, scolded, and loved each other through an amazing transition. We've watched so many sunrises and sunsets on the beach together that if you were a guy I'd marry you.

Mia would also like to thank:

Dad, I'm so grateful for this extra time we've had together. You are and always will be my hero, my best friend, and my rock.

Bubbie, I love you for your sense of humor, your compassion, your bravery, the poppy-seed pastries you've baked, and the blankets you've knitted me since birth.

Grandmaude and Grandpa, you gave me childhood memories that I cherish, and I love that every visit is somehow more fun than the last.

Richard, for your nourishment and support, for bringing Florida to life, and for keeping me laughing throughout.

Soraya, for being my steadfast guide and anchor. You're the kind of true-blue friend we happen upon so rarely.

Nina, for your ongoing friendship and support. The humanitarian work you've done over the years has been such an inspiration.

Guenn and Alanna, for being the best roomies a New York newcomer could ever want.

Peter, thank you for showing me the city and the countryside that I never saw, and returning me to a place that changed my life.

To the RYLA crew and the Nelson clan, thank you for creating weekends that I look forward to year after year. Sean Nelson, you're truly inimitable, and your dedication and passion for youth continuously amaze me.

Sarah, I'm pretty sure that whatever we exist as before we're born was halved in two and delivered forty years apart. Your love and friendship are lifelines for me. Lee, thank you for bringing her the love and light she's always deserved.

I am especially grateful to Catherine Cordell of Artistay for her generosity and expertise. Artistay (www.artistay.org) is a remarkable resource for established writers and artists seeking a residency in France.

About the authors

About the book

Insights,
Interviews
& More . . .

Read on

Meet the Authors

Claire Fontaine is the author of two memoirs, a national public speaker, and a former screenwriter. She's also a certified life and relationship coach. She lives in South Florida and France, most recently in Paris, where she spent five months researching a historic novel for her next project.

Claire has degrees in film, design, and art history. She enjoys running, fencing, hiking, and yoga. Her hobbies include travel, reading, film, art, and knitting. She's having way more fun in her fifties than she ever did in her twenties.

Mia Fontaine is an author, writer, and motivational speaker whose past appearances include *Good Morning America, The O'Reilly Factor,* and *The Montel Williams Show.* She has spoken nationally about overcoming adversity and the long-term cost of child sexual abuse.

In addition to the memoirs she's coauthored, she has written for the *New York Times,* the Huffington Post, the Atlantic online, and *Ms.* magazine digital. She resides in Brooklyn and is currently at work on a narrative nonfiction book. She's also continuing her commitment to understanding and stopping child sexual abuse as she prepares to work toward a Ph.D. in neuroscience and child studies.

A talented sculptor, Mia also enjoys biking, reading, scuba diving, cinema, mentoring teens, and of course, exploring new cultures, cuisines, and countries. ◌

Mad Dash for Mah-Jongg

As ADVENTURE-FILLED as this book is, especially the first half, we couldn't begin to include everything we did on the scavenger hunt. Each day was packed with challenges from the moment you charged out of the hotel at dawn, eager to take on the world. To give you a sense of a typical day, and how creative Bill is, here's a page from our Malaysia scavenge book, complete with our scribbled notes.

Some look deceptively simple. For example, the last scavenge on the right

SINGAPORE SCAVENGES:

50. While in SIN try at least two of the following:
a) The city's signature dish? (35)
b) Try some *hokkien nee.* (15)
c) Try some *bak kuah.* (15)
d) Try some *babi pongteh.* (15)
e) Try some *nonya.* (15)
f) Try some *teh tarik.* How is it served? (15)
g) Have the house specialty at the Banana Leaf Apolo. What's unique about this eatery? (25)
i) Enjoy a traditional *rijsttafel* dinner. (25)
j) Try something strange at the Imperial Herbal Restaurant. (25)

51. Take a spin on The Singapore Flyer. (30)

52. Explain Singapore's gum restrictions? (15)

53. Can you name the so-called "seven seas"? (10)

54. Obtain a photo of an Airbus A-380. (25)

55. What is the civil fine for first-time spitting? (10)

56. What is the fine for not flushing? (10)

57. What happens when a taxi cab goes over the speed limit? (10)

58. What are the "8 Habits for OK People"? (10)

59. Take a bumboat from Boat Quay to Clifford Pier.

60. Attend Shermay's Cooking School (100)

61. Bonus (125): *Not for the faint of heart!* On the island of Sentose you will find an Underwater World. One of you must swim with a bull shark! Prove it.

62. Locate and visit the oldest building in Singapore. What is it? (15)

63. Singapore is one of the smallest nation-states on earth. Can you name 5 smaller nation-states? (10)

64. Attend an event associated with the World Gourmet Summit taking place in SIN these days. Prove it. (35)

65. See if you can locate a traditional *kampong.* What is it? (25)

66. What does "Pikir dahulu pendapatan, sesal kemudian tidak berguna," mean? (10)

67. It is the mythological guardian of Singapore. What is it? Photograph one. (15)

68. Why is Kwan Im Thong Hood Cho Temple so popular? Visit it. (15)

69. Locate the wet market near the Chinatown complex. If you take the trouble to force your way through the cheap clothing and chopstick stalls at the front you'll find a large fish butcher with a tattoo across his shoulders. What does it say? Ask him nicely for a photo! (25)

70. Buy something at Punjab Bazaar. (25)

71. Find folks playing mah-jongg and ask to play. Prove it! (25)

page says to join a game of mah-jongg in Singapore. Sounds easy enough—but where do you find folks in the act of playing mah-jongg? Well, the same way you start most of the scavenges—keep asking strangers until you find out, which in most countries meant ▶

Mad Dash for Mah-Jongg *(continued)*

communicating with gestures, drawing pictures, enacting, and so on. Turns out the mah-jongg action was in Chinatown, usually in private clubs on a tiny, out-of-the-way street.

We did the Singapore leg with Rainey and Zoe (who, by the way, went on to win first place in 2009, 2010, *and* 2011.) Just imagine a group of elderly Singaporeans in their dimly lit club staring in surprise and disapproval as four foreigners burst in, red-faced from running, and trying desperately to communicate (we didn't speak Chinese, they, no English), to say, not the normal "We're lost" or "Can we please use the bathroom?", but something ridiculously complex: "We're in a big competition like *The Amazing Race* on TV and we have to learn how to play mah-jongg— would you be so kind as to teach us how to play? Like, right now?"

Thankfully, a man named Mr. Lee came from the back, basically asking, in good English, what the hell we were doing. Miraculously, it turned out that Mr. Lee had a son in L.A. who lived near our old apartment, and that he did indeed watch *The Amazing Race*. After translating what was going on to his scowling cohorts, he offered to teach us how to play. By then we'd gotten used to things like this; "miraculously" and "as if by magic" had become a daily occurrence. We truly are part of a global community of souls who, given the opportunity, usually delight in connecting with their fellow man. Or at least watching them make fools of themselves (see page 93).

Their goodwill did not extend, however, to allowing us to photograph them or the club. Either mah-jongg is taken very seriously in Singapore or more than mah-jongg was going on down there. But as you can see in the photo, we did get Mr. Lee to write in our notebook, in Chinese, that he'd taught us to play so that we could prove the scavenge to Bill! ∾

Mother-Daughter Magic

WE REALLY TOOK TWO JOURNEYS. The first was chronicled in this book. The second was during the writing of it. To broaden our understanding of the mother/daughter relationship, we read and researched extensively, interviewing women in the United States and in other cultures; we also sent surveys to hundreds of women from ages sixteen to eighty. It's been an illuminating and moving experience, confirming the significance and power of this most primal relationship in a woman's life.

We found differences between generations and between cultures. However, when asked what advice their mothers gave most, mothers of all ages and nationalities tended to give the same advice on the three big M's in our lives—money, men, and motherhood. And that was: Don't settle, *know your worth*; men can leave, make sure you can take care of yourself; the years pass all too quickly, enjoy your kids when they're small, then let them go and live life for yourself.

The thing that stood out most powerfully in the surveys was also the most sobering, especially for Claire. When daughters were asked what they most wanted for their mothers, the vast majority, in *all* age groups and countries, answered that they wish

YOU WILL TAKE A PLEASANT JOURNEY TO A PLACE FAR AWAY

PANDA EXPRESS • PANDA INN

You are about to embark on a most delightful journey.
Lucky Numbers 11, 17, 18, 19, 41, 43

Two weeks before we left on the scavenger hunt, we each opened fortune cookies, a thousand miles away from each other, with these messages. Prophetic!

6

their mothers were happier. If we think we've come a long way since women had little choice in their lives, think again. Choice hasn't brought us greater happiness. In reading the stories women so generously included in the surveys, what seemed to lie beneath the dissatisfaction, yearning, and frustration in so many mothers' lives were *approval needs*.

Women still, whether they are stay-at-home moms or bank presidents, give up chunks of themselves to be liked, to belong, to be loved, to be cool, to be whatever their culture defines as "enough." As if just being who we are isn't. It's one reason Claire chose to include Kristin's story about the journalist. How can we as mothers inspire our daughters to be enough, throughout their lives? As daughters how can we be with our mothers in a way that honors her as enough, as a mother and a woman?

Given our power to impact each other's lives, and that whether strong or strained, our mother/daughter relationship is a mirror for every other relationship in our life, why not make this relationship an *intentional* one? Why not consciously create the relationship you really want with your mom and/or daughter—and with yourself (which happens naturally, an added bonus). We promise it will be one of the most gratifying and important journeys you will ever embark upon!

To get you started on this journey, Claire will put on her coaching hat and offer one of the most powerful ways to ▶

shift your relationship—enhancing your listening and speaking skills. Women are verbal creatures; you could almost say our mother/daughter relationship is a lifelong conversation with each other. Language can be words, silence, body language, tone, facial expression.

We all remember learning to speak; even as adults we seek to learn new words and phrases. Very few of us have learned to listen, deeply and *neutrally*. Neutral means removing your own agenda and worldview and listening solely for the other's experience; it means *tuning in*.

Mothers and daughters usually listen to speak; without even thinking about it, we have a simultaneous inner dialogue, usually about our response, about advising, judging, disagreeing, blaming, educating, denying, rebutting, reacting, dismissing, and so on. All of which is a way to make it about you. Even just *agreeing* is about you; it's about *your* experience of her experience. Or chiming in with our own similar experience—we think it's a way to bond or show understanding, and it can be, but, again, the focus went from them to you.

It can be very challenging to listen without injecting ourselves into it. The most powerful understanding and connection happens when we listen in a way that creates a space for discovery and awareness—*theirs*. This kind of listening, also called active listening, builds trust, respect, and confidence, not just between you, but also of her in herself. It's being with her in a way that allows her to tap into her own power and inner being, to remember who she really is. Which is one thing mothers and daughters very much want for each other.

So how do we begin to do this?

First, **make the commitment**. Recognize that making any internal change and changing your relationship's dynamic takes time and practice. Commit to bringing the same dedication and energy you do to staying fit, changing your diet, planning a vacation. Declare when you rise each day that you will listen differently. It can be helpful to **use an anchor** to keep you focused on your goal; a special ring or bracelet, sticky notes in conspicuous places, or doing something like touching your belt buckle. I find that a physical reminder of my commitment works best—for me it's a big aqua ring. You can work on this yourself or the two of you can work on it together.

Before a conversation, take a moment to **ground yourself**. Take a few breaths, **still your inner voice and leave your own agenda behind**—as you listen, silence your opinions, judgment, blame, any inner conversation. You can always process it in your head later, alone.

Put aside feelings or thoughts from the past or fears for the future with regard to what she's saying. Stay focused on *her* and **stay in the present moment**. Listen as if you're hearing and seeing her anew. If it's a phone call, I find it useful to keep my eyes closed so that no visuals take my attention away from Mia's voice. Sometimes I also sit on one hand to remind me not to interrupt, give an opinion, or advise.

Seeing her anew means you **assume her strength and capability**, and that she has all the resources she needs within her to be and create what she wants in life. Active listening holds a mirror up, reflecting who she really is back to her. Of course, part of the beauty of being with her this way is that you get to learn more of who she really is, too.

As she speaks, check in with her that you're clear on exactly what she's saying by occasionally repeating what she said; for example, "So you felt you expressed yourself clearly to your colleagues, am I correct?" "Okay, just so I'm clear, my expecting x, y, z from you created pressure for you last week, but a, b, and c did not, do I have that right?" You're not asking to respond or react, just to let her know that you heard exactly what she said, not your slant, version, or interpretation of it.

Listen beyond the words, for the emotions, for what she may not be saying, for what the experience or situation really means to her. When she's done talking you can explore any meaning or emotions behind the words by saying something like, "It sounds as if you're still uncertain about your colleague's perception of you and that's scary for you, am I right?" Or "It seemed as if you were hesitant to tell me x, y, z—is that true? Is there more you'd like to say?"

Be curious. Not so much for more information or content, that's usually not why someone shares with you, though you ▶

may ask if you need more clarity on content. It's more important to be curious about what the content *means* to them.

In a situation where she's come to you with a dilemma, always ask first if she wants you to just listen or if she wants your advice, opinion, or help finding a solution. In which case, first listen as described above to be sure you're clear on her communication.

When speaking, remember that language is powerful. By our choice of words we can convey whether we assume weakness, dependence, incapability, or a negative intention, even unconsciously—or if we assume strength, belief in her abilities and a positive intention. We want our words to create possibility, respect, trust, and connection. Banish *you should, you never, you always, you can't.* They are about you, your fears, your need to control or to be right, your opinion, they focus on history, and on limitations. These words cut off possibility. "You always overeat" states a *fact.* "You've often overeaten in the past" states a *past* behavior and allows for choice and new possibility.

Listen to the difference in the following: "I hope you get into your first-choice college," or "I hope you know what you're doing," which are about *your* fears—that she won't and she doesn't—versus, "I trust that you're going to have an amazing experience wherever you go to school," and "I believe in you."

Don't echo complaints. Women's conversations are often a chorus of complaints—nothing could be more disempowering and energy-draining. If, for example, she's complaining about her horrible job, yet again, you can contribute to her playing victim by saying, "I can't believe what an idiot your boss is," or "I don't know why you took that job to begin with, it's so beneath you," both of which focus on how helpless and foolish she is (that's the unspoken message). Or you can simply say, "It sounds as if you're still pretty unhappy there." Period, nothing more. You've acknowledged that you've heard her without feeding the negative energy that's keeping her stuck. Silence can sometimes be the best response to chronic complaining.

Recognize that a complaint is just a request in disguise; listen for it. If she didn't want you to just listen—if she's asked you for advice, an opinion, or your thoughts—speak to the unexpressed request, to any unmet needs she may be unconscious of or afraid to ask for.

Here are examples of what you might say:

- "Would you like me to brainstorm some ideas with you for moving forward?" Let her throw out a couple, then you add to them. You'll be co-creating ideas rather than advising. Play out the possibilities of each idea.
- "So, what choices are available to you now that will change the situation?" or if she's not willing or able to change the situation, "Have you explored what you might change in yourself to make the situation work for you?"
- A great question for moving someone forward (and stopping a whine fest) is "So, what's next for you?" Again, you're focused on moving her forward without injecting your agenda—you're calling upon her own smarts and creativity.
- "What if taking this job turned out to be perfectly designed for your own growth, what would you say you've learned?"
- "I wonder if there is a way any of these problems can be turned into possibilities—have you explored that?"
- If you're sure you have a good idea she may not have thought of, hear the difference between "You should . . ." or "Why don't you try . . ." versus "Would you find value in exploring x, y, z?" The second empowers her, it assumes her ability to assess and be resourceful.

If she's so used to your "helping" her with your opinion, advice, judgment, worries, admonitions, and so on, she may get annoyed that you're suddenly not being "helpful". Don't fall for it; **take a stand for her strength**, believe in her when she may not believe in herself. If you've always been the brains behind the operation, she may not have developed those muscles. Your constant "helping" also gives her the opportunity to blame you with what isn't working in her life. Once you remove yourself from the equation, you encourage two things: She'll become accountable for her own life, and feeling your trust fosters her trust in herself and her ability to make positive choices. And if things don't work out, it will be *she* who created those results. ▶

Mother-Daughter Magic *(continued)*

Use your new listening skills, let her own that, to feel what she feels, to be proud of the lessons that she's learned, and to make new choices moving forward.

Of course there are times when she's genuinely suffering—experiencing pain, sorrow, fear, grief. Don't tell her it will be okay or chime in with how you remember when you went through the same thing. Your suffering last year is of no help to her now; few things make someone feel more invisible than dismissing their feelings or minimizing them by maximizing yours. It's also about you, often your inability to deal with her pain. It's okay to say very little, or sometimes say nothing. If you're uncomfortable (which can be a normal response, especially if someone's crying) you can simply say, "You're really hurting now, I'm so sorry," or "I'm here for you." Don't tell her it will pass—it's not the future yet, she's hurting *now*, so be with her right now, just as she is. Only she will know when it passes or when it will be okay.

Listening and speaking this way is about holding her in high, unselfish regard, about compassion, stillness, kindness, love, and above all, trust. It's a skill that takes time.

At the end of each day, take time to reflect. First, acknowledge yourself for doing something that's pretty amazing if you think about it—how often do we take on *being* in a whole new way? You might explore any feelings and thoughts that came up for you while you were listening (and perhaps biting your tongue). As you reflect, what did you notice was different for you? For her? What opened up for you? What opened up between the two of you? Reflect on what worked and commit to continuing that. Now, with the same neutrality and lack of judgment you offered your mom or daughter, reflect on what didn't work, and what you'll do differently moving forward.

If you stick to your commitment and this becomes not just a new skill, but a new way of being, you'll begin to notice all of your relationships shifting. You and your mother or daughter will feel more ease and pleasure in being together, more openness and trust, more willingness to share. You'll also notice that you're more tuned into someone else more deeply—yourself! ∿

More from Claire and Mia Fontaine

COME BACK

A National Bestseller
How does a Los Angeles honor student from a loving home end up shooting speedballs in rural Indiana?

What does a desperate mother do when she learns that her runaway daughter has been living a secret life for more than a year?

In powerful parallel stories, a mother and daughter give mesmerizing first-person accounts of the nightmare that shattered their family and the amazing journey they took to find their way back to each other. Claire Fontaine's relentless cross-country search for her missing child and ultimate decision to force her into treatment in Eastern Europe is a gripping tale of dead ends, painful revelations, and, at times, miracles. Mia Fontaine describes her refuge in the seedy underworld of felons and addicts as well as the jarring shock of the extreme, if loving school that enabled her to overcome depression and self-loathing. Both women detail their remarkable process of self-examination and healing with humor and unsparing honesty.

Come Back is an unforgettable true story of love and transformation that will resonate with mothers and daughters everywhere.

More from Claire and Mia Fontaine
(continued)

"A testament to the power of the love between a mother and daughter."
—*New York Times*

"Best mother-daughter memoir."
—*Glamour*

"Beautifully written and inspiring, it speaks compellingly to women of all ages. This is an extremely important book."   —Susan Forward, Ph.D., author of *Toxic Parents*

Don't miss the next book by your favorite author. Sign up now for AuthorTracker by visiting www.AuthorTracker.com.